STATE OF STRUGGLE

LOIS HARDER

Feminism and Politics in Alberta

STATE OF
STRUGGLE

The University of Alberta Press

Published by
The University of Alberta Press
Ring House 2
Edmonton, Alberta T6G 2E1

Copyright © Lois Harder 2003

All rights reserved.

No part of this publication may be produced, stored in a retrieval system, or transmitted in any forms or by any means, electronic, mechanical, photocopying, recording, or otherwise, without the prior written consent of the copyright owner or a licence from The Canadian Copyright Licensing Agency (Access Copyright). For an Access Copyright license, visit www.accesscopyright.ca or call toll free: 1–800–893–5777.

NATIONAL LIBRARY OF CANADA CATALOGUING IN PUBLICATION DATA

Harder, Lois, 1966–
State of struggle : feminism and politics in Alberta / Lois Harder.

Includes bibliographical references and index.
ISBN 0-88864-401-9

1. Women's rights—Alberta—History. 2. Women's rights—Government policy—Alberta. 3. Women—Alberta—Social conditions. 4. Alberta—Politics and government—1971– I. Title.
HQ1459.A4H37 2003   305.4'097123   C2003-910590-3

Printed and bound in Canada by AGMV Marquis Printing Inc., Monmagy, Quebec.
First printing, 2003.
Copyediting by Carol Berger.
Book design by Alan Brownoff.

The University of Alberta Press is committed to protecting our natural environment. As part of our efforts, this book is printed on Enviro paper: it contains 100% post-consumer recycled fibres and is acid- and chlorine-free.

The University of Alberta Press gratefully acknowledges the financial support received for its publishing program from The Canada Council for the Arts. In addition, we also gratefully acknowledge the financial support of the Government of Canada through the Book Publishing Industry Development Program (BPDIP) and from the Alberta Foundation for the Arts for our publishing activities.

For my mother, Anne, and my father, Eric.

Contents

IX   *Preface*

XIII   *Acknowledgements*

1   CHAPTER 1
      Sites of Engagement

19   CHAPTER 2
      The Big Boom and a "Resounding Thud of Nothingness"
      Feminist Claimsmaking in the Context of Affluence

45   CHAPTER 3
      Disparate Strategies and Expedient Responses
      The Acquisition of Political Legitimacy in Troubled Times

79   CHAPTER 4
      Feminists and Family Values
      The Crisis of Alberta's Welfare State

119   CHAPTER 5
      Learning Neoliberalism

153   CHAPTER 6
      Oil, Sex, and Power

163 *Notes*

193 *Bibliography*

219 *Index*

Preface

IN THE COURSE of my research, a common response to learning that I was writing about feminist organizing in Alberta was, "Well, that should be a short book." The less glib have assumed that I must be writing about the "Famous Five," those remarkable Alberta women who did so much to advance women's voting rights and representation in Parliament and in provincial legislatures during the early part of the twentieth century. Of course, the foundation laid for women's political participation by Nellie McClung, Irene Parlby, Emily Murphy, Louise McKinney, and Henrietta Muir Edwards is certainly present in these pages. Without their work and that of many lesser known women, the struggles recounted here would not have been possible. But it is the more recent struggles of feminism's second and third waves and the insights these struggles provide into the inter-relationships among the economy, state, and society that are the central concern of this book.

One of the truisms of Canadian politics is the significance of the regions to the definition of our national identity. Alberta's contribution to this definition is to provide the conservative end of the country's political spectrum, a conservatism borne out of the province's economic roots in ranching, large-scale crop farming, and, of course, oil and gas production. Albertans have developed a reputation for individualism and for a frontier mentality that promises great rewards to anyone willing to work hard. This reputation belies a more complex social realm. It turns out that the rugged individualist will give you the shirt off his back while muttering about the need for welfare recipients to stand up on their own two feet. Video lottery terminals, casinos, and Sunday shopping coexist with a robust commitment to Christian faith. And Alberta's feminists, many of whom believed the land of opportunity mythology and took seriously the provincial government's commitment to formal equality, have had their ambitions thwarted by *Ozzie and Harriet* notions of women's proper place. Contradictions are the lifeblood of political research and Alberta certainly offers a rich supply.

This book casts Alberta's recent political history in a new light. At least since the publication of C.B. MacPherson's *Democracy in Alberta: Social Credit and the Party System* in 1952, the province has been characterized by monolithic politics. One-party dominance, weak legislative opposition, and a long-running antipathy towards central Canada and particularly the federal government have been key elements in this characterization. But while these features cannot be ignored, they only tell part of the story. The complexities surrounding feminist efforts to secure resources and recognition for women, as well as for racial and ethnic minorities, the poor, and the disabled, demonstrate that things are not entirely what they seem. Opposition did and does exist. Alberta's elected officials and state agents have had to seek consensus and broker compromise. The interests of the dominant commodities—oil and gas—are never far away, but there are, in fact, moments when the outcomes of political struggles have been unpredictable.

Feminism, too, is not necessarily what one might presume. The popular stereotype of feminists as man-hating lesbians is quickly discounted by the analysis of feminist activism presented here. But even for those more familiar with feminist organizing, Alberta offers a few surprises. As the following pages attest, despite the province's often hostile climes, there is, or certainly has been, incredible dynamism in Alberta's feminist community.

The campaigns considered in these chapters are representative rather than comprehensive. Many other stories could and should be told. My choices were driven by the information available in various archives, resource libraries, and the memories of activists and state agents. The choice was further restricted by a desire to limit the claimsmaking initiatives under investigation to those concerned with the Alberta state, or the Alberta provincial context. Alberta feminists have, of course, been active in campaigns surrounding free trade, the Constitution, the status of Aboriginal women, and the sale and distribution pornography, among others. Because these issues are of a federal character, however, they have not been included here.

Much of the material from which I have reconstructed accounts of feminist claimsmaking belongs to activist groups and, as such, presents a particular analysis of their activities. In order to ensure the accuracy of these descriptions, I have attempted to acquire additional accounts of particular events. Further, in order to indicate how feminist claimsmakers understood their activities and their strategies, the language in which they expressed their objectives has been retained. In some cases, then, the terms of struggle may appear dated and insensitive to more recent developments in the language of feminist activism. The purpose of preserving the language in its original form is not to deride these early organizing initiatives but to provide a discursive sense of the development of feminist claimsmaking in Alberta.

Acknowledgements

THIS BOOK WAS PUBLISHED with the generous support of the Canadian Federation for the Humanities and Social Sciences, through the Aid to Scholarly Publications Programme, using funds provided by the Social Sciences and Humanities Research Council of Canada. Research support was provided by the Ontario Graduate Scholarship Program, and the Brenden Rule/Harriet Snowball Winspear fellowship from the University of Alberta. I am also indebted to many people for their help in the completion of this project.

In terms of resources, I wish to thank Linda Trimble and Sylvia McKinley for access to their personal papers, and Nanci Langford for her enthusiasm for the project, contacts, and for her work with the Northern Alberta Women's Archive Project. Additionally, I am grateful for the help of the tireless archivists and librarians at the Provincial Archives of Alberta, the Glenbow Archives, and the Alberta Legislature Library.

The women interviewed in the course of my research were enormously generous with their time and their knowledge. Many people have offered helpful comments on various drafts. My thanks to Isabella Bakker, Janine Brodie, Ken McRoberts, Abby Bakan, Judy Garber, Sue Hamilton, Susan

Smith, and Lesley Cormack, as well as the staff at the University of Alberta Press including Carol Berger, Alan Brownoff, Michael Luski and Leslie Vermeer. For their intellectual friendship and support I would particularly like to thank Catherine Kellogg, George Pavlich, and Dave Whitson. My family has been incredibly supportive, with particular thanks owed to my parents for their regular goading and constant faith in me; to my brother, Lawrence, for his mentoring and psychic life preservers, and to my sister-in-law, Dale Hensley, for sharing her firsthand knowledge of feminist activism in Alberta. My sisters also deserve hearty thanks: Marilyn for her generosity and intuition and Doris for her perspective and her ready laugh. I would also like to thank Noah and Alec for reminding me how important it is to play. And finally, and most whole-heartedly, I would like to thank my partner, Curtis, for his patience, his devotion, and his love.

1

Sites of
Engagement

SINCE THE 1970S, there have been profound transformations in the relationship between the Alberta state and feminist activists, within the Alberta state itself, and within the feminist community. These transformations have occurred as a result of the boom-bust cycle of the provincial economy; shifts in the views of legislators, policymakers, and feminist activists concerning both the nature of the relationship between state and civil society and the management of that relationship; and demands for greater inclusiveness within the feminist movement. This analysis of feminist struggles in Alberta disrupts prevailing views of the constancy of the province's conservatism. But more broadly, the many stories recounted here provide an empirical grounding to the concept of state forms and evidence for the varying effectiveness of different strategies of governance and claimsmaking. They also represent an effort to forge an alliance between discourse analysis and political economy methodology. For those less interested in the theoretical and methodological debates of political science, the book reveals a little-known but extremely colourful dimension of Alberta's political history.

I have chosen to use the term "claimsmaker" and its derivatives to denote people and organizations whose desire for change extends beyond the limited and self-serving objectives that are the hallmark of "interest groups." The objectives of claimsmakers could be characterized as emancipatory and the realization of those objectives has, or is anticipated to have, far-reaching effects on the structure and functioning of social life. The term "claimsmaker" also indicates a belief that democracy is enhanced by the participation of social groups within the policymaking process and a desire to avoid the disparaging connotations now associated with interest groups or "special interests."

The following four anecdotes provide some grounding for the abstractions of state form and strategies of governance and claimsmaking. These examples provide a context for the exploration of the book's central theoretical concepts as well as providing some indication of the book's analytical trajectory and the rationale behind its periodization.

■ OIL WEALTH, FEMINIST OPTIMISM, AND STATE INSULARITY

In the early 1970s, the Supreme Court of Canada ruled that, upon legal separation, Irene Murdoch, a farmer from Nanton, Alberta, had no entitlement to the farm that she and her husband had operated for over twenty years. The court argued that "the work of an 'ordinary' ranch wife and of a homemaker and mother was not sufficient contribution to establish that she had a beneficial interest in the property."[1] This ruling became the basis of a demand for the reform of provincial matrimonial property legislation throughout Canada and was a central focus for feminist organizing in Alberta in the late 1970s. The majority of voices advocating for legislative change, including those of both radical and mainstream women and the Alberta Institute of Law Research and Reform, supported the idea of deferred sharing. This was a concept that presumed marriage to be an equal partnership, and hence, in the event of separation, property acquired over the course of a marriage should be divided equally between the marriage partners. By contrast, the Alberta government argued that judicial discretion should prevail in the distribution of marital assets. This was to be done on the basis of nineteen criteria, including a homemaker's contribution to the welfare of the family, but also including financial contribution and conduct of the spouses. When confronted by the disjuncture between public opinion, which overwhelmingly supported deferred sharing, and the provincial government's proposed course of action, government members stood firm. As the deputy premier at the time, Hugh Horner, stated,

> My hope is that none of the women who are now achieving notable places for themselves in the work world and who are accumulating possessions of considerable material value, will ever be forced automatically by law to forfeit one-half of their possessions to useless partners who have contributed nothing to the marriage property.[2]

■ FALLING PRICES, DISCORD, AND DAWNING RECOGNITION

In the early 1980s a coalition of mainstream, Alberta women's groups came together to pressure the Alberta government to establish an advisory council on women's issues. At that time Alberta was one of only two provinces that had not yet established such an arms-length advisory body. This was not the first attempt to persuade the provincial government to adopt an advisory council. Indeed, the experience of ten years of activism had persuaded some women's groups that such an advocacy effort would fail, or, if successful, would result in an ineffective or co-optive agency. In the initial stages of the coalition's efforts it seemed that failure was the most likely outcome. Although government representatives indicated some support for the principle of the council, one cabinet minister advised the coalition to change the demand for an advisory council to, simply, a council on women's affairs, since the term "advisory" implied an obligation, on the part of government, to take the council's advice.[3]

After several years of advocacy, a weakening economy, and increasing disenchantment with the condition of provincial governance, the Alberta government finally agreed to establish the Alberta Advisory Council on

Women's Issues. Its first chair, Margaret Leahey, had no history of women's organizing. Her work as a journalist for television news had captured the attention of government leaders because it showed an apparent sympathetic attitude towards the policies of the Conservative Party.[4] Among her first acts as chair was to announce that, in filling the positions on the council, she would be looking for "a very strong male...someone with a lot of influence over women's lives."[5]

■ FURTHER FALLING, DISILLUSIONMENT, AND AMBIVALENT INCORPORATION

By the late 1980s women's organizing in Alberta, as elsewhere in Canada, was characterized by fragmentation. Groups organized around specific issues, often for limited periods, and with an attitude of thoroughgoing skepticism regarding the state as a facilitator of social change. At the same time, the structure of the Alberta state offered women an unprecedented number of access points, including the Women's Secretariat, the Advisory Council on Women's Issues, and an Official Opposition that viewed the government's historical approach to women's issues as a point of vulnerability. However, the policies of the government often contradicted this appearance of openness.

Notable among the many discrepant actions of the Alberta state was the simultaneous development of the Plan for Action for Alberta Women and the emergence of family-values discourse, articulated most explicitly in the establishment of the Premier's Council in Support of Alberta Families. Although the plan suggested a relatively progressive approach to addressing inequities faced by women in various social and economic policy areas, reality had a more conservative pallor. Employees of the Women's Secretariat and Career Development and Employment, for example, were informed that they were not to use the phrase "pay equity" in any of the correspondence sent to ministers' offices or in any reports of preparations for committee or cabinet meetings.[6] Additionally, the premier frequently voiced his intentions to support the "traditional family" headed up by a sole, male, income earner. Premier Don Getty asserted that the government's intention was "to strengthen the family, to provide reasons why the family is stronger, why mothers will stay in the house, in the family while not having care outside of the house."[7]

■ ECONOMIC RECOVERY, DESPAIR, AND THE CAMPAIGN TO DISPLACE POLITICS

Among the first and most enduring controversies to confront the Conservative government under the leadership of Ralph Klein was the issue of human rights protection on the basis of sexual orientation. In late 1992 the Alberta Human Rights Commission (AHRC) was in the process of studying the frequency of acts of discrimination against gays and lesbians in the areas of tenancy, employment, and services. In response to the AHRC's decision to accept sexual orientation complaints, Diane Mirosh, Klein's newly appointed minister responsible for the AHRC, forbade commission staff from undertaking such investigations and made a series of public statements advocating the abolition of the provincial human rights agency. The ensuing controversy compelled the government to undertake a review of the commission and human rights legislation in Alberta—a process that was widely regarded as designed to provide justification for dismantling the AHRC. Many community groups, including women's groups, were skeptical about devoting increasingly limited resources to a public consultation whose conclusions were predetermined. Nonetheless, they did participate and were successful in persuading the government to maintain the human rights commission and to make some minor alterations to the existing legislation. Predictably, sexual orientation as a protected ground of discrimination was not included in the amendments. It would take a ruling by the Supreme Court of Canada to ensure this outcome. Even then, however, the Conservative caucus was deeply divided over whether to accept the Court's ruling or invoke the notwithstanding clause of the Canadian Constitution. Ultimately, the Court's ruling was upheld but controversy surrounding sexual orientation has persisted, with subsequent challenges to discriminatory practices pursued in the areas of adoption and the recognition of spousal status for same sex partners. Despite the leadership's desire to remain focused on achieving the economic fundamentals for a flourishing investment climate, the controversies of political life seem destined to persist.

■ FRAMING ABSTRACTIONS

The interrelationships between Alberta's contemporary political economy and feminist struggles for political legitimacy demonstrate the possibilities and constraints imposed by particular arrangements of power, political strategies for claimsmaking, and significant social and economic events. I have chosen to represent these relationships through the lens of "state forms" in order to underscore the dynamism and fluidity of the interactions among particular practices of governance, economic priorities, and strategies of claimsmaking. The concept of state form is taken from Philip Corrigan and Derek Sayer's ground-breaking examination of the formation of the English state. This work was later adapted by Janine Brodie as a means of understanding the discursive structures through which the form of the state affects and is affected by the character of citizenship. State form denotes a particular, historical configuration of political, productive, and social relations that are regulated and enforced by the state and socially reproduced through "our shared understandings…of what is natural, neutral and universal."[8] A considerable degree of enforcement is required in order to ensure that these shared understandings maintain their "natural" character. Moreover, as Corrigan and Sayer observe, social consensus around a particular state formation is never complete. Indeed, "state formation is something that has ever been contested by those whom it seeks to regulate and rule. It is first and foremost, their resistance that makes visible the conditions and limits of bourgeois civilization, the particularity and fragility of its seemingly neutral and timeless social forms."[9]

In the case of Alberta, the concept of state form is used to distinguish between welfare and neoliberal configurations. As Chapters 2 through 4 demonstrate, a reorientation in the relationship between state agents and advocacy groups can occur within the context of a single state form. As

6 STATE OF STRUGGLE

Corrigan and Sayer observe in the quote above, the persistence of political contestation and efforts to diminish its disruptive effects are integral to the articulation of a particular state form. However, there are limits to the extent to which both refusals to address demands as well as accommodations between claimsmakers and state institutions can be taken. As Nancy Fraser observes, reorganizations of social relations have a tendency to illuminate the shortcomings of the state's capacity to regulate social life, to emphasize contradictions within state agencies, practices and policies, and to incite further challenges to prevailing relations of power.[10] When these challenges become sufficiently intense, the form of the state itself is called into question. If the old state form cannot address the challenges with which it is faced, as has been asserted regarding the welfare state, a struggle ensues to reassert social control under the auspices of a new state form. The extraordinary contrasts between the 1970s and 1980s, when state interventionism in the Alberta economy and a reluctant willingness to acknowledge the legitimacy of claimsmaking were standard features of governance, and the drastic minimization of state functions and vilification of "special interests" in the 1990s and 2000s underscore the saliency of the concept of state forms for making sense of contemporary Alberta politics.

This analysis also owes a debt to the contributions that feminists have made to our understanding of the state. Feminist theorists have pointed to the articulation and policing of the gender order, or the differentiated articulation and organization of men's and women's roles in society, as a central state activity in reinforcing "common sense" understandings of social life. The policies and practices of both welfare and neoliberal state forms have dramatic, though differing, effects on the conditions of women's lives and in how women seek to change those conditions. As feminist welfare state theorists have argued, the state has been an agent of both emancipation and oppression for women. On the one hand, welfare state policies enabled women to escape their personalized dependency on men by providing alternative means of support in the form of social assistance, family allowances, and child care, and through employment within state agencies. On the other hand, welfare state policies, particularly in Anglo-American

Sites of Engagement   7

democracies, continued to reinforce the link between women and caring and resisted substantive recognition of the contribution this caring work made to the health of the economy.

With regard to the neoliberal state, feminist theorists have drawn our attention to the ways in which the resurgence of the market and the diminishment of the state "simultaneously erodes and intensifies gender."[11] As the process of social regulation has shifted from the state to the market, the capacity of individuals to provide for themselves through their participation in the labour market has become the central requirement of citizenship. This requirement pertains equally to men and women. Single mothers, for example, can no longer lay claim to social assistance on the basis of their caring responsibilities. In this universal expectation of labour market participation then, the neoliberal state erodes the significance of gender. However, with the withdrawal of the state from the provision of public services, clearly witnessed in the decreased length of hospital stays and expectations of increased parental involvement in children's education, the need for family members to provide care has increased. In the absence of public policies that support men's participation in this work and as a result of the persistence of the association between care and femininity, gender is intensified. Perversely, it is the diminishment of the state through spending reductions, program elimination, and the explicit pursuit of policies to ensure the state's decreased fiscal capacity that most clearly exposes its significance, since this diminishment of the state forces people, particularly women, to reorganize their lives in order to accommodate the privatization of social goods.

For the purposes of this exploration, the interrelationships between the form of the state—the particular organization of power and objectives of policy making—and the strategies of feminist claimsmaking can be broken down into four distinct periods. The first three periods are marked by changes within the dynamics of the province's welfare state while the fourth concerns the attempt to consolidate a neoliberal state form. The narration of Alberta's contemporary political economy and feminist struggles for legitimacy provides an opportunity to explore the possibilities and constraints imposed by particular arrangements of power, political strategies for claimsmaking and managing claimsmakers, and significant social and economic events. From the perspective of a progressive politics, it is a kind of "we laughed, we cried" drama, but most importantly, it is a drama that is unresolved. The achievements of the struggle for social justice are notoriously and frustratingly unstable. But the struggle is never completely closed off, and certainly never finished.

The first period under investigation in this study is discussed in Chapter 2 and corresponds to the 1970s. In Alberta these years were marked by a strong social consensus, a widely shared understanding of an interventionist role for the state in the economy (though in the Alberta case, this interventionism was skewed towards facilitating the expansion of the oil and gas economy rather than legitimating the state through public provision of social programs), the flow of windfall revenues to the provincial treasury, and a lack of experience among government officials in addressing the demands of claimsmakers, especially feminist claimsmakers. Under these conditions, agents of the Alberta state chose to ignore women's demands for policies that ensured workplace equality and recognized women's contributions to their families and to the economy, and strongly resisted demands for the development of state agencies to protect women's interests.

In these early days of second-wave feminist claimsmaking, the provincial state's response to the conciliatory, partnership-based approach adopted by feminists came as a rude shock to Alberta women. In part, this shock stemmed from the contrast between the approach of the Alberta government to the rise of feminism and that of the federal government. While the Alberta state insisted that women's subordination could be addressed through the formal equality clause of the province's human rights legislation, the federal government, particularly after the United Nations declared 1975 International Women's Year, responded much more positively to feminist claimsmakers.[12] A number of state agencies were established under federal auspices, including the Women's Bureau in the Department of Labour, the Office of Equal Opportunity in the Public Service Commission, the Canadian Advisory Council on the Status of Women, and the Women's Program of the Secretary of State.[13]

The Alberta government's intransigence towards feminist claimsmakers weakened as the price of oil began to collapse in the early 1980s. This shift in the province's relationship to feminists is the focus of Chapter 3. It was at this point that the strength of the social consensus surrounding the preeminence of the oil and gas sector on Alberta's political agenda began to break down. State agents recognized that the government, if it was to sustain its legitimacy, would have to address a broader array of concerns appealing to a wider cross-section of the electorate. In substantive terms, this shift required an expanded arena of political actors and new methods for managing these disparate groups while maintaining a political agenda that remained centred on the strength of the economy. These new methods fit under the general rubric of distributive justice and the politics of liberal pluralism.

A central contradiction within the welfare state form is the necessity of ensuring the success of the capitalist economy while realizing some measure of social justice within the policy agenda. On the one hand, the state must facilitate sufficient private accumulation to keep capital content while simultaneously redistributing wealth through taxation and the implementation of social programs. On the other hand, state agents must appear to be responsive to equality-seeking groups without undermining capital accumulation and without incurring serious challenges to the prevailing social consensus.[14] For many welfare states, a key mechanism in resolving this dilemma was the adoption of liberal pluralism.

Although commonly advanced as a theory of the state in which the state itself is devoid of interests and state agents act as neutral arbiters, adopting policy on the basis of the competitive outcome of popular demands, I argue that liberal pluralism is a strategy of governance rather than an accurate characterization of the policymaking process. Rather than facilitating vibrant democratic exchange, the operation of liberal pluralism within the welfare state largely involved private interactions between groups and state agencies, with few connections between groups or co-ordination among state offices. Success in securing public resources resulted from a correspondence between particular demands, timing, and their fit within a narrow political program rather than being the product of competitive interaction within the marketplace of ideas. In this environment, as Iris Young has observed, an appeal to justice is simply one more strategy in the attempt to gain access to state resources. Normative claims for justice are easily collapsed into the selfish desires of an interest group, the claims of that group then being delegitimated.[15] Indeed, it is this inherent tendency towards delegitimation within the practice of liberal pluralism that created the conditions in which neoliberal legislators were able to discount the political concerns raised by claimsmaking groups as the self-interested grasping of "special interests."

In the specific case of women and the Alberta state, a significant contributor to the adoption of liberal pluralism was the emergence, in the early 1980s, of a vocal antifeminist movement. This movement was embodied primarily in the Alberta Federation of Women United for Families (AFWUF). Largely oblivious to the disenchantment of feminist organizations regarding state-centred claimsmaking, antifeminists viewed the provincial state's appointment of a minister responsible for women's issues and, subsequently, cabinet and interdepartmental committees on women's issues and a Women's Secretariat as further indications of the seriousness of the threat posed by feminism to the traditional gender order and social cohesion. The women of AFWUF proved to be keenly adept at manipulating pluralist politics for their own gain, regularly insisting, for example, that they should receive funding equal to that provided to their primary feminist rival, the Alberta Status of Women Action Committee (ASWAC). While state agencies concerned with women generally assessed AFWUF's views as anachronistic if not dangerous, AFWUF did have significant support among a number of elected officials. Moreover, its presence as one of the sole voices of organized opposition to feminism ascribed the group a significance on the political landscape that was disproportionate to the popularity of their views within Alberta society.

It is an interesting and significant paradox that at the same time that the Alberta state became more willing to acknowledge the political legitimacy of feminist claimsmakers, many progressive women's organizations began retreating from state-centred claimsmaking.[16] In part, this retreat reflected frustration with the inadequacy of the provincial state's responsiveness to women's demands for equality and a growing skepticism regarding the federal state's willingness and capacity to act as a catalyst for social change on a meaningful scale. Despite the existence of a variety of federal agencies whose mandates were directed at improving the status of women, and a widely held perception among feminist activists throughout English-speaking Canada that advocacy could produce change, particularly in the realm of social policy,[17] feminist organizations were also increasingly concerned by the constraints on the activities and objectives of feminist organizations created by the federal granting structure. The tension between the need for federal funding to maintain the work of feminist advocacy and the restrictions that this need placed on feminist organizations also contributed to a reconsideration of, and skepticism regarding, state policies as the focus of feminist organizing.

Additionally, the internal dynamics of feminist organizations, particularly the challenge to the predominance of white, middle-class women in positions of power within organizations and the reorientation of some feminist activism towards therapeutic models of self-understanding and increasingly personalized analyses of patriarchy, led many women's groups to become more introspective and less attentive to state-focused claims-making. While few groups totally abandoned the state as a target for their activism, its importance was certainly diminished. In Alberta, the notable exception to this trend in the early part of the 1980s was the establishment of the Provincial Coalition for a Council on Women's Affairs, which was predominantly composed of mainstream women's organizations. Years of pressure, the example of virtually every other Canadian province, and the "respectability" of the women's groups involved in the coalition, eventually resulted in the creation of the Alberta Advisory Council on Women's Issues. However, the fact that the advisory council's chair and the majority of its members had little understanding of women's issues or connection with the feminist movement only reinforced the skepticism towards the state that had already taken hold among the province's feminist organizations.

Chapter 4 continues the discussion of changes in Alberta's welfare state in the late 1980s. In this period, liberal pluralism was consolidated as a technique of governance, though many examples of feminist organizing and the incorporation of feminist demands within state agencies demonstrate its inconstancy and inadequacy as a method for addressing the demands of feminist claimsmakers. As the 1980s proceeded, Alberta's fiscal crisis intensified, while feminist groups continued to fragment and antifeminists became increasingly well-organized and vociferous in their attacks. Although discontent with the provincial government was not sufficient to result in a Conservative electoral defeat, the ranks of the legislative opposition swelled and the Conservative Party itself attracted some relatively progressive people among its candidates.

For women, Alberta's increasingly contestatory political environment and the use of liberal pluralism to manage this environment posed substantial challenges. A variety of initiatives were undertaken to improve the economic position of women within Alberta society. However, each of these initiatives was marked by a unique, Alberta approach to gender equity that foreclosed systemically targeted policy initiatives and insisted, despite the occasional acknowledgement of the persistence of sexism, on individual responsibility for women's subordination in the labour market.

The Alberta state was relatively responsive to women's demands for adequate resources for women's shelters, although this responsiveness was not immediate and not always generous. Women found their right to reproductive choice compromised under the auspices of budget balancing, but successfully revealed the centrality of conservative morality to this strategy and regained medical coverage for sterilization and birth control counselling, as well as relatively improved access to abortion. The Alberta state's sharpest contradiction with regard to feminist legitimacy, however, was the simultaneous development of a feminist-inspired Plan for Action for Alberta Women at the same time that government members were explicitly articulating "family-values" discourse in the creation of a statutory holiday known as Family Day and the establishment of the Premier's Council in Support of Alberta Families.

"The family" represents a peculiarly vexed institution for feminist analysis. While the family has been a central location of women's oppression, participation in family life has been and continues to be extremely

meaningful and rewarding. Michelle Barrett and Mary McIntosh contextu-
alize the self-fulfilling attributes of the family as the limited reward for
participating in an otherwise highly atomized society. While their argument focuses on the ways in which the reification of the family is antisocial,
as it prevents the strengthening of broader social bonds, they also recognize that existing historical conditions make participation in the family a
compelling and rational choice for women.[18] In a less radical theoretical
intervention, Mimi Abramovitz qualifies her critical position on the family
by arguing:

> The critique of the family ethic is not meant to devalue the experi-
> ence of sharing one's life with a partner or that of bearing, raising,
> and loving children. Rather it suggests that institutionally enforced
> rules of family organization do not necessarily enhance family life and
> they frequently disadvantage women.[19]

The usefulness of "the family" as a tool in delegitimizing the demands
of feminists also, ironically, stems from the strategies of feminists themselves. Feminist theorists and activists have struggled over whether to
articulate women's needs in such a way as to obtain treatment equal to that
of men, or to make claims on the basis of women's difference from men:
that is, in women's capacity to bear children and in their socially assigned
responsibility for care-giving.

The problem with adopting the equality strategy is the tendency for
equality to be equated with sameness. When women are treated as "the
same" as men, the specificity of women's various experiences within the
gendered organization of social life and the particular expectations for
women that this social organization implies, cannot be addressed. The oft-
used illustration of this problem is the inclusion of maternity leave under
"disability" compensation in the framework of an employee-benefits
package. Further, the equality strategy also risks homogenizing all women
and all men, such that class and racial inequalities among women and
between women and men are obscured.

14   STATE OF STRUGGLE

Demanding that needs be interpreted on the basis of difference, however, poses its own set of difficulties for feminist struggles. In the context of this discussion, the primary risk of the difference strategy is the institutionalization of the existing gendered division of labour and women's subordinate position within that structure. When feminist claimsmaking is structured around addressing women's needs for child care, elder care, respite care, protection against the objectification of pornography, and freedom from domestic violence, women enter the debate from a position of subordination. These issues are "women's issues" because women are responsible for activities that are undervalued and to which formal polit-ical power does not accrue. Of course, feminist campaigns in these areas are focused on re-valuing "women's work" and sharing the burden of care among all members of the household. But as long as the gendered subtext is maintained, so too is the possibility that opponents may use women's difference as a justification for conservative retrenchment.

By the early 1990s, the contradictions of liberal pluralism and the acknowledgement of difference as strategies for managing an increasingly contestatory political environment became sufficiently sharp to inspire a rethinking of the Alberta state's approach to governance. After having regularly posted budget surpluses between 1971 and 1986, Alberta accrued a substantial debt throughout the latter half of the 1980s. Mounting public debt and revelations concerning the Alberta government's use of public money to support failing business ventures provided the basis for the argu-ment that the provincial state was a poor fiscal manager and had lost control of spending. However, as this analysis of Alberta's fiscal situation was developed, the emphasis shifted from the public subsidization of private business ventures to spending levels in the areas of health, educa-tion, and social services. And not only did these services represent the state's greatest expense, their associated ministries were also the most directly involved in claimsmaking and the most familiar with the politics of pluralism.

Out of this situation emerged the impetus for a dramatic transforma-tion in the form of the state itself. It is this transformation that provides the focus of discussion in Chapter 5. For those arguing that the Alberta state had lost control of its fiscal management capacity and that spending reductions were the means to reassert that control, political contestation was viewed as a divisive process, one that was not conducive to efficient public management, and a distraction from the facilitation of the effective functioning of the market. A neoliberal project of state restructuring was, thus, highly attractive since it involved the evacuation of politics from the realm of the state. This discounting of the liberal democratic state's implicit obligation to ensure the equality and well-being of citizens, or at least engage in some debate about how well-being might be achieved, represented a radical departure from the welfare state form. It was not simply that some, specific claimsmakers had temporarily lost their political legitimacy, but rather that state agents no longer considered access to, provision of, and debate over public resources to be a matter of citizen entitlement.

The impetus for the adoption of a neoliberal state form was twofold. First, fiscal crisis brought on by economic recession, falling oil prices, and developments in the international political economy propelled decision-makers to address the provincial state's weakening fiscal health. Second, the expanding reach of the political realm that accompanied the incorporation of social movements and their demands within the ambit of state policy initiated a reaction, both from the social movements themselves, the members of which were uncomfortable with the skewing of their demands when operationalized in state policy, and by opponents of these groups who viewed the expansion of the state as an infringement on the freedom of the individual and the market.[20] As a result, the state's capacity to articulate social consensus was challenged and the need for a rearticulation of the state's role was intensified.

Sociologist Anna Yeatman argues that the evacuation of politics from the public realm is a central motivation and function of the neoliberal state. The rationale for this evacuation is as follows:

Where there can be no consensus derived from a shared culture of orientation to…transcendental grounds, the consequence for truth and justice is simple. Some other approach than that of basing them in shared transcendental grounds has to be found. If this approach is consensualist in the sense of requiring agreement on how to approach decisions concerning truth and justice, there is no guarantee that this agreement is anything more than a highly provisional and pragmatic adaptation to the conditions of contestation over these values, and how they are to be interpreted.[21]

If the probability of on-going conflict is viewed as negative, it follows that ridding the state of its redistributive functions and, hence, of the need to articulate some inevitably contestatory notion of "the good," will allow proponents of the neoliberal state to reimpose a more lasting consensus around an apparently apolitical and minimalist notion of the state. If the state is no longer the site at which claims for democracy, equality, and justice are to be made, it need no longer concern itself with the difficult moral questions with which politics is so intimately concerned.

The adoption of a neoliberal state form and its ensuing techniques of governance have had an enormous impact on the practice of claimsmaking generally, and feminist claimsmaking in particular. Formal equality and liberal pluralism are pale cousins to neoliberal practices of delegitimation. The branding of claimsmakers as "special interests," the lack of accountability for public-service delivery resulting from restructuring and privatization and the adoption of private-sector performance standards have overwhelmed long-range concerns for well-being, equity, and a more democratic and inclusive polity.

The development of the neoliberal state in Alberta has not, however, been entirely successful in evacuating politics from the realm of the state. Organizing on the part of socially progressive and morally conservative groups, particularly around issues of health care, education, and human rights, as well as Supreme Court decisions on sexual orientation and gun control, have ensured the continued presence of moral issues on the province's political agenda. Additionally, as much as the Klein government has been remarkably impolitic in its denunciation of various social groups, including women, there is also some evidence of a grudging acknowledgement of the political liabilities associated with an overly zealous approach to the elimination of programs directed at vulnerable Albertans. For example, despite the certainty that the Klein government would disband the Alberta Advisory Council on Women's Issues, as per the sunset clause in the council's founding legislation, the Klein government nonetheless felt compelled to hold a public consultation with Alberta women concerning alternative means of communication between women and the provincial state. Similarly, after announcing that kindergarten funding would be reduced by 50 per cent, the Klein government was forced to backtrack when it became clear that the public would not tolerate budget restraint on the backs of five-year-olds, particularly when the government was also announcing a budget surplus. The development of a new state form in Alberta, then, cannot simply be read as a straightforward, unimpeded stripping of welfarism for neoliberalism. Popular resistance and electoral politics have seen to this.

The recent history of feminist organizing in Alberta demonstrates the complexity of the relationships between power and resistance. Even in a province noted for its lack of meaningful political contestation, it has not been a simple matter for the state to rebuke demands for greater inclusion. Shifts in economic fortunes, the influence of alternative approaches to governance, and the persuasiveness of claimsmakers have disrupted the most single-minded legislators in the pursuit of their political agendas.

In insisting that Alberta politics are more contentious than is popularly understood, I do not wish to suggest that my refutation is as simple as noticing that feminists have put their shoulders to the wheel of the Alberta state and, after much resistance, made it budge. The political dynamics explored in this book operate both within and among the state, feminist organizations, and civil society. State forms and strategies of governance may help the political observer to narrow the range of possibilities, but they cannot assure, with accuracy, what is to come. It is this unpredictability that gives one hope that, even under a government on autopilot, the struggle for equality will continue.[22]

The Big Boom and a "Resounding Thud of Nothingness"

FEMINIST CLAIMSMAKING IN THE CONTEXT OF AFFLUENCE

THE *CALGARY HERALD* reported on 8 December 1970 that the Royal Commission on the Status of Women (RCSW) had been received with "a resounding thud of nothingness [that] stirred the city's women into a buzzing mass of lethargy."[1] With regard to feminist activists, the *Herald* spoke too soon. But if one was to characterize the response of the Alberta state to women's demands during this first decade of feminism's second wave, the thud metaphor is profoundly accurate.

In the summer of 1971, the Conservative Party, led by Peter Lougheed, defeated the long-standing Social Credit government. This was the first election in Alberta's history in which the representation of urban voters surpassed that of rural voters within the legislature.[2] Throughout the postwar period, the province had enjoyed the benefits of its oil wealth. The dramatic increase in oil prices that followed the Organization of Petroleum Exporting Countries (OPEC) cartel in 1973 ensured that Alberta's economic growth in the 1970s would be unprecedented. The Lougheed Conservatives ushered the province into a new-found secularism and cosmopolitanism associated with the rapid expansion of the province's cities and the wealth generated by the oil boom.[3] In some respects, the philosophy of governance embraced by the Conservative Lougheed government was not markedly different from its Social Credit predecessor. However, the intensification of state interventionism over which the Conservatives presided and the social dynamics that emerged as a result of rapid population growth and a booming economy represented a significant shift in the social and moral fabric of the province.

For Alberta's feminist movement, the growing political salience of urban areas, economic growth, the expansion of the provincial state, the impetus of federal initiatives, and the inspiration of feminist organizing throughout the country, suggested that the time had finally come for women to challenge their social and economic subordination within society. The emergence of "status of women" groups throughout the province and efforts to lobby the government for the establishment of an advisory body on women's issues are indicative of the structures and targets deployed by early organizations of Canadian feminism's second wave. Despite the growth of the state and public spending that characterized this period, however, public compensation for social and economic inequality was not a significant objective on the provincial state's agenda. The ambitions of feminists were circumscribed by the provincial government's insistence that formal equality, as enshrined in provincial human rights legislation, should be sufficient recognition of women's political legitimacy. The state's failure to acknowledge the force of sexual difference in the organization of social life regularly frustrated feminist claimsmakers in their efforts to persuade the state that equality was not "sameness" but would require responses particular to the needs of marginalized groups. Further, Ottawa's position as friend to women's groups and foe to the Alberta government bestowed an additional challenge on the province's feminist organizations.

For the Alberta government, Ottawa had assumed the status of "the enemy" in the federal-provincial struggle over oil revenues and pricing. Ottawa's loathsome reputation had two significant implications for feminist activism in Alberta. First, the assessment of the federal government as thwarting the realization of Alberta's economic potential by attempting to keep the price of oil below world levels inspired the formation of a social consensus around the sanctity of provincial state policy. The possibility of democratic debate within the province was stifled in the interests of maintaining a united front with which to "fight the feds."[4] Second, many feminist organizations in Alberta chose to counter the recalcitrance of the provincial state to recognize their political legitimacy and the worthiness of their initiatives by availing themselves of federal funding, provided, primarily, through the Secretary of State Women's Program. In an era when siding with the federal government was akin to treason, this alliance between Alberta feminists and the Canadian government, tenuous though it was, likely further undermined the legitimacy of provincial feminists.[5]

The emergence and growth of the welfare state have often been associated with policies designed to ensure a level of equity among citizens. A concern for social justice, however, did not figure in the expansion of the Alberta state during the oil boom. Instead, the growth of the state was fuelled by the needs of oil producers, the various service industries that the oil and gas sector supported, and the increasingly affluent members of the middle class whose work allowed them to benefit from the province's growing prosperity. This focus was justified on the basis of the regional character of the province's economy and on the inadequacy of the markets on which that economy relied.[6] By contrast, those people subjected to the social displacements that emerged out of rapid population growth and economic expansion found their crises framed in terms of individual fallings or were simply ignored. The seeming ease with which wealth was accumulated during this period could be used to support the view that systemic inequality could be alleviated by working harder, pulling up one's bootstraps, and taking advantage of the opportunities of a booming economy.

Still, for feminists and social critics, the connection between rapid growth and the problems of social dislocation was clear. Alberta soon had the inauspicious honour of having Canada's highest rates of suicide, divorce, abortion, and teenage pregnancy.[7] As historians Howard Palmer and Tamara Palmer argued, "Many individuals and couples, lacking family support systems, could not stand the stress of a boom-bust economy that fostered big dreams, and produced confused values and identities."[8] Yet, despite the mounting statistical evidence and the enrichment of provincial coffers, provincial state spending on income and social supports for those in need remained inadequate. A letter from a minister without portfolio to the chairmen [sic] of the province's Preventive Social Services Boards provides ample illustration of the government's stinginess:

> The government has made it abundantly clear it intends to restrict its expenditures…There is…a growing concern for the need to evaluate what we are doing as there seems to be almost an insatiable appetite for all forms of social services. Considering the overall effects of budget restraint, of annualizing the present projects, of a continuing inflation factor, as well as the concern for cost effectiveness, I am anticipating that there will be little or no money available for new projects in the next fiscal year.[9]

In addition to the weakness of the social supports that characterized the peculiar shape of Alberta's welfare state, provincial officials were also slow to recognize that incorporating equality-seeking groups within the policy-making process was a logical extension of the moral framework supporting the welfare state. Unlike both the federal and Quebec governments, Alberta did not entertain the strategy of enhancing the provincial state's legitimacy through a process of social inclusion and expanded social entitlements. Instead, most elected representatives and some civil servants resisted the adoption of the techniques of governance, such as liberal pluralism, that were characteristic of the welfare state. In the context of an economic boom, the political costs of alienating groups perceived as marginal were minimal. Still, the continued exclusion of legitimate groups tended to draw the state into growing controversy, as its policies were increasingly revealed as benefiting the privileged. After the world price of oil plummeted in the early 1980s, the government lost its capacity to gloss over social strife and political exclusion with the balm of growing wealth.

The following examples of feminist encounters with the Alberta state during the oil boom of the 1970s demonstrate women's efforts to insist on the welfare state's implicit promise of equality and the various articulations of resistance that greeted their initiatives. These encounters demonstrate the intensity of the resistance to feminists' modest demands but also reveal the provincial state's slow acknowledgement that governance of a modern welfare state must at least appear to be considering the concerns of a wider array of citizens.

■ FEMINIST CLAIMSMAKERS

Perhaps what is most remarkable about many of the feminist organizations that emerged during the 1970s in Alberta is the limited character of their demands. While clearly committed to the goal of women's equality, their initial approaches to the provincial state were, for the most part, conciliatory, patient, and measured. The influence of the Royal Commission on the Status of Women (RCSW) can be seen in their initiatives. Feminist organizations appeared confident that the reasonableness of their objectives would be apparent to provincial policy makers. It would not take many encounters with the state, however, to deflate their hopefulness, inspire more radical positions, and set in motion a reconceptualization of how best to achieve sexual equality.

■ CALGARY STATUS OF WOMEN ACTION COMMITTEE AND THE *CALGARY WOMEN'S NEWSPAPER*

In 1974 the Calgary Status of Women Action Committee (CSWAC) was formed to act as a steering committee for the establishment of a provincial advisory council on the status of women. However, the provincial government's objection to the formation of such a council persuaded CSWAC to shift its focus to specific issues of concern to women and to serve a co-ordinating function among local women's groups.[10] Its primary mechanism for this effort was the publication of a monthly women's newspaper, an endeavour that lent the organization a stature incommensurate to its actual active membership.[11]

CSWAC's small size and limited funds meant that the newspaper budget was a constant concern for the organization. Funds from government sources were certainly available but, as feminist groups throughout the country would eventually recognize, the stipulations of the granting body could skew the recipient's objectives and strategies. CSWAC's decision to raise funds for the *Calgary Women's Newspaper* through participation in casinos, as a nonprofit charity, landed the group on the horns of this dilemma. Although the province did not articulate clear rules with regard to the granting of casino applications to nonprofit groups, its unofficial policy was to ensure that only the most politically benign of organizations would be successful.[12]

One indication of this policy is provided in the Alberta Attorney General Department's explanation for the initial rejection of CSWAC's casino application in 1977. According to CSWAC, the "legal department of the Attorney General declared that improving the status of women was not of benefit to the community and therefore, not charitable."[13] CSWAC successfully appealed this decision, but later applications were consistently rejected, with unofficial reports that the group's politics were to blame. Indeed, the group's lack of political focus may, in fact, have resulted from this confrontation between CSWAC's need for substantial sums of money to maintain the *Calgary Women's Newspaper* and this undeclared requirement for apoliticism on the part of the Attorney General's department.[14]

In the early days of CSWAC, members frequently contended with the degree to which political action would frame the group's activities. The minutes of a board meeting in May of 1979 note that a member's request that CSWAC endorse candidates running for the New Democratic Party had to be refused because it would be a violation of CSWAC's status as a "non-political charitable organization."[15] A *Calgary Herald* article from 1978 observed that some of CSWAC's members "wondered if CSWAC wasn't spending too much time in political lobbying and frightening away the everyday woman...[while other] members were concerned that more women learn how to lobby and explain the issues comfortably without becoming angry and defensive in everyday encounters."[16]

Ultimately, the demands of the paper would contribute to a serious crisis for the organization. The constant pursuit of funding sources, as well as the presence of paid staff whose duties were solely directed to the production of the paper, created a situation in which other issues identified by CSWAC as priorities were often sidetracked. Board meetings were consumed with newspaper business. In January of 1979, in response to rapidly falling attendance, the organization decided to replace its monthly general membership meetings with quarterly socials.[17] This shift away from involving the membership in the political work of the board precipitated a further decline. In February 1983, an emergency meeting was held to consider disbanding the CSWAC.[18]

As long as the publication of the Calgary Women's Newspaper remained viable, CSWAC's difficulties surrounding its political focus were a secondary concern to the organization. However, with the reduced availability of financial resources and the threatened closure of the newspaper, the group was forced to reconsider its objectives. The lack of a focus beyond the paper brought the organization to a crisis. Interestingly, this crisis was not precipitated by disillusionment with the project of exacting social change through claimsmaking with the state, although the provincial government's repeated rejection of CSWAC's casino applications was, doubtless, a disheartening experience. Rather, while publishing insightful feminist analyses of current political issues, thus raising expectations surrounding the possibility of exacting change, the organizational capacity to realize those expectations was weak. The group had failed to articulate and achieve clear goals. CSWAC would retreat from the brink of collapse, but it would not reclaim its centrality to the Calgary feminist community.

■ OPTIONS FOR WOMEN AND MATERNITY LEAVE

The Edmonton-based group Options for Women (OFW) was similar to CSWAC in the breadth of its mandate, but considerably larger in terms of membership and more directly concerned with the process of claims-

making with the state. The OFW grew out of a western Canadian conference on women held in 1973. The organization was founded in October of
that year as a nonprofit, nonpartisan group. Its objectives were to promote
greater awareness of the status of women, press for the implementation of
the recommendations of the RCSW, and initiate and co-ordinate action
aimed at increasing options for women in Edmonton.[19] Among the priorities identified by the organization were amending the federal Indian Act to
ensure equality of status for Aboriginal women, revising matrimonial property legislation, developing a nonsexist curricula for Alberta school boards,
and improving the situation of women in the workplace.[20] The founding
members of the organization felt that the best approach to advancing their
concerns was to be nonthreatening, conciliatory, and conservative. As
noted in the minutes of the founding meeting of the organization, "Options
for Women should work on good public relations using conservative diplomatic means to avoid the labeling as a radical group, and thereby gain
'respectable' public recognition."[21]

Among the most notable initiatives undertaken by the OFW was its
campaign for maternity-leave legislation for women employed in the
private sector. Unlike so many other feminist campaigns in the 1970s,
maternity-leave legislation was actually passed, and within a very short
period after the initiation of efforts to persuade the government to undertake legislative change. Yet the feminist victory surrounding maternity
leave would also underscore the on-going weaknesses of the province's
human rights code, the Individual Rights Protection Act (IRPA), in ensuring
equality rights for women, and would illuminate the limits of the provincial
government's willingness to intervene in the private sector in order to
achieve a social good.

The catalyst for the OFW's maternity-leave campaign was a 1973 amendment to the Labour Act in which a discretionary power of the Industrial
Relations Board to implement maternity-leave provisions was withdrawn
from the Act on the basis that maternity leave was discriminatory. Since
maternity leave provided an unequal benefit to women, it contravened the
IRPA.[22] Because the provincial government insisted that individuals rather
than groups should be the focus of human rights protection, women found

their campaigns for equality confronted by the argument that a program designed to redress group oppression was illegal because it treated some individuals differently than others. The fact that women's capacity to bear children did, indeed, make them different from men, was of little consequence. All people were to be treated the same way, even if that meant that all people were to be treated like men.

The OFW chose 1975, International Women's Year, to lobby the government to reconsider its position on maternity leave. The OFW argued that maternity-leave legislation should protect women from dismissal on the basis of pregnancy, that women should be assured their jobs with the same salary and benefits upon returning from leave, and that they be paid during their maternity leave.[23] By autumn the lobbying efforts of the OFW and other women's groups and growing discontent with the government's inactivity surrounding International Women's Year finally pushed the government to reverse its amendment to the Labour Act. The Board of Industrial Relations was given the discretion to order employers to provide maternity leave notwithstanding the IRPA.[24] Overcoming the limits of the IRPA by carving out exemptions to the Act would prove to be a favoured, though dubious strategy for dealing with rights-based claims.

With the potential impediment of the IRPA set aside, the Cabinet moved quickly to pass maternity-leave legislation. In uncharacteristic fashion, particularly in an area concerning women, the government pushed the bill through the legislative process in only fourteen working days.[25] Not surprisingly, however, the legislation was both inadequate and unpopular.

The legislation provided women with fourteen weeks of unpaid leave and stipulated that maternity leave could not exceed twelve weeks immediately preceding the estimated date of delivery and six weeks following the birth of the child.[26] Critics of the legislation focused on the brevity of the leave, the lack of discretion to be exercised by the employee in determining when she would take maternity leave, and the lack of any provision for paternity leave or for adoption.[27] The speed with which the legislation was passed, however, did not allow for these concerns to be addressed in the Act. Mothers of new-borns employed in the paid workforce would be forced to comply with the terms of the legislation or forfeit their jobs.

The particular formulation of the legislation provided the government with the appearance of addressing social policy needs but without incurring any associated costs. Additionally, the legislation allowed the government to address the needs of women in a framework that posed little challenge to "traditional" notions of women as mothers. While maternity leave ostensibly addressed the needs of women who were both workers and mothers, the limitations of the legislation suggested a strong bias in favour of a single-income, two-parent family model. The fact that maternity leave was to be unpaid indicated the government's belief that the income women earned in the paid workforce was not essential to family income. A woman with a new baby, and perhaps other children as well, was to be supported solely by her husband's income. Certainly the absence of provisions for paternity leave indicated the government's thinking on who bears the responsibility for caring for children. But most revealing of the nuclear-family model operating underneath the government's maternity-leave legislation was the dearth of government-subsidized infant care in the province.[28] In the absence of good-quality and accessible child care, the Alberta government's maternity-leave provisions would not ensure that women had equal opportunities in the labour force.

■ ALBERTA STATUS OF WOMEN ACTION COMMITTEE– JOINT INITIATIVES

The Alberta Status of Women Action Committee (ASWAC) was formed out of OFW as the co-ordinating body for a series of regional meetings sponsored by the Secretary of State Women's Program. The objective of the meetings was to determine unmet needs in the various regions of the province, strategize for the attainment of those recommendations of the RCSW that had not yet been met by the province, decide whether improving the quality of life for the province's women would best be achieved through legislation and programs or through education, and recommend the type of structure that would be most suitable for realizing women's equality.[29] The regional meetings were held in the spring of 1976 and culminated in a provincial conference at which ASWAC was officially founded as Alberta's first provincial feminist organization.

The provincial meeting of 1976 also produced the raw material that would form the basis of *Joint Initiatives: A Goal for Women and Government in Alberta*. This extensive brief to the provincial government articulated a series of recommendations involving the state, women's groups, and society in the achievement of women's equality. In a conciliatory style indicative of the optimism of the early days of second-wave feminism, ASWAC asserted:

> The route to change is one of joint initiatives between the individual on the one hand and the government on the other. Obviously, the full responsibility for expanding choices cannot rest on government, but in our view it must do something and it must do something more than to legislate in areas of concern. It must initiate policies, programs and structures, and it must be prepared to treat the problems most associated with women as social rather than family concerns.[30]

The main objective of *Joint Initiatives* was to propose a set of structures through which the needs and demands of women could be addressed at both the political and bureaucratic levels of the state. These structures included:

1. A cabinet committee on equal opportunity and the appointment of a minister responsible for the status of women;
2. A bureaucratic link to the cabinet committee in the form of a secretariat, "the members of which would be drawn from existing senior positions in relevant departments and agencies";
3. A Women's Secretariat that would oversee the review of all government policies affecting women;
4. A Citizen Council on the Status of Women to "allow for meaningful citizen input at a time when sensitivity to women's experience and existing inequities is urgently needed."[31]

These proposed structures were almost uniformly rejected by the Lougheed government, then enjoying strong electoral popularity and economic growth. They would eventually, in more precarious political and economic times, be established.

One of ASWAC's primary objectives in proposing these structures was to ensure that the government would not dispense with its concerns through the tokenism of setting up a single agency to deal with women's issues.[32] A sex-specific government agency would allow the government to claim that it was taking steps to ensure women's equality, and might thus allow elected officials to avoid questions surrounding the more difficult challenges involved in improving the everyday lives of women. More dangerously, a single agency might also serve as a quarantine for feminist activism, thus restricting claimsmaking to a potentially isolated, poorly funded, and politically powerless agency.

The government's response to ASWAC's brief was initially congenial, at least in the context of private meetings with government ministers.[33] However, the tone of ASWAC's relationship with the provincial state was ultimately set by the government's official response to *Joint Initiatives* as delivered by Hugh Horner, the deputy premier, at the organization's first annual meeting in October of 1976. Predictably, the deputy premier sang the praises of the Individual Rights Protection Act, reiterating its significance as legislation to which all other provincial laws must comply. While recognizing that equality could not be achieved through a legislative act, he nonetheless claimed that "we have equality in Alberta." He continued, "Fortunately, attitudes eventually do change and in retrospect, society looks back at the original issue and doesn't really remember what the fuss was all about in the first place!" In response to ASWAC's proposals for government structures directed at ensuring women's equality, Horner stated that the government already had the necessary mechanisms in place in the form of various cabinet committees and, moreover, that a minister responsible for the status of women would be an act of discrimination against women. He stated:

Such a Ministership would suggest that women are incapable of looking after themselves and would suggest that they need special protection. My understanding of the aspirations of the women in Alberta is one which indicates to me that they do not want "special status" but equality! Further I believe that women can take care of themselves and that they do an excellent job in getting their views across to all segments of society, including Government.[34]

The afternoon was marked by a number of other unfortunate comments and heated altercations between the women in attendance and Horner, not the least of which included the exchange concerning matrimonial property cited in Chapter 1.[35] It was an inauspicious beginning for ASWAC, at least in terms of the government's receptivity to the group's ideas. Nonetheless, the animosity generated by the encounter was a catalyst for action.

ASWAC persisted with its demands for government structures designed to address the concerns of the province's women. In February of 1977, ASWAC met with Lou Hyndman, minister of federal and intergovernmental affairs. Hyndman proved to be a more diplomatic emissary than the deputy premier, inspiring ASWAC members to inform Hyndman that they would recognize him as their link to the Cabinet Committee on Social Planning and as the unofficial minister responsible for the status of women.[36] Hyndman responded, however, that he could not be considered the unofficial minister responsible for the status of women since, in the government's view, "all ministers have an awareness of and sensitivity towards equal opportunity issues."[37] Further, he stated:

> We do not see the desirability of a Cabinet Committee on Equal Opportunity because the Social Planning Committee and other committees are now performing this function. It also follows that an enlarged bureaucracy involving an ad hoc secretariat, a women's secretariat and a citizens' council would not be necessary.[38]

Nearly a year later, however, Hyndman was more favourably inclined towards ASWAC. Although still resisting cabinet and bureaucratic structures, the need for provincial representation at national meetings of provincial advisory councils on women led Hyndman to suggest that ASWAC members serve as the province's representatives.[39] ASWAC refused to allow the government to address its national obligations so easily. Instead, it continued to press for an advisory council, arguing that, as a young organization, ASWAC lacked the funds to send representatives to national meetings and, in any event, members would not be able to vote at these meetings since ASWAC itself did not constitute a government-appointed Advisory Council on the Status of Women.[40]

Perhaps sensing a thaw in the provincial government's position surrounding the appointment of an advisory council, ASWAC stepped up its lobbying campaign in the first half of 1978. The organization printed several thousand postcards to be distributed to its members and supporters, who would in turn mail the postcards to their MLAs and to the premier. Valentine's Day and Mother's Day served as the focus for this campaign, with the cards proclaiming: "Love is not enough, Alberta women need an advisory council on the status of women."[41] While the campaign was certainly innovative and attracted a great deal of media and public attention to the cause, the government remained steadfast in its opposition to the establishment of an advisory council.

ASWAC was slightly more successful, however, in its efforts to persuade the government to appoint a minister responsible for the status of women. Early in 1979, Hyndman asked ASWAC to provide him with a rationale for creating such a cabinet responsibility.[42] In May of that year the Cabinet agreed to set up a rotating system of responsibility in which the ministers of social services, labour, advanced education, and the Attorney General would each take the mantle of women's issues for one year.[43] While the government supported this rotating structure with the argument that "all ministers and all departments should constantly be aware of and sensitive to the needs of women to ensure equality of opportunity in all policies and laws," feminists were unsure about how to read the government's sudden willingness to concede some ground to their demands. Lougheed's practice in managing his Cabinet was to appoint ministers who would maintain their portfolios for the duration of the government's term of office in order to build consistency and expertise into the conduct of the province's affairs. The use of a rotating structure in the case of the new portfolio thus suggested that women's issues was not an area that required the development of expertise or one that would benefit from constancy in political representation. Certainly, the practice of rotating responsibility proved very frustrating for those involved in the province's women's groups, who were forced, on an annual basis, to educate a new minister regarding the history of their struggles with the province, as well as the issues with which they were currently concerned.[44] Hence, while the government's concession was a breakthrough, the limitations surrounding the government's particular approach to the establishment of the portfolio lent a sense of precariousness to their achievement.

■ MATRIMONIAL PROPERTY CAMPAIGN

The struggle to reform matrimonial property legislation was the primary object of feminist activism in Alberta in the 1970s. Virtually every women's group in the province submitted briefs on the issue and all of them, from the most conservative to the most radical, advocated implementation of legislation based on the principle of deferred sharing—that property acquired over the course of a marriage should be divided evenly between the marriage partners upon the dissolution of the marriage.[45] ASWAC's role in educating the public about the issue and in grassroots organizing was central in bringing pressure to bear upon the provincial government. Less inspiring, was the manner in which the Alberta government chose to address this campaign for women's equality.

As noted in Chapter 1, the issue of matrimonial property appeared on the national political agenda in response to a Supreme Court ruling asserting that financial contribution should form the basis of entitlement to property upon the dissolution of a marriage. Since Irene Murdoch had only provided her labour, she was not entitled to half of the farm that she and her husband had operated over the course of their relationship. The resulting outcry from women's groups and the legal community and a recommendation from the RCSW persuaded Alberta's Social Credit government to ask the Institute of Law Research and Reform to "study the feasibility of legislation which would provide that, upon the dissolution of the marriage, each party would have a right to an equal share in the assets accumulated during the marriage."[46]

The Big Boom and a "Resounding Thud of Nothingness" 33

On the basis of responses to a provincially distributed questionnaire and the Institute's own study, the Institute released its report in the fall of 1975. The majority of the report's authors recommended that the Alberta government enact deferred sharing with some provision for the exercise of discretionary power by a judge. In the view of women's groups, however, the Institute's report fell short in that it recommended that the new law should not apply retroactively.[47] Without retroactivity, they argued, the contributions of women like Irene Murdoch would continue to be unrecognized by the courts.[48] CSWAC suggested that couples married previous to the enactment of a new law should be given the opportunity to opt-out of the deferred sharing scheme.[49]

The level of public activism that the Institute's work had generated created high expectations that the government would act quickly on the report's recommendations. But lack of consensus within the Conservative caucus, delayed the introduction of legislation until the end of the spring legislative sitting of 1977.[50] Ignoring the Institute's recommendations, the government proposed an elaborate form of judicial discretion involving nineteen criteria for the division of marriage property. The government's bill provided no indication as to how the various criteria were to be weighted, nor did it propose that the courts begin from the premise that marriage is an equal partnership.[51] Particularly remarkable, however, was the government's desire to have the bill die on the order paper, encourage public discussion over the summer, and draft a new bill in the next legislative session. As a member of Options for Women pointed out:

> There has already been more public concern evidenced on this issue than any matter dealt with by this government. The alleged lack of public opinion cannot continue to be used by this Government as an excuse for their own lack of action. We must guard carefully against an attempt to wait until the public is so discouraged and frustrated that this Government can safely do nothing; or introduce piece-meal legislation that attempts to put a band-aid on a festering sore.[52]

Despite its stated desire for public input, the government did little to inform the public about the proposed legislation. By contrast, Women's groups, undertook an impressive public education effort. Over the summer and fall of 1977, and with the financial support of the Institute for Law Research and Reform, the Norwood Women's Collective and ASWAC organized 104 workshops, collected 5,000 names on a petition, inspired a flurry of brief writing, co-ordinated an extensive media campaign, and, through the deployment of another postcard campaign, deluged the premier's office with more mail on a single issue than the government had ever received.[53]

The outcome of this intensive organizational initiative was a rapid increase in ASWAC's membership and in the organization's profile throughout the province. Yet in terms of legislative change, the results were insignificant.[54] Government ministers continued to insist that deferred sharing was unfair. In an argument reminiscent of that provided by Hugh Horner to ASWAC in the fall of 1976, Al "Boomer" Adair wrote to CSWAC:

> An arbitrary fifty-fifty split would cause varying degrees of injustice in most cases. For example, an arbitrary fifty-fifty split would mean that an industrious woman married for years to an alcoholic who did not work at all and had accumulated nothing would be forced to give him one half of her property. A wife who married a millionaire solely to get his property could divorce him after a short time and take half of his holdings.[55]

Despite Adair's comments surrounding the unfairness of the "arbitrary fifty-fifty split," he stated, in the same letter, that "it is likely…that Alberta judges will start from the basis that a fifty fifty split is desirable and then modify their positions as the particular case dictates."[56] The Murdoch case, however, gave ample evidence that Alberta judges could not be relied upon to presume equality between spouses.

Ironically, the government also argued that deferred sharing was too complex and that it would involve cumbersome legislation. Further, the government refused to consider amending the legislation to apply retroactively, arguing that retroactivity was unfair and that opting out of the legislation would be an unsatisfactory resolution to the problem since many people would be unaware of the option to do so.[57]

The Big Boom and a "Resounding Thud of Nothingness"   35

Seven years after the Social Credit government asked the Institute of Law Research and Reform to study the feasibility of deferred sharing, the Alberta government finally passed new matrimonial property legislation. The new law, however, bore few marks of the concerns that had given rise to its formulation. It did not acknowledge marriage as an equal partnership and only slightly modified the significance of financial contribution to the determination of the ownership of matrimonial property. If the success of feminist claimsmaking was to be judged solely on the basis of impacts on policy and legislation, the effort amassed around reform of the matrimonial property regime could only be interpreted as a bust. The government shunned the findings of surveys and workshops and ignored petitions in support of deferred sharing. Yet the public education efforts of ASWAC and many other women's groups in the province, while not achieving the desired legislative change, substantially increased awareness surrounding the issue itself. Women's activism around matrimonial property helped to increase support for and membership in feminist organizations. The response of the government clearly demonstrated its disregard for the results of grassroots activism and revealed the disjuncture between the government's rhetorical claim regarding the sanctity of equality and its unwillingness to ensure equality in its own legislation.

For ASWAC, though, the failure of its efforts to obtain significant changes to matrimonial property legislation pushed the organization to reconsider its objectives and identity. The idea that social change could emerge through joint initiatives between the state and social movements seemed increasingly unlikely. While the desire to organize for change remained, the target of that activity would be reassessed.

■ ROADBLOCKS TO THE STATE

As the previous discussion made clear, the Lougheed administration was strongly resistant to redressing women's inequality through the incorporation of women's concerns within the institutions of the state. While other provinces set up women's directorates and advisory councils and instituted programs to address the underrepresentation of women in male-dominated workplaces and in the public sector, Alberta chose to address women's demands through recourse to the Individual Rights Protection Act and the Alberta Human Rights Commission (AHRC), which administered the Act. Although the province started the 1970s with a Citizens' Advisory Council, appointed to examine those aspects of the report of the Royal Commission on the Status of Women that fell under provincial jurisdiction, it was disbanded shortly after the passage of the IRPA.

Alberta did have a Women's Bureau, but its purpose was to disseminate information to the public rather than to act as an advocate within the agencies of the state.[58] Moreover, its two employees had a limited understanding of the obstacles facing women in their struggle for equality. In response to a query regarding the wage gap between male and female workers, for example, the director of the Bureau stated that "the trouble with some of the girls is that they won't complain. I advise them to report things to the Board of Industrial Relations. But they say they fear they will lose their jobs."[59] Typically, the fault was said to lie with the individual rather than the structures within which she worked.

■ EQUALITY AND INDIVIDUAL RIGHTS

During the oil boom, the IRPA and the Alberta Human Rights Commission, through which it was administered, were the primary sites where the social justice elements of the welfare state were manifested in the governance of Alberta. The Lougheed government was fiercely proud of the fact that human rights legislation had constituted its first legislative act. Yet the emphasis on individualism, the commission's inability to enforce its decisions, and its inability to investigate discrimination in the absence of a formal complaint are strongly indicative of the shortcomings in the Conservative government's integration of equality principles within public policy.[60]

According to the terms of the IRPA, provincial residents who felt that they had encountered discrimination in the workplace, in the securing of housing, or in the provision of service could seek redress through the complaints process administered by the AHRC. The AHRC was restricted to examining acts of discrimination against individuals rather than groups and had only a weak mandate. The provincial government resisted calls to expand the powers of the AHRC and the relationship between the AHRC's commissioners and their political overseers was cool.

The AHRC articulated its displeasure with the government in several instances. In the commission's annual report for 1974–75, for example, its authors stated:

> If this province is to alleviate the extreme stress placed on the poor, the ignorant, the handicapped, and other disadvantaged groups, it may well be that our government will have to embark on major affirmative action programs, programs that will willingly and knowingly discriminate in favor of these groups. Since no other course of action is likely to alleviate such suffering, the people of Alberta should normally deem affirmative action programs to be programs involving acceptable discrimination.[61]

Yet the government opposed the implementation of such programs and thus forced the commission to judge such initiatives as contraventions of the IRPA.[62]

The AHRC also expressed its displeasure with its political masters through its recommendations for amendments to the IRPA. Changes proposed in 1976 and again in 1978 included:

1. That the Act be broadened to prohibit discrimination on a number of additional grounds: physical characteristics, source of income, sexual orientation, and all ages above sixteen, as well as marital status in all categories;
2. That the Act provide for programs of affirmative action, or reverse discrimination;
3. That the Act streamline the complaint procedure by creating a tribunal that would combine investigative and enforcement powers.[63]

When the government ignored these recommendations in 1976, the commission chose to keep its proposals confidential and "work with the Government in trying to get the changes implemented."[64] In 1978, however, the AHRC abandoned this conciliatory approach and made its frustration with the government a public matter. In a press release in May of 1978, the commission alerted the public that

> although the Speech from the Throne indicated that changes to the Individual's Rights Protection Act would be introduced in the current session of the Legislature, the AHRC has reason to believe that only minor changes, if any, will be made and that the major recommendations, as included in the submission made to the Minister of Labour in December of 1976, will not be made.[65]

Cabinet was unmoved and again rejected the commission's recommendations, this time on the grounds that the Act, though in effect since 1 January 1973, had not had time to "mature."[66] In 1979 the commission opened its monthly meetings to the media and to groups advocating for social change.

Despite the seeming logic, the coolness between the AHRC and its political masters did not give rise to an alliance between the commission and the province's feminists. Indeed, the commission was often hostile to women's demands, particularly around pay equity. ASWAC, in particular, was involved in efforts to persuade the government to implement pay- and employment-equity policies and the AHRC, given its role as guarantor of equality for the province, was the logical target for these initiatives. A study commissioned by the AHRC to examine the status of women in the Alberta public service served as one particular instance of contention. While the study found that there were no formal discriminatory policies within the Alberta public service, its authors also argued that, having accounted for differences in education and job experience between men and women, there remained a considerable discrepancy in the wage rates between the sexes:

> A difference of about $3097 remains which cannot be attributed to differences in qualifications and which is therefore associated with

the sex of the employee. That is, women who are of the same age as men, in the same occupational category, with similar levels of education and years of experience earn about $3097 less per year than men.[67]

The government's response to this report was to dismiss its findings as unsubstantiated due to "technical deficiencies in the study."[68] By 1979, women's groups were not surprised by the government's unwillingness to take the study seriously. The AHRC's reaction was a greater disappointment, however.

Although the commissioners agreed with the report's recommendation that "an office of Equal Opportunity be created ... to oversee the creation of Departmental Affirmative Action Programs," they were less enthusiastic about the implementation of a pay-equity scheme.[69] It was the commission's view that "a meaningful and measurable definition [could not] be given for the concept 'equal pay for work of equal value.'"[70] Moreover, the commissioners argued that such a proposal would never be accepted by the Alberta government because it would go against the free market system, since employers should be able to bargain freely concerning wages and employees; it would impinge on the rights of employers; and it would be opposed by the business community as being too expensive and unworkable.[71]

Yet each of these objections could also be applied to the affirmative action programs that the commission so readily supported. When considered in light of the commissioners' assertions that women had to accept the blame for their unequal position in the labour market since they did not have to accept low-paying jobs, could upgrade their education, and could unionize, it becomes increasingly apparent that the AHRC was either ignorant of or ill-disposed towards the particular plight of women in Alberta society.[72] As long as the unequal treatment faced by women could be viewed in the broad strokes of discrimination that affected a variety of identifiable groups, the commission would be supportive. But in instances of discrimination that were particular to women, the commission was resistant.

An additional example of the commission's perplexing attitude towards women can be found in the AHRC's reluctance to read sexual harassment

40   STATE OF STRUGGLE

as an instance of sexual discrimination within the IRPA. While the commission supported legislative protection against sexual harassment, its commissioners argued that it would be better addressed by criminal sanction rather than the IRPA.[73] This position was justified on the grounds that

> an employer who denies a woman employment or promotional opportunities because of her sex is generally applying this discriminatory policy to *all* women. However, the employer who sexually harasses a female employee will not necessarily harass each and every female that is in his employ. For example, a supervisor might make indecent advances to one female secretary, and not to another. Incidents of sexual harassment generally involve blackmail or indecent assault as opposed to discrimination. For this reason, it may be more appropriately dealt with under the Criminal Code than under the Human Rights Legislation.[74]

There are a number of peculiar elements to this argument. First, while sexual harassment in the workplace may not happen to all women in that workplace, the same might be said of the denial of employment or promotional opportunities. Discrimination occurs when the denial of employment or sexual harassment is consistently directed at members of an identifiable group. The commission's argument would seem to suggest that sexual harassment is not discrimination on the basis of sex, but rather on the basis of desirability or attractiveness. This suggests that the harassment of "desirable" women is not an infringement of human rights. Second, given the emphasis on protection of the *individual* from discrimination, so rigorously underscored in the government's objections to affirmative action programs, the commission's argument that sexual harassment occurs on an individual basis rather than being uniformly targeted at an identifiable group would seem to be at odds with the intent of the legislation.

In any case, sexual harassment was, ultimately, determined to be discrimination on the basis of sex and hence within the purview of the commission. Not surprisingly, however, women bringing sexual harassment complaints to the commission were required to provide evidence of wrong-doing far in excess of that required for other complaints addressed by the AHRC.[75]

While both the government and the AHRC would remain intransigent on the issue of pay equity, the government began to rethink its position on the desirability of "special" programs and, in a very troubling move, amended the IRPA in 1980 to allow the Cabinet to approve exemptions from the Act.[76] While the amendment was apparently intended to work in favour of marginalized groups, women's groups, among many other organizations concerned with human rights, saw this legislation as providing the government with the opportunity to reinforce the existing structure of dominance and subordination, notwithstanding its own human rights legislation. The president of the Canadian Advisory Council on the Status of Women described the new exemption to the IRPA as "an escape clause as big as a barn door"[77] and the Cabinet's acceptance of the proposed change prompted the resignation of three staff members of the AHRC's education wing.[78]

■

BY THE END OF THE 1970S, Alberta's feminist claims-makers had acquired considerable experience in confronting the state and having their demands rejected. Of course, the province's politicians could not completely ignore the emergent women's movement since support from the federal government allowed these groups to sustain their campaigns and women's councils established under federal auspices created an imperative of representation that the provinces had some obligation to address. Additionally, the persistence of the province's organized women's movement persuaded the government to make some concessions, however inadequate. Nonetheless, for all the optimism with which women began the decade and undertook their campaigns for social change, the province's meagre response was, indeed, assessed as a "resounding thud of nothingness."

The disappointment and frustration that resulted from this experience of claimsmaking provoked a reassessment of the state as a target for femi-

42   STATE OF STRUGGLE

nist organizing. If, in a period in which the provincial state had amassed such wealth, its agents could not be persuaded to undertake programs that would improve the lives of the province's least fortunate citizens and establish mechanisms to ensure equality of opportunity for all, it seemed unlikely that these objectives could ever be accomplished. Yet, as social theorists Iris Young and Nancy Fraser have pointed out, in the context of the welfare state, the moments of greatest potential for social change do not lie in times of stability and affluence, but in crisis and uncertainty. But when the first moment of crisis emerged with the collapse of oil prices in 1981, both ASWAC and CSWAC were in organizational disarray and hence ill-disposed to seize the moment.

In insisting that formal equality would meet the needs of the province's women, that women's disadvantages in the workplace could be overcome through individual initiative rather than policy measures, and that women's differences were unimportant to the development of public policy, ministries of the Alberta state resisted feminists' claims for equality and for recognition of the legitimacy of their demands. As the 1970s progressed, however, greater efforts to address women's demands were undertaken on the part of state agents. The cases of maternity leave and matrimonial property legislation can be seen as rough attempts to incorporate women's needs within the ambit of a public policy regime that fostered its strongest ties with oil and gas and agricultural constituencies.

This chapter has introduced a number of the characters and themes that will replay in various states of transformation throughout the remainder of this book. A conservative and co-operative approach to the state and a response characterized by a resort to formal equality and values of self-reliance and liberal individualism, however, are particular to a period when social consensus within the province was strong and a particularly unchallenged form of welfare state prevailed. Given the success of the provincial state in containing political contestation, this was not a period when an inclusive politics or liberal pluralism were needed to maintain the state's legitimacy. As the material conditions underlying Alberta's social consensus began to break down, though, a new dynamic of claimsmaking began to emerge.

Disparate Strategies and Expedient Responses

THE ACQUISITION OF POLITICAL LEGITIMACY IN TROUBLED TIMES

NINETEEN EIGHTY-ONE MARKED the end of Alberta's oil boom. The price of oil reached a peak of $44 a barrel that year before falling in a rapid decline to $39 a barrel in 1983 and $10 a barrel in 1986.[1] Of course, from the vantage point of 1981, it was difficult to know how precipitous this decline would actually be, and what political liabilities might attach themselves to such a profound shift in the fortunes of the provincial economy. Certainly, the ability to enforce social consensus around resistance to the incursions of the federal government on the province's oil wealth was weakened, but it would take some time before provincial policymakers softened their position towards groups whose concerns for social justice challenged the preeminence of the oil and gas sector on the provincial state's political agenda.

The period between 1981 and mid-1986 was characterized by a fragmentation in feminist approaches to the state and a shift in the state's responsiveness to claimsmaking. While there were issues and legislative initiatives that harkened back to the process of claimsmaking in the previous decade, the trajectory of claimsmaking in the first half of the 1980s was more notable for an increased willingness to address the demands of feminists, at least in terms of establishing mechanisms within government to ensure the consideration of sexual difference in the formation and implementation of state policy, and, paradoxically, for the onset of a moral retrenchment around gender identity.

This increasing contestation surrounding the prevailing social order and the challenge to the state's integrity as the guardian and enforcer of social consensus also inspired a more rigorous commitment to fair process on the part of provincial policymakers. The emergence of the antifeminist women's organization, the Alberta Federation of Women United for Families (AFWUF), was a central contributor to this new-found appreciation for clear and consistent rules governing the relationship between state officials and claimsmakers. Procedural fairness allowed state agents to avoid revealing their normative commitments by taking refuge in procedural requirements that were to be applied to all women's groups, whether or not their activities advanced women's equality.

In some instances, however, fair process did not provide a safe haven for policymakers. The passage of the Canadian Charter of Rights and Freedoms and the signing of the United Nations Convention to Eliminate All Forms of Discrimination Against Women (Copenhagen Convention) pushed the provincial government into making a more explicit articulation of its position on women's equality than it might have preferred. The province proved to be very conservative in its audit of statutes requiring revision as a result of the Charter's passage and interpreted the pay-equity clause of the UN Declaration in a very narrow way. Nonetheless, each of these documents required politicians and bureaucrats to consider government policy and legislation in light of their obligations to uphold the terms of these agreements. Rather than simply dismissing feminist demands for the implementation of pay equity as too costly and an impingement on the rights of employers, policymakers now had to provide a justification that directly addressed a provision within the UN Declaration and confront the opposing interpretations offered by feminist advocates. Thus, in the presence of a formal agreement, the provincial state was less able to retreat to the apparently apolitical position of guarantor of fairness and determiner of the public interest in the face of competing demands. To the extent that the provisions of the Charter and the Copenhagen Convention made the substance of justice clear, its signatories were assumed to share the normative underpinnings of the agreement's provisions. If these norms were not shared, or if ambiguity tinged the interpretation of a clause, there was an increased demand on the state to clarify its interpretation.

Another significant contribution to the shift in the provincial state's approach to claimsmaking was its decreased capacity to enforce social consensus around the province's antipathy towards the federal government. While the National Energy Program (NEP) might have borne some of the blame for the weakening of the provincial economy, the federal government could not be scapegoated for the collapse of the world price for oil. In any case, the NEP was effectively dismantled with the signing of the Western Accord in 1985.[2] As well, the 1984 election of the federal Conservatives on a platform of pro-western initiatives, and with the backing of every federal constituency in Alberta, effectively ended the Alberta government's efforts to use the federal government and its focus on Quebec as a means to quash dissent within the province.[3]

In addition to the various campaign promises targeted at western Canadians, the federal Conservatives' campaign strategy was significantly focused on women. This acknowledgement of women's political legitimacy, attributed, in part, to the profile achieved by the women's movement in its advocacy around the Charter's equality rights provisions and manifested in the participation of the federal party leaders in a public debate on women's issues during the election campaign of 1984, helped to undermine the Alberta government's insistence that granting women formal equality would suffice in addressing the conditions associated with women's subordination. Had the Alberta Tories' own political fortunes been more secure, the federal government's commitment to women might have had a weaker demonstration effect for the province. However, the unravelling of political consensus in Alberta recommended that the provincial Conservatives expand their base of support. The province's women, 51 per cent of the population, made a compelling target.

Evidence of Alberta's new-found responsiveness to its federal counterparts with regard to women's issues can be seen in a memo from the minister responsible for women's issues to the premier. The memo stated:

> In light of the new federal government's commitment to act to improve the status of Canadian women, it would seem imperative that, in the near future, we make policy decisions on some of [these] issues [child care, maintenance enforcement, education and training, homemakers' pensions, pay equity]. Those items relating to the Charter of Rights and Freedoms, such as the statute audit and Alberta's position on affirmative action, should receive urgent attention.[4]

While traces of the government's "formal equality" posture in regard to women's issues would continue to be operative, it was clear that a greater willingness to substantively consider the claims of women was now emerging in Cabinet.

Interestingly, as the political necessity for the state to respond to the demands of claimsmakers increased, those groups that had fostered a public profile as claimsmakers in the 1970s became increasingly skeptical about the process of exacting social change by attempting to influence the policymaking process. At the same time, however, antifeminists emerged with the express purpose of countering the growing influence of feminists within provincial politics. Clearly the work of the province's feminists in building on a generalized societal push in the direction of enhanced social and economic power for women was viewed as a significant threat to those invested in maintaining a more conventional and less egalitarian gender order.

Of course, the inward turn and growing skepticism of ASWAC and CSWAC towards the state did not preclude other groups from taking advantage of the improved conditions for claimsmaking or from adopting those conservative lobbying techniques espoused in ASWAC's *Joint*

Initiatives brief. Indeed, even ASWAC, despite being enmeshed in a radical rethinking of its structure and objectives, chose to reaffirm the principles of *Joint Initiatives* at its annual general meeting in 1982.[5] The group most active in pursuing a conventional approach to feminist claimsmaking, however, was the Provincial Committee for a Council on Women's Affairs.[6] Made up of a broad cross-section of women's groups, the committee's campaign for an advisory council would serve as the focal point for women's organizing in the province, much as matrimonial property had done in the previous decade.

This chapter explores the first of a series of shifts in the province's approach to the politics of claimsmaking. The Alberta state's transformation from a position of intense resistance to feminist claimsmakers to a more conciliatory posture is shown through a discussion of the increasing introversion of the feminist movement, the beginnings of antifeminism, and the campaign for, and realization of, state structures directed at the concerns of women. The tensions among formal equality, procedural fairness, and more explicit articulations of support or resistance to demands for women's equality are a unifying theme among the examples presented. They bear witness to early attempts to manage the increase in political contestation that was to become a hallmark of the welfare state.

■ FRAGMENTATIONS AND RECONFIGURATIONS— ALBERTA STATUS OF WOMEN ACTION COMMITTEE

ASWAC and CSWAC began the decade by engaging in thoroughgoing analyses of their objectives and structures. While CSWAC's motivation for this period of reflection resulted from the need to reorient the organization after the demise of the *Calgary Women's Newspaper*, ASWAC's contemplative moment grew out of its frustration with the inertia of the Alberta state. One of the organization's strategists described the impetus for this shift in focus:

Women's understanding of the vast and increasing gap between "their terms" and our own has evolved incredibly...Many of us can no longer stomach the forms of lobbying for legislation and legislative reform which conventionally were based on the deceitful assumption that one simply had to convince decision-makers of the justice of requested changes and that corrective action would follow.[7]

This frustration prompted ASWAC to reorient its activities towards grass-roots organizing. However, this organizational transformation could not be manifested instantaneously. ASWAC had to undergo a rethinking of its organizational structures in order to ensure that the principles it would foster in its interaction with the community would be mirrored within the organization itself.

Among the organization's subsequent structural innovations were the abandonment of *Robert's Rules of Order* and voting procedures and their replacement with a consensus decisionmaking model, the replacement of competitive elections for board positions with a self-selection process, and an attempt to bridge the gap between the organization's volunteer board and its paid staff by including staff members in the administrative decision-making structure, which was renamed the "stoard." The motivation behind each of these changes was to create a more supportive, responsive, and conciliatory process through which to channel the organization's work.

ASWAC members had mixed responses to these organizational initiatives. While many members supported the implementation of alternative structures, they also felt that they had been implemented at the expense of public, political, and educational work.[8] Other ASWAC members took issue with ASWAC's adoption of a consensus decisionmaking model. Their concerns stemmed from the difficulties involved in achieving unanimous agreement in an organization with over 600 members who were widely dispersed throughout the province.[9] Ultimately, however, although the transition to new structural forms was painful and tumultuous, the outcome was an enhanced sense that ASWAC's decisionmaking processes, as well as its activities, conformed to its feminist principles.

In addition to the internal tensions derived from ASWAC's structural reorganization, its new processes also attracted the attention of external bodies. The federal Secretary of State Women's Program, for example, upon observing the dramatic changes in ASWAC's structure, tied the granting of a funding request from ASWAC in 1984 to a review of the organization and its relationship to the Alberta Secretary of State program.[10] The province also found itself unwittingly enmeshed in the consequences of ASWAC's reorganization.

The lack of formality in ASWAC's new structure opened the organization's name to abuse. One notable incident occurred in 1984–85, when a woman from Lethbridge, Flores Langeslag, contacted ASWAC regarding the operation of a referral phone service in that city. ASWAC accepted her on its board with the understanding that she would operate the service in co-ordination with other community groups.[11] Langeslag, however, had other ideas. In a contribution request sent out on ASWAC letterhead, Langeslag transformed the referral service into a nonprofit agency that she claimed was partially funded by the provincial government. The activities this agency was to be involved in were wide-ranging. The letter stated that, while the agency was starting out as a referral service for employment, self-improvement courses, and local and provincial agencies, greater plans were in store. It read, in part:

We also intend to promote and provide training through various courses and workshops; such as, a cottage industry in various creative arts and handicrafts which can be sold province-wide; to begin a cooking school for native women to provide training in cooking techniques from basic to advanced, including nutrition; a driving school for women; to acquire and operate a nursing home; to assist any woman involved in a troubled situation and to expand on other services as required and as our capacity to fulfill needs evolves.[12]

The fact that Langeslag was soliciting funds and promising tax receipts on behalf of an agency that did not exist put ASWAC at risk of being charged with fraud. Moreover, the fact that a number of Lethbridge citizens wrote the minister responsible for women's issues querying provincial funding for such a peculiar agency did not enhance ASWAC's credibility with the minister. While the Women's Secretariat conveyed ASWAC's attempts to disavow the activities of Langeslag to the minister, it was clear that the government was displeased that it was being dragged into a potential scandal on the basis of ASWAC's irresponsibility.[13] To make matters worse, AFWUF seized on the contribution letter as an attempt to catch the government in a contradiction over its claim to the organization that it had not provided money to ASWAC in the previous year. The minister assured AFWUF that no money had been provided to ASWAC or the Lethbridge-based agency and that the letter had been released without the consent of the ASWAC board.

Despite ASWAC's various difficulties, the organization did undertake a number of important challenges to provincial policy in this period. Once the organization's catharsis of 1982–83 had passed, ASWAC embarked on a number of educational and claimsmaking initiatives, notably a campaign to include single and divorced women in the province's widows' pension program, an effort to secure more resources for after-school care, a public education program around pay equity that included lobbying the AHRC, and an attempt to increase the provincial state's involvement in ensuring the payment of maintenance orders. Each of these initiatives incorporated grassroots organizing and coalition building into the process of claims-making as a means to build support for the movement and, in the long run, increase the political force of ASWAC's demands.

In terms of achieving policy change, ASWAC's greatest success lay in its maintenance-payments campaign. In large part, this success rested on ASWAC's ability to convince the provincial government that enforcing maintenance orders would result in a savings to public coffers, since women would be less reliant on social assistance. Moreover, the state's involvement in overseeing the payment of maintenance would help to compel compliance from men who refused to heed the repeated requests of their former partners.

ASWAC devoted energy to the issue of maintenance enforcement in 1984 and 1985. Using Manitoba's program for maintenance enforcement as an example, ASWAC argued that a computerized system that notified debtors of their obligation to pay and tracked payments would help ensure that women actually received the money to which they were entitled. By the fall of 1984, the Attorney General was quoted in the *Edmonton Journal* as stating that, although the government had "concerns" regarding police involvement in civil disputes over maintenance orders, the government was "caving in" to the demands of women's groups to take action on the issue.[14] By August of 1985, a computerized maintenance-enforcement program had been announced and would become operational in February of 1986.[15] The program was to be implemented in two phases with the first phase restricted to the registration of women on social assistance, thereby providing an economic justification for implementation of the new program, while other women would be integrated into the system by January of 1987.[16] ASWAC organized a public information campaign around the program that encouraged women requiring the program to participate and to report back to the organization on their experiences. ASWAC was aware of the limits of such a program in addressing the financial needs of divorced women, especially given the disparity among judicial rulings and the limited capacity of some spouses to meet their obligations due to rising levels of unemployment. Nonetheless, ASWAC applauded the actions of the government.[17] It would take several years before the government would reconsider its advocacy of women in disputes over maintenance enforcement and threaten to link maintenance to access.

For ASWAC, the early 1980s was a turbulent time. Nonetheless, the shift in focus from lobbying the state to a more socially integrated form of claimsmaking based on coalition building and community outreach was seen as a goal worthy of the associated risks. Complicating this new approach, however, was an increasingly heated political environment resulting from the formation of AFWUF. Still, the provincial state's more conciliatory approach towards feminist claimsmakers, although not uniformly responsive to their demands, did create a new context in which to advance a feminist analysis of social provision and initiate campaigns for social change.

■ ALBERTA FEDERATION OF WOMEN UNITED FOR FAMILIES

The early 1980s witnessed the debut of the antifeminist, "pro-family" women's organization Alberta Federation of Women United For Families

(AFWUF), formed in direct response to the threat its members perceived in the feminism of ASWAC. Indeed, ASWAC was a central reference point in AFWUF's attempts to discredit feminist campaigns for women's equality and to advance its "traditional" views on the gender order.

The emergence of AFWUF and its antifeminist objectives can be traced to ASWAC's 1981 annual conference. The conference was a weekend event in which various community groups were asked to lead workshops in their areas of expertise. As part of what was later revealed as an organized strategy, three pro-life women joined ASWAC with the intention of attending a workshop on strategizing against pro-life forces led by members of a Calgary group, Abortion By Choice. The workshop moderator chose to cancel the session, however, upon learning that there were pro-life women in attendance. The moderator argued that the workshop was not intended as a forum for debating the abortion issue, but rather as a discussion of strategy, and that she was not willing to share her strategic insights with these pro-life women.[18] Shortly thereafter, Kathleen Toth, one of the pro-life women, and the president of Campaign Life, announced to ASWAC's president that she would "destroy this organization [ASWAC] if it's the last thing I do. Just watch me."[19] Toth and her associates then left the conference. In light of Toth's threat as well as "past attempts to discredit ASWAC and her statements regarding plans to approach ASWAC's funding sources to have ASWAC funding cut off," the ASWAC membership voted, that afternoon, to revoke her membership.[20]

Given the drama of the event, it is not surprising that it was quickly picked up by the press and that several versions of the story were soon available.[21] Toth contributed to the misinformation, communicating through a Campaign Life press release that "pro-life women from three different areas of the province were told that ASWAC did not welcome their membership" and that "twenty women who had each paid at least $15 registration and membership fee, were told that because of the presence of 'pro-lifers in the room' the workshop was cancelled."[22] The press release also expressed Campaign Life's intention to inform ASWAC's funding sources that ASWAC did not represent pro-life women.

The usefulness of Campaign Life to Toth's ambitions regarding the destruction of ASWAC was, however, limited. Because Campaign Life was focused on a single issue, it lacked the capacity to challenge ASWAC on the breadth of the feminist organization's concerns and initiatives. Moreover, Campaign Life was not a women's organization and hence could not be credibly recast in the mould of an organization representing the many women whose views could not be accommodated by ASWAC. As a result of these practical limitations, Toth joined with several other women to form Alberta Women of Worth, which then changed its name to the Alberta Federation of Women United for Families.

AFWUF borrowed a large portion of its agenda and analysis from the right-wing women's movement in the United States. With the help of Phyllis Schlafly, credited with leading the campaign against the American Equal Rights Amendment, AFWUF developed a definition of the family that was restricted to "two or more people living together related by birth, marriage or adoption."[23] The organization initiated an educational reform campaign specifically targeted at sex education and the morally ambiguous "humanist" curriculum, which it felt should be replaced by both a stricter attention to "the facts" and an increased emphasis on religious education.[24] AFWUF also undertook an effort to promote the career of homemaker primarily through challenging the expansion of child-care facilities, persisted with advocacy around pro-life initiatives, and undertook a multipronged attack against the perceived growth of feminist influence on public policy.[25] AFWUF's most significant and enduring legacy in its campaign against feminist gains, however, resided in the group's espousal of fiscal conservatism. In the early 1980s this emphasis was manifested most productively in the area of funding for women's groups. It was here that AFWUF proved itself most adept in using the logic of pluralist politics for its own ends.

Rather than challenging the legitimacy of public funding for ASWAC, AFWUF argued that because it was a women's organization it should receive funding equal to that of its rival organization.[26] This insistence put government decisionmakers in a difficult position. If they wished to avoid articulating a normative standard regarding the substantive meaning of women's equality, they would have to take up the mantle of being a fair and neutral arbiter among competing claims, and would likely have to provide funding to all groups who met the basic granting criteria. If, instead, they chose to reveal a normative standard, they risked a radical intensification of the politics of claimsmaking as various groups were sure to challenge this standard, regardless of whether it favoured feminists or their opponents.

The response to AFWUF's first salvo in the game of pluralist politics reveals that this new method of managing claimsmakers was not entirely supported by elected officials. The minister responsible for women's issues, Les Young, attempted to avoid the pull of pluralism entirely by proposing that the money provided to ASWAC be withdrawn and that all further requests for funds from women's groups be refused.[27] The minister evidently felt there was greater political gain in removing the state from this particular site of political contestation than in becoming more deeply embroiled within it.

The minister's views, however, were overridden by his political colleagues and staff. In their view, Alberta women were becoming increasingly conscious of the provincial state's refusal to address the limited demands of feminist groups. Given the increasing opposition to the government and an appreciation by party strategists that an intensification of the government's hard line on feminist demands was unlikely to improve the party's position among women voters, support grew for a new, pluralist regime of interaction between the state and civil society. Young's proposal was rejected by the Cabinet Committee on Social Planning, and he was requested to draft a policy proposal for the funding of private organizations and groups.[28] Ultimately, it was decided that funding would be provided to ASWAC, as to other groups, on the condition that the provincial auditor would have the right to ensure that the grant had been dispensed in accordance with the objectives of the organization and the Financial Administration Act.[29] Additionally, it was recommended that the province provide itself with an escape clause giving the minister responsible for women's issues the prerogative to review the process of funding women's organizations.[30] This prerogative would allow the province to alter the rules of claimsmaking should the particular context of the game of pluralist politics in Alberta require either a clearer articulation of a normative frame, or a radical retreat from political contestation.

Unlike the Secretary of State Women's Program, whose funding requirements included a commitment to improving the status of women, the Alberta state made no such stipulation. In avoiding the articulation of a normative standard, a gesture the federal state was willing to make in this instance, Alberta neatly avoided the political maelstrom that would entangle the Secretary of State program once AFWUF and its national variant, Realistic, Effective, Active for Life (REAL) Women, began their campaign to contest the federal government's interpretation of the activities involved in working towards improving the lives of women. Interestingly, once confronted with this demand to substantiate the normative basis on which the Secretary of State program operated, the federal state also sought refuge in the pluralist framework, eventually providing AFWUF with $8,000 for a conference on pornography.[31] However, this retreat was less easily achieved by the federal government as feminist groups were ill-disposed towards allowing the Secretary of State Women's program to revoke its explicit commitment to ensuring that its funds were directed towards activities devoted to the improvement of the status of women.[32]

Drawing from the financial restraint rhetoric of the Reagan administration and plugging into an increasingly generalized feeling in Alberta that the oil wealth of the 1970s had been squandered, AFWUF's nostalgic cry for a return to the days when people lived within their means and relied on their families to attend to their needs was suggestive of a political program that the state could actually afford. While some of the group's initiatives would clearly not be tolerated in an increasingly secular society, the fiscal responsibility portion of their claimsmaking agenda and the commitment to individual responsibility that it implied were compelling to some Alberta policymakers. In the early 1980s, however, the political moment was not yet ripe for AFWUF's message. The group's legitimacy would increase in the second half of the decade, however, when support for deficit reduction began to grow.

■ PROVINCIAL COALITION FOR A COUNCIL ON WOMEN'S AFFAIRS AND THE DEVELOPMENT OF GOVERNMENT STRUCTURES FOR WOMEN

The experiences of the Provincial Coalition for a Council on Women's Affairs, in its efforts to persuade the Alberta government to establish an advisory council, round off this discussion of the Alberta state's shift away from formal equality and towards a pluralist approach in its interactions with feminist claimsmakers. While the coalition would realize its objective, its achievement would also prove to be a radicalizing experience.

The provincial coalition was formed in 1981 as a result of organizational efforts by the Social Issues Committee of the Calgary YWCA. The impetus for the initiative came from the committee's reflections on "the unmet needs of Alberta women, their lack of a unified voice, their lack of access to government, and the lack of research on Alberta women."[33] Despite their awareness of previous, failed efforts to establish an advisory council, members of the Social Issues Committee felt that a concerted effort would have a more positive outcome. However, the perception, particularly on the part of ASWAC, that the Social Issues Committee and the coalition it organized were insensitive to the history of advocacy around an advisory council weakened the capacity of the coalition to present a unified voice. Moreover, in neglecting the experience of these groups, the Social Issues Committee also closed itself off to the lessons these groups had learned about the character of the state's resistance to their demands. Although the province would be more receptive to the coalition, elected officials also ensured that the advisory council, once it was finally established, would serve their political purposes rather than meeting the concerns of the women who organized for the council's formation.

Unlike the members of ASWAC, the original organizers of the coalition were single-minded in their identification of the coalition's objective and were considerably less concerned than their feminist sisters about the process they chose to reach their goal. This single-mindedness and, indeed, the conservative character of the women involved in the initial stages of the initiative inspired a strategy that, at least at the outset of the organizing drive, was uncharacteristic of other feminist groups in the province.

The Social Issues Committee launched its coalition-building initiative in the summer of 1981 by holding meetings with provincial cabinet ministers "regarding the desirability of establishing a Provincial Advisory Council on the Status of Women in Alberta."[34] Over the course of these meetings, the committee learned that the minister of labour was unreceptive to the potential requirement of accepting the advice of an "advisory council." In response, the committee reframed its objective as a "council on women's affairs."[35] The minister also advised the group to consider how representatives to the council would be chosen as, in his view, the failure to devise a selection process that ensured the representation of all women's interests had "severely flawed the Federal Advisory Committee, which is now looked upon as very partisanly political."[36]

This implied desire for inclusiveness, however, had its limits. Women who were considered radical feminists, for example, were not the intended beneficiaries of the minister's cautions and were largely excluded from the coalition's early organizing initiatives. Organizers of the coalition, for example, felt that part of ASWAC's failure in its campaign to establish an advisory council could be explained by the perception, on the part of government, that the group was a radical and lesbian organization.[37] The fact that ASWAC was not invited to early organizational meetings of women's groups in northern Alberta points to the coalition's desire to maintain some distance from groups that might sully its efforts to establish an image of reasonableness.[38] Even in 1985, when the coalition had become increasingly vociferous in its critique of the provincial government's inaction in establishing an advisory council, its organizers continued to maintain a nonthreatening image for the group. One coalition member was quoted in the *Edmonton Journal* as stating: "The difference with our particular committee is that we're not radical—we're just ordinary people. We're wives and mothers and working women."[39]

An additional outcome of the committee's preliminary consultations with state officials was an undertaking to solicit support for the initiative from all regions of the province.[40] To that end, approximately sixty groups representing 40,000 women joined the coalition. There were, however, some complications in this membership drive.[41] Four Jewish women's groups, for example, observed that the coalition's Saturday meetings effectively excluded them from participating. In response, regional organizations of the coalition were asked to consider rescheduling their meeting times in order to accommodate members of the Jewish faith.[42]

A notable lack of support for the coalition's initiative emerged from the United Nurses of Alberta. Contentious labour disputes between the province and nurses did not incline the union to view any positive government gesture towards women as being undertaken in good faith. The union stated that it

> would have a particular concern with a Council of Women's Affairs dependent in any way upon the present Alberta government. As you may be aware, our relationship with the government has been one of confrontation. I believe this type of relationship has been the direct result of this government's apparent inability to recognize or accept, the changes in women today, as well as this government's apparent lack of respect towards organized women workers.[43]

The union also objected to a gender-specific structure on the grounds that it would segregate women and marginalize their concerns as "women's issues" rather than societal issues.

Predictably, the AFWUF was also opposed to efforts to establish an advisory council. AFWUF's objections were leveraged by the presence of "pro-abortion" groups among the coalition's members. Although the coalition itself did not take a stand on the abortion issue, AFWUF's position was that "you can tell the nature of an organization by the company it keeps."[44] In AFWUF's view, disagreements over abortion would result in a lack of clarity in an advisory council's work and underscored AFWUF's argument that "one council cannot represent all Alberta women. The issues which divide us are too profound to admit of compromise."[45]

In a letter to the premier, AFWUF President Kathleen Higgins asserted that "women are not an oppressed group in Alberta" and did not require an advisory council to inform the government of women's needs.[46] AFWUF also attempted to subvert the coalition by challenging its membership. In this regard, AFWUF made a presentation to the annual convention of the

Catholic Women's League, a supporter of the coalition at that time. AFWUF argued that the failure of the coalition to take a pro-life stand made it impossible for AFWUF to join. It encouraged the Catholic Women's League to take a similar stand and withdraw its support for the coalition.[47] While a member of the provincial committee provided a justification for its neutral position on the abortion question, the Catholic Women's League voted to withdraw its support for the coalition for one year.[48]

The coalition also came under attack for allegedly exaggerating its membership in order to increase the group's influence with the provincial government.[49] A story in the *Calgary Herald* quoted Ernestine Lisoski as stating that the provincial committee appeared to be "the instrument for promoting the interests of a small number of extremists," and that feminist groups in the province were setting up multiple organizations with overlapping memberships in order to inflate their support.[50] Dennis Anderson, the minister responsible for women's issues, was also quoted in the story as expressing his support for the presentation of opposition, if not for the content of the opposition itself. The coalition responded to these accusations by asking each of its member organizations to provide additional written confirmation of their support.[51]

Despite these various examples of resistance to the provincial committee, its efforts to push the government towards the establishment of an advisory council gained increasing support among provincial politicians. One of the early signs of this growing responsiveness was the termination of the rotating system of ministerial responsibility for women's issues. The announcement of this change was made on the eve of the annual meeting of the Canadian Advisory Council on the Status of Women, held in Edmonton in 1983, as part of the coalition's strategy to pressure the provincial government.[52] The announcement was taken as a sign of the Alberta government's increasing willingness to concede its weakness among the Canadian provinces in acknowledging the legitimacy of women's concerns regarding their position of inequality in the social, political, and economic life of the country.

While the new minister was willing to concede that Alberta had avoided a range of issues by concentrating its administrative focus on managing the oil and gas sector, and that the time had come to shift its attention to other issues, the provincial government would make no apologies for "letting certain issues drift."[53] The fact that Alberta lagged behind the rest of the country in dealing with women's concerns was attributed to the fact that Alberta was compelled to take a leadership role in the areas of energy, the Constitution, and economic growth. Moreover, these leadership responsibilities "[had] been foisted on us by the same people who are criticizing us for not having a very good strategy on women's issues. … We've had to take a defensive position when we would rather have been doing other things."[54]

As the new minister responsible for women's issues, Dick Johnston was willing to take the demand for an advisory council seriously but his efforts to bring the council to fruition were cautious and methodical. An investigation into alternative forms of presenting the concerns of women's groups to the government would have to be undertaken before an advisory council could be seriously considered.[55] Moreover, more time and lobbying were required to increase the perception, on the part of MLAs, of the need for a "better system to respond to women's concerns."[56]

The establishment of the Women's Secretariat and the Cabinet and Interdepartmental Committees on Women's Issues might be read as an attempt to put this "better system" into place without establishing an advisory council. These initiatives were announced in February 1984 and were to "signify the Government's intention to accelerate women's integration into the mainstream of Alberta life."[57] The new secretariat was to act as a liaison between government departments, ensuring that women's concerns were considered in the formulation of government policy. It was also to serve as a link to the community. Additionally, the Interdepartmental Committee on Women's Issues was to take on responsibilities that were "expected to approximate some of those that might be carried out by an advisory council."[58]

Evidence for the government's attempt to offer the secretariat as a stalling tactic, if not a replacement for an advisory council, are plentiful. In mid-1983 the director of the Women's Bureau was asked to draft a proposal for an expanded bureau that would serve as "an alternative to an advisory council on women's affairs."[59] The chair of the caucus committee on health and social services wrote to the coalition that "in reviewing your draft

62　STATE OF STRUGGLE

proposal to our committee, it appears that the major functions of the Secretariat described by the minister can accommodate the mandate desired by your committee."[60] Further, while the minister responsible for women's issues conceded that the coalition's arguments for an advisory council had "considerable merit," the fact that the secretariat and the two committees had just been established required that "any decision to define yet another structure must be approached with caution."[61] At the second annual meeting of the provincial coalition, however, Johnston quoted from a *Chatelaine* article that allegedly stated that advisory councils were outmoded.[62] In a departure from the coalition's earlier, conciliatory tone, the chair of the provincial committee responded that Johnston reminded her of "someone quoting the Bible out of context" and cited another quote from the article arguing that advisory councils were important, though new and imperfect.[63]

The secretariat itself, though understaffed, employed women who were well informed on women's issues. The director, Sheila Wynn, had a scholarly as well as professional interest in women's issues and had chaired the Alberta Committee on Wife Battering. Another staff member had served as the chair of ASWAC's steering committee. Certainly, correspondence between the secretariat and the minister, as well as other politicians and bureaucrats, attests to a desire to assume a position of advocacy for the claims of progressive women's groups. However, the secretariat's efforts to address women's marginalization were circumscribed by the limits of its mandate. As the coalition observed, the secretariat did not meet the needs of Alberta women because it was not autonomous, representative, or legislated, and did not make its research public.[64]

Despite the provincial government's efforts to distract advocates for an advisory council through the secretariat and the committees on women's issues, calls for an advisory council persisted. As a result, the provincial government decided to test the sense of the legislature on the issue through the introduction of a private member's bill. While the majority of MLAs supported the initiative, the discussion surrounding the motion, introduced in the spring of 1984 and further debated in the fall 1984 sitting, provided an opportunity for the full range of positions on the council to be

Disparate Strategies and Expediant Reponses 63

aired. A number of MLAs voiced their concern over the continuing inequality of women, pointing to the need for affirmative action and pay equity as well as the election of more women to the legislature, and expressing the hope that the work of an advisory council would help to heighten public awareness of these matters.[65] Attention was drawn to the importance of the independence of such a council to ensure that it could be both critical and supportive of government initiatives, without having to concern itself with the imperatives of electoral politics.[66] Less thoughtful orations, however, queried the perceived lack of effort on the part of women's groups to lobby their MLAs[67] and suggested that women's groups provide financing for an advisory council.[68]

The debate around the private member's bill also revealed the influence of "family values" in the approach of some MLAs to women's concerns. One MLA argued that, while he did not oppose an advisory council, it could only be seen as part of a larger program to ensure the well-being of the community.[69] In his view, the larger project could not be achieved unless women stayed home to raise their children. As he said, "If we as members of this Assembly were sincere about the future of Alberta in terms of our young people, our men and our women, we would seriously consider putting emphasis on the family, the value of the mother who stays home to look after those children."[70] While this MLA's position represents the conservative extreme in the expression of elected officials' views on the role of women in society, Lougheed's successor to the premiership, Don Getty, would increase the acceptability of such views within the Conservative Party in the latter half of the decade.

The provincial government's lethargy in establishing an advisory council provoked a radicalization in the coalition's approach to claimsmaking. Departing from the conciliatory and co-operative tone adopted in the initial stages of the committee's organizing initiative, its queries to government officials became increasingly pointed. Dick Johnston's presence at the committee's annual meetings provoked hostile challenges to the sincerity of Johnston's interest in women's issues.[71] The coalition also undertook an aggressive phone campaign, targeting MLAs and their spouses in an attempt to place the advisory council on the personal agenda of MLAs.[72]

The coalition's most daring move, however, was to attend the March 1985 Conservative Party convention with the express purpose of embarrassing the premier into taking action on the establishment of an advisory council. The three women participating in the action targeted the question-and-answer session for the premier, which had characteristically been reserved as a time to express appreciation for his work and to articulate the party's support of his leadership.[73] The questions posed by the women from the provincial committee, however, disrupted the premier's moment of adoration by pointing to the meagreness of the government's programs for women. While this line of questioning elicited hostility from the majority of convention delegates, it did succeed in securing the premier's first announcement that an advisory council would be established.[74]

On various occasions throughout the provincial committee's campaign, its supporters were informed that, should the requested council be established, it would be done at a time that was politically advantageous for the government.[75] Despite Lougheed's promise at the Conservative convention, this moment of political expediency did not arise prior to his resignation as premier. The prospect of a leadership race introduced the possibility that a new leader might oppose the idea of an advisory council. In fact, while two of the leadership candidates supported an advisory council, the third, Julian Koziak, offered no indication of his intentions, stating only that he preferred to avoid discussing narrow issues.[76] Of course, support for an advisory council did not necessarily mean the establishment of a council of substance. Ron Ghitter, another leadership hopeful, argued, that while he supported a council, it should be staffed by volunteers and should not have an independent research budget. The *Calgary Herald* reported that Ghitter had told the provincial committee that

> as premier he'd expect the council to cooperate with government and not go "crying out loud" when problems arose. "I don't look on an advisory council as being an activist lobby group running to the newspapers every time there's a problem," said Ghitter, adding that problems cannot be resolved by "shrill activism," but through consultation.[77]

Less colourfully, Don Getty, the front runner, announced that he would establish a council once he assumed the premier's office, though he offered no indication as to its mandate.[78]

Six months after Getty's successful leadership bid, the new premier finally announced that a council would be established. The premier also announced that the council's chair would be Margaret Leahey, a journalist known to be sympathetic to the Conservative Party.[79] Additionally, the fact that the council was to be established under the Women's Secretariat Act without independent status, a research budget, or provision to make research public prompted one Edmonton journalist to comment that the government had proposed an agency "with the clout of a Tupperware Party."[80] The provincial committee was so disheartened by the government's proposal that, having asked interested women to submit their resumes to the minister responsible for women's issues in anticipation of the appointment of a council, the committee strongly urged women who had done so to remove themselves from consideration.[81] AFWUF, by contrast, was delighted with the government's proposal. The organization's newsletter noted:

> If we have to have a council at all it is refreshing to see a woman appointed who has no ties to the radical-feminist fringe. Margaret Leahey is a wife, a mother, a successful career woman and...a woman who appreciates the contribution of women who [choose] to be wives and mothers full-time.[82]

Although the government's 7 April 1986 announcement of an advisory council was deflating for the coalition, the legislature's dissolution and election call three days later provided a window of opportunity for proposing changes to the government's plan. The vigour of the reform campaign was sufficient to ensure that the Alberta Advisory Council on Women's Issues was ultimately established as an independent body under its own legislation, though it lacked the power to publish research independent of the minister responsible for women's issues.[83] Additionally, while the capacity

66   STATE OF STRUGGLE

of the legislature to disband the council was weakened with the new legislation, it would, nonetheless, operate under a sunset clause of ten years.
Finally, appointments to the council were relatively representative of the
province's regions and ethnic diversity, but did not include any members
of the coalition or any prominent feminists.[84] Moreover, council members
evidenced strong ties to the Conservative Party.

With the passage of the legislation establishing the advisory council and
the announcement of its membership, the provincial committee decided
to disband.[85] The task of holding the council accountable to its constituency
was left to the groups that composed the coalition and to the women of
Alberta. In the end, it seemed that all the words of warning regarding the
state's propensity to act in its own interests and the ineffectiveness of advisory councils for advancing the concerns of feminist claimsmakers should
have been taken more seriously. Certainly, the key organizers of the coalition recognized, by the time of the council's announcement, that its
establishment would do little to alter the material conditions of women's
lives.[86] Nonetheless, in their letter to the new minister responsible for
women's issues, the co-chairs of the provincial committee wrote that the
decision to dismantle the coalition was taken "in recognition and support"
of the new council, and "with a feeling of accomplishment."[87]

■ THE PERPETUATION OF INTRANSIGENCE

In addition to reviewing the institutions established in response to the
activism of the Provincial Coalition for a Council on Women's Affairs, a
more detailed consideration of the work of the Interdepartmental Committee
on Women's Affairs, as well as the relationship between women and the
Alberta Human Rights Commission, provides greater insight into the
perceptions of state agents regarding women's demands. The approach of
these structures to issues of sexual equality sharply demonstrates the frac-
tiousness that existed within the Alberta state regarding the legitimacy of
women's demands and how best to address them.

Disparate Strategies and Expediant Reponses 67

■ EMPLOYERS' RIGHTS ARE HUMAN RIGHTS: THE ALBERTA HUMAN RIGHTS COMMISSION

The propensity of the AHRC's commissioners to assess the viability of rights-based claims against the anticipated response of Alberta employers intensified during the 1980s. Particularly illustrative of this tendency were debates within the bureaucracy surrounding the inclusion of pregnancy and sexual orientation as protected grounds within the Individual Rights Protection Act (IRPA), as well as the issues of employment and pay equity. These debates emerged in response to a series of recommendations and amendments to the IRPA inspired by the necessity of ensuring that Alberta's statutes, but particularly its human rights legislation, were in accordance with the Charter of Rights, and as the result of an Alberta Court of Queen's Bench ruling that the IRPA's protection against discrimination on the basis of sex did not extend to pregnancy.[88] The explicit inclusion of pregnancy as prohibited grounds for discrimination would represent a small victory for feminist efforts to persuade the commission that prohibiting discrimination simply on the basis of sex was inadequate. However, the refusal of the government to include sexual orientation as a prohibited ground of discrimination, despite the recommendations of the commission, and the commission's increasing hostility towards affirmative-action programs, voiced most vociferously by its chair, Marlene Antonio, were notable disappointments for feminist claimsmakers.

The debate concerning protection against discrimination on the basis of pregnancy centred on whether such protection should be addressed in provincial human rights legislation or the Employment Standards Act. Both the AHRC and the Women's Secretariat rejected the Employment Standards Act option because it did not apply to provincial employees.[89] Moreover, the secretariat argued that, under the terms of the Employment Standards Act, violations in regard to pregnancy could only be addressed as they related to a job termination and that the only recourse available to the dismissed employee was to make a complaint and receive damages.[90] Reinstatement was not an option unless the employee was willing to incur the costs of a legal proceeding.[91] The assistant deputy minister of labour,

68   STATE OF STRUGGLE

however, argued that "in the interests of efficiency and effectiveness for the targeted client group, the Employment Standards Act is the best option."[92] Ultimately the views of the AHRC and the secretariat prevailed.

The debate over which statute would best insure protection against discrimination for pregnant women presented an opportunity to revise the maternity-leave provisions of the Employment Standards Act. These revisions were fairly modest, providing for an unpaid leave of eighteen weeks with the distribution of the leave determined by the circumstances of the pregnancy, and were passed at the same time as the amendment to the IRPA to include pregnancy as a prohibited ground of discrimination.[93]

In the cases of both of these amendments, the state's concern to ensure the accommodation of employers was central. The Women's Secretariat noted:

Some people believe that small businesses would be disproportionately affected by legislation prohibiting discrimination on the basis of pregnancy without requiring a period of service beforehand. In our view, an exemption on the basis of "undue hardship" or "business necessity" cannot be justified, although we accept as reasonable the twelve month qualifying period before a woman is eligible for maternity leave.[94]

In regard to maternity leave, the AHRC argued:

The provision of this coverage need not create any undue hardships on any business as the benefits provided for a pregnancy leave come through unemployment insurance. No employer would be caught with the requirement to pay two people simultaneously. Even in the case where a pregnant person does not qualify for unemployment insurance there is no other legislative requirement to pay for any period of leave. It is the Commission's position that a pregnant person should receive the same leave related benefits as are available to any other employee.[95]

Disparate Strategies and Expediant Reponses 69

Although both the Women's Secretariat and the AHRC argued that the proposed amendments would not result in undue hardship for employers, one might have presumed that these offices would be more concerned with the substantive effects of these amendments on the lives of women. Even more problematic is the language used by the commission to express its position on employers and maternity leave. By conceptualizing pregnancy as something that happens to "persons" rather than to women and by insisting that women employees not be entitled to any "additional" benefits, the AHRC ignored the socially significant and identifiable characteristics of women, reducing these characteristics to individual traits. This conceptual position served to further undermine the commission's, albeit limited, capacity to ensure that its guardianship of equality would have some substantive meaning for women in Alberta.

Despite the perplexing assumptions in the arguments surrounding the inclusion of pregnancy in the IRPA, there was some achievement to be acknowledged in the fact that the failure of the courts to associate pregnancy with discrimination on the basis of sex had compelled the commission to undertake a review of the IRPA. Moreover, even if the commission was locked into a conceptual framework that dissociated pregnancy from women, most Albertans were not so inclined. On the issue of including sexual orientation as a protected ground within the IRPA, however, there was no success and the problematic assumptions that underscored arguments on both sides of the debate were less easily countered by common sense.

With regard to the issue of sexual orientation, the primary argument in the AHRC's case for its inclusion within the IRPA was that homosexuality "appears to be an immutable condition—in other words, research indicates it is firmly established at an early age and cannot be changed by therapy."[96] The commission also argued that the right to employment was fundamental and, hence, to permit discrimination on the basis of sexual orientation was to deny gays and lesbians "many things most people take for granted."[97] As additional support for their position, the AHRC argued that the majority of the Canadian population believed that homosexuals should be entitled to protection from discrimination, that the United

Church was considering a recommendation that would permit ordination to the ministry without regard to sexual orientation, that its inclusion in the Act would be an important first step in "eroding prejudiced attitudes," and that "prohibition of discrimination in employment on the basis of sex does not apply to homosexuality."[98]

The commission's argument that homosexuality "appears to be an immutable condition" suggests that the absence of immutability would justify discrimination. That if sexual orientation were a matter of choice rather than biological hard-wiring, the social expectation that everyone must be heterosexual would be justified. This position also suggests a presumption that the sexuality of gays and lesbians impacts on their behaviour in the workplace in a way that the heterosexuality of straight people does not. Such a presumption is apparent in the position of a bureaucrat in the department of personnel administration who argued that "bona fide occupational concerns relating to sexual orientation do exist in respect of a few occupations (e.g., child-care worker, teacher)."[99] Finally, the commission's strategy of basing its support for the inclusion of sexual orientation on immutability undermines the inclusion of other provisions that do not rest on the immutability argument such as marital status and source of income.

Whatever the weaknesses of the AHRC's rationale for the inclusion of sexual orientation, they were of little concern to the overseeing minister and his assistant deputy. In their view, the proposed amendment was a nonstarter, regardless of the rationale. In response to the commission's observation that "it has been found in various reputable studies that up to 10 per cent of the adult population is homosexual," the assistant deputy minister noted: "Delete, is debatable."[100] In response to the commission's argument that sexual orientation may be protected under the provisions of Section 15 of the Charter, the same official asserted, "Can use notwithstanding clause."[101]

The position of the minister of labour was that social acceptance of homosexuality had increased and that it would continue to increase through the provision of information and the fostering of understanding. In the minister's view, a homosexual person had the same protection as anyone else. Simply because sexual orientation was not enumerated in the Act did not mean that the Alberta state endorsed discrimination. After all, it would be impossible to enumerate every existing difference. Further, the absence of sexual orientation as a specified ground was not to be "interpreted as ignorance and bigotry by legislators."[102]

While the minister of labour and the AHRC disagreed on the necessity of including sexual orientation in the Act, they were of one mind on the issues of affirmative action and pay equity. Although the commission had supported the necessity of "special" programs at the end of the 1970s, the appointment of Marlene Antonio to chair the commission reversed the AHRC's position on this matter. As a result, the commission's perplexing animosity towards women's struggles for equality intensified.

Antonio's position on affirmative action (the provincial state did not use the term "employment equity"), was marked by her belief that individuals had to take responsibility for the situations in which they found themselves. While she conceded that women continued to experience discrimination in the workplace, the weight of her argument lay in the view that "women must accept the fact that career choices and preparation are important tools in lessening the amount of discrimination."[103] Parents and schools bore some responsibility for steering girls into programs that would ensure their employment in low-wage jobs, but, she argued, "Final responsibility rests on the individual."[104] Antonio insisted that if women were to be valued in the labour force they would have to abandon their romantic dreams of being stay-at-home mothers. She stated:

> Many young women are still victims of the "Cinderella Syndrome," choosing occupations that require little preparation or education and viewing them as "something to do" until Prince Charming comes along to support them forever. Unfortunately, things are seldom that simple.[105]

Nowhere in this argument for individual responsibility, however, is there an appreciation of the role of the state and the market in ensuring that women remain dependent on a second income, though a variety of examples were readily available to the commission. Certainly, some of the policies of the Conservative government, including the widows' pension and the spouse-in-the-house rule rested on the presumption of a man's superior earning power and its necessity for the well-being of families. Moreover, legislative debates also provided evidence of the view that married women should be required to surrender their jobs to unemployed men.[106] Moreover, the acknowledgement that discrimination does occur might have suggested that at least some employers devalue the work of women.

The chief commissioner's embrace of individual responsibility as the solution to workplace discrimination was shared by her boss, the minister of labour. In the minister's view, affirmative action and pay equity unjustifiably extended the power of the state in the marketplace.[107] He argued that the "social engineering" associated with affirmative action and pay equity was an infringement on both the rights of individuals and employers, asking, "Is it for us to say what the values of a particular individual or group of individuals should be? Are we to set ourselves up to be the social engineers who apply the procrustean bed to groups of individuals who share a common characteristic regardless of their personal values?" and "Why should we impose a contract on an employer which forces that employer to employ some pre-established arbitrary number or proportion?"[108] Further, the presumption that various groups had been systematically denied access to adequate wages and jobs and that this denial required compensatory measures risked creating a situation in which "the notion of debt to a group may quickly lead to a shifting of responsibility—to the idea that 'society owes us.'"[109] Rather than incurring this risk and the expansion of the state that it implied, Young insisted that social inequities could, again, be addressed by individuals who felt "a moral obligation as their brother's keeper, especially when that brother appears to be disadvantaged."[110]

Regardless of what Albertans might have felt morally compelled to do for their brothers, Alberta's obligation to comply with the provisions for affirmative action included in the Charter meant that the province was required to undertake statutory reform in this area. Predictably, however,

Disparate Strategies and Expediant Reponses 73

the statutory changes reflected the minister's resistance to positive measures on the part of the state. The minister proposed the removal of the 1980
special measures amendment that allowed Cabinet to permit exemptions
to its human rights legislation and its replacement with a "reasonable
limits" clause. Thus,

> discrimination [would] be deemed not to have occurred where the
> action was reasonable and justifiable in the circumstances. Thus,
> special projects, such as those for natives and disabled persons,
> should not be found to be unacceptably discriminatory, nor should
> they need formal and specific authorization.[111]

However, if people were concerned about what constituted "reasonableness," the AHRC was authorized to provide *nonbinding* recommendations
on specific cases.[112]

If the "special measures" section could be characterized as providing
the province's human rights legislation with "an escape clause as big as a
barn door," its replacement with a "reasonable limits" clause that required
no approval process and was not subjected to any binding regulation might
be likened to wiping out the barn entirely. Even though the espoused intention of the "reasonable limits" clause was to permit the existence of programs
that would be limited to specific groups, this intention continued to be
locked within the belief that everyone was to be treated in the same way,
regardless of their differences. Thus, ironically, the force of the province's
human rights legislation was uniformly diluted so that its provisions could
be thwarted by everyone, regardless of their rationale for "violating" the
Act.

In the first half of the 1980s, the continuing impenetrability of the AHRC
to arguments that located inequality in systemic forces effectively erased
the commission as a site for feminist claimsmaking. Certainly, symbolic
importance could be attached to the inclusion of pregnancy in the 1985
amendments to the IRPA, and the AHRC's continued support for the inclusion of sexual orientation within the provisions of the Act. However, the
commission's enduring commitment to individual responsibility truncated

its capacity for innovative responses to the demands it confronted. The significance of the AHRC's relative inaccessibility to women was mitigated by the opportunities for feminists to engage in claimsmaking at multiple sites within the state. Although examples of a rhetorical commitment to less state intervention were evident in the early 1980s, inclusion through pluralism was the strategy preferred by an increasing number of state agents. The quality and delivery of social entitlements would animate the politics of claimsmaking in Alberta throughout the period of decline in the province's economic growth.

While the Human Rights Commission demonstrated the persistence of formal equality and individual responsibility in its approach to women's inequality, the attempt to ascribe a community liaison function to the Interdepartmental Committee on Women's Issues illustrates one of the Alberta state's early attempts to manage claimsmaking through pluralism. It would be a fiery baptism for this managerial innovation.

■ THE INTERDEPARTMENTAL COMMITTEE ON WOMEN'S ISSUES

The Interdepartmental Committee on Women's Issues undertook its first meeting with the women's community at the request of Premier Lougheed. The AFWUF president contacted the premier and requested a meeting with him and the Cabinet Committee on Women's Issues to outline AFWUF concerns regarding the policy direction of the provincial government and the AFWUF's perception that feminist groups had undue influence in the policymaking process.[113] The premier declined and offered the interdepartmental committee as an alternative structure to which AFWUF could express its views.

Education, social services, employment, and pay equity were among the issues AFWUF raised in its presentation to the interdepartmental committee. With regard to education, the AFWUF representatives stressed that parents should be acknowledged as bearing primary responsibility for their children's education. They also urged the Department of Education to adopt a sex education curriculum that promoted chastity.[114] In the area of social services, AFWUF argued that only parents in need should be eligible for child-care subsidies and that parents who surrendered their children for adoption should have the right to refuse to allow their child to be adopted by a homosexual or a single parent. AFWUF also expressed its opposition to the Women's Secretariat, arguing that the secretariat could not represent the concerns of all Alberta women, especially since its staff had been appointed rather than elected, and asserted that representatives of the feminist lobby were overrepresented in government appointments.[115]

Not surprisingly, the Women's Secretariat was particularly concerned with AFWUF's appearance before the interdepartmental committee. While the secretariat appreciated the requirement to appear both inclusive and neutral, its staff was also committed to a very different understanding of women's place in society. As a result, the secretariat was determined to ensure that other women's groups would also be invited to make presentations to the interdepartmental committee's monthly meetings. Indeed, shortly after AFWUF's presentation, the secretariat received a letter from Planned Parenthood requesting information about the interdepartmental committee. A memo attached to the letter read, "This couldn't have come at a better time. This group should be scheduled for our consultations. May have to travel to Calgary to accommodate them."[116] Additionally, four days after AFWUF's presentation, the director of the Women's Secretariat asked one of her staff members to send a letter to the Provincial Committee for a Council on Women's Affairs, ASWAC, the Local Council of Women, a Native women's group, and an immigrant women's group, inviting them to make presentations to the interdepartmental committee.[117]

The interdepartmental committee's engagement with AFWUF did not end, however, with their meeting's final round of handshakes. In the aftermath of the meeting, AFWUF wrote to the Minister of Federal and Intergovernmental Affairs to complain that the ministry's representative on the committee had "snickered at the suggestion that chastity be promoted as a way of fostering individual and community health."[118] In AFWUF's view, the Federal and Intergovernmental Affairs representative was not qualified to comment on the practicality of promoting chastity in sex education courses. He had "every right to disagree with us but we have the right to expect that he avoid displaying discourtesy and bias during a presentation by members of the public."[119]

76   STATE OF STRUGGLE

Further, AFWUF mistakenly presumed that it had secured the secretariat's agreement to photocopy, compile, and distribute AFWUF's resolution book to all MLAs. The secretariat was only willing to supply the material to the Cabinet Committee on Women's Issues, asserting that it would be an inappropriate use of resources to fulfil AFWUF's request.[120] AFWUF managed to marshal support from the minister responsible for women's issues but, in the end, the secretariat only extended its efforts to the cabinet committee and to MLAs with whom AFWUF had frequent contact.[121]

Ultimately, the experience of dealing with AFWUF and other groups convinced the director of the secretariat to ask the minister responsible for women's issues to amend the mandate of the interdepartmental committee regarding its obligation to meet with community groups. In the view of the interdepartmental committee, the inability of public servants to take action on the issues raised by women's groups meant that the committee's usefulness as a vehicle for interaction between the state and the women's movement was limited.[122] The committee's role and that of the secretariat was further limited by the failure of government departments to consult with them in the development of policies, programs, and legislation, again suggesting that the authority of these state instruments would require enhancement or revision.[123] In fact, it was not long after these concerns were expressed that the new premier disbanded both the cabinet and interdepartmental committees in anticipation of the establishment of an advisory council.[124]

■

IF ONE WAS SIMPLY to note the transformation in the Alberta state's approach to women's issues from its espousal of formal equality to the establishment of a Women's Secretariat and the Alberta Advisory Council on Women's Issues, the early 1980s would appear to be a period of impressive achievements for feminist claimsmakers in their encounters with the province. Indeed, the recognition of women's political legitimacy that the creation of the secretariat and the advisory council denoted should not be discounted. However, the state's shift from straightforward resistance to the claims of feminists to the more normatively obscurantist politics of liberal pluralism created a new set of obstacles and compromises for feminist claimsmakers.

These new impediments complicated the politics of claimsmaking both for feminists and for the state. In both cases these complications emerged as a result of the disjuncture between the appearance of attentiveness to women's demands and the reality. In the court of public opinion, the state's new-found responsiveness to women's concerns diluted feminist charges that the province's policies continued to contribute to the subordination of women. On the other hand, elected officials who resisted a more congenial approach to feminists appeared to sanction the work of these new institutions. The inability of the Women's Secretariat and the Alberta Advisory Council on Women's Issues to develop and implement policies that would substantially improve the lives of women was obscured by the novelty of the Alberta government's apparent willingness to look beyond the oil and gas sector in its calculation of the public interest.

To further complicate matters, the feminist movement was becoming increasingly fragmented. Divisions emerged over issues of organizational focus and inclusivity. Feminists began to reconsider their strategy of seeking social change through claimsmaking with the state. Groups with varied agendas and approaches emerged, making the concept of *the* feminist movement problematical. Co-operation among groups became the subject of intense negotiation. Already in the process of being reconstituted due to the fragmentation of the feminist movement and the collapse of Alberta's social consensus, the politics of claimsmaking was intensified by the emergence of an organized antifeminist group with a keen appreciation for the rules of pluralist politics and a strong aversion to critiques of patriarchy. By the mid-1980s, the terrain on which feminist organizations struggled to improve the lives of women had been reshaped. While the state had, in its fashion, finally established instruments that would ensure that women's concerns were considered in the crafting of policy, there was considerable skepticism that these instruments would meet even their limited promise. The remainder of the decade would witness a growing complexity in the character of this skepticism.

4

Feminists and Family Values

THE CRISIS OF ALBERTA'S
WELFARE STATE

IN ALBERTA, as in Canada generally, the welfare state crisis reached its zenith in the late 1980s. It was apparent that the rules of political engagement that prevailed during the oil boom were unsuitable to the new economic and social conditions. However, the adoption of a more inclusive, pluralist approach to governance, initiated in the first part of the decade, had its own shortcomings. From the perspective of Alberta feminists, the province's new approach to governance was simply old wine in new bottles. The government's understanding of the gender order was unreformed and, hence, the inadequacy of public policy in addressing feminist concerns for equality, particularly in matters of women's economic independence, persisted. Feminist activism was more successful with moral issues, especially reproductive rights, but even here women were regularly confronted with "traditional" notions of women's roles. The provincial government's embrace of family-values discourse was only the clearest indication of this continued adherence to a patriarchal gender order.

Feminist groups also faced internal crises during this period. The implementation of feminist norms within group administrative structures ignited debates regarding the degree to which organizational practices reproduced masculinist norms of hierarchy and power, whether feminist groups should continue to make claims on the state and accept state funding, and the failure of organized feminism to include women outside of the white, middle class. Additionally, inconsistencies in state policy resulted from the play of power within the provincial Cabinet and federal obligations to maintain an active women's file. These inconsistencies created opportunities for feminist activists to advance their claims but they also stoked feminist cynicism as to the authenticity of their hard-fought and newly won political legitimacy.

The late 1980s marked a significant, if temporary, cracking of the stranglehold that oil and gas producers had exercised on democratic governance in Alberta. Oil prices had fallen to $10 a barrel,[1] the province's unemployment rate sat at over 10 per cent,[2] and demands on the province's social services, which had been under strain since the beginning of the decade, were intensifying. Albertans were angered by the mounting evidence of economic mismanagement implicit in the lavish bail-out packages offered to the Conservatives' business constituency at the same time that government departments faced budget cuts.[3] Environmentalists and Aboriginal peoples were outraged by the province's willingness to sell off Alberta's forests, without the appropriate assessments or consultations, as part of its efforts to diversify the province's economy.[4] Workers were horrified by the province's approach to labour disputes involving nurses and employees of the Gainers meatpacking plant. Organized feminist groups were disillusioned by the limited mandate of agencies such as the Women's Secretariat, the weak appointments to the Alberta Advisory Council on Women's Issues (AACWI), and the disproportionate effects of the government's budget-reduction measures on women. This swelling of public discontent was manifested in a number of sites and activities, though most obviously in the growth of the ranks of the legislative Opposition, whose member-ship expanded from four to twenty-two in the 1986 election, and then to twenty-six in 1989, and in the necessity of a by-election for the premier to regain his seat after he was defeated in the 1989 election.

It is imperative to underscore, particularly in light of the social policy initiatives and cutbacks undertaken by its successor, that the Getty govern-ment continued to assert a role for the state in the management of the province's social and economic life. The tensions that existed within Cabinet circulated around the extent to which the province could resist acknowl-edging the political legitimacy of an expanding array of social movements. The fundamental understanding of the state as interventionist, however, was not under debate.

■ WOMEN AND CLAIMSMAKING

In the late 1980s, incongruity was a feature of both public policy concerning women and the women's movement itself. The dramatic points of differ-ence between broadly defined feminist organizations and the antifeminist, "pro-family" group, the Alberta Federation of Women United for Families (AFWUF), is the crudest example, though one that found its parallel in Alberta's public policy regarding women. Additionally, however, significant fissures in the process of claimsmaking were also appearing within the feminist movement itself. Disengagement from the state, introspection, and concerns for feminist process were paralleled by project-oriented, time-limited organizing by small groups of long-acquainted and like-minded individuals. Inclusiveness and antiracism initiatives within multi-issue organizations led to the formation of groups concerned specifically with issues pertaining to women of colour and immigrant women. Although the feminist movement in Alberta was never encapsulated in a single organi-zation or organizational strategy, the late 1980s represented a unique moment of diversity within the province's feminist groups and a burgeoning in their numbers. Indeed, in 1988 the Alberta Women's Secretariat listed 300 women's groups in the province compared to seventy-five in 1974.[5] The causes, forms, and implications of this diversity bear some examination.

Feminists and Family Values

■ ALBERTA STATUS OF WOMEN ACTION COMMITTEE

By the middle of the 1980s, ASWAC had begun implementing far-reaching administrative reforms. Board meetings that had formerly taken a few hours per month and been targeted to the achievement of specific initiatives, now involved an eighteen-hour retreat every six weeks, with much time devoted to the expression of personal crises and the lived experience of sexism.[6] This organizational innovation attracted women with particular needs and objectives to the board while screening out action-oriented women. Although challenges were made to this shift in the organization's focus from within the board itself, the challengers eventually resigned.[7] By the end of the decade, interviews with Alberta feminists collected for the Northern Alberta Women's Archive Project contained multiple references to ASWAC's reorientation. These expressions ranged from ASWAC's "celebration of the beauty and pain of women" to the organization's takeover by "feminist flakes" who preferred to "hold hands and hum" and engage in "collective, sisterhood, touchy feely, let's feel good together shit."[8]

Of course, ASWAC could not completely reinvent itself on a therapeutic model since a substantial portion of its membership saw the organization's primary role as claimsmaking.[9] Moreover, if ASWAC was to maintain its access to public funding, its primary source of sustenance, it was required to draft proposals that would be acceptable to government granting bodies and account for the spending of public funds. Indeed, the imperative of undertaking equity initiatives that could be readily evaluated and justified by the granting body became all the more acute as conservative women's groups intensified their campaign to either gain access to federal funding dollars or have the federal Secretary of State Women's Program dismantled.[10] Under this onslaught, and as a result of budget cuts more generally, feminists perceived growing pressure to represent themselves to the state as acceptable and nonthreatening.[11]

Not surprisingly, the pressure to conform to the guidelines of granting bodies inspired debate within ASWAC, as well as many other women's organizations, regarding the advisability of continued reliance on public funding. Some ASWAC members felt that the organization should disengage from the public funding process because the cost of compromise was too dear.[12] Others, however, feared that replacing government money with private funds would result in the capture of the organization's agenda because members' energy would have to be expended on fundraising campaigns.[13] Ultimately, two events dampened the debate. First, in an attempt to rebuild membership support, ASWAC launched its Women Against Poverty campaign, the scope of which required substantial funding and, second, sources of public funding began to disappear.

In an attempt to reinforce the provincial character of the organization, to expose women outside of Calgary and Edmonton to feminism, and to provide support for local feminists who felt politically isolated, ASWAC decided to hold its 1987 annual conference in Camrose, a small city in central Alberta. The meeting attempted to address political issues and provide opportunities for personal accounts of sexist oppression.[14] Additionally, ASWAC attempted to conduct the business portion of the meeting in an informal manner. The structure of the meeting, then, reflected the various strains at work within the organization.

For women who were unfamiliar with or unsympathetic to feminist organizing, the radical elements of the conference program were overwhelming. At the level of process, it became clear that participatory decisionmaking was, actually, quite alienating. As an article in ASWAC's postconference newsletter observed, "Collectively run business meetings which are open to the membership are often wonderful, but they can also be chaotic as compared to the terse rules of meetings run according to *Robert's Rules of Order*. For new women, unfamiliar with collectivity, much of what went on was bewildering."[15]

Even more perplexing to some women in Camrose was the ease with which conference speakers and participants discussed patriarchy, pagan spirituality, lesbianism, and neoconservatism. Indeed, the shock evoked by these discussions was conveyed to the area's MLA and Alberta's Solicitor General, Ken Rostad, as well as to the local newspaper. One woman wrote: "One of the self-selected board members stated that society tries to control women in different ways. To them this was a horrible thing. They are forgetting that for a society to function there have to be controls." She also mentioned the "strange things that went on at the spirituality workshop with talk of witches and [a] witch camp." Although she confessed that

Feminists and Family Values 83

she did not actually know what had occurred, she stated, "I do know it is something that I do not support nor do I support government funding supporting these activities."[16]

In a similar tone of moral anxiety, an editorial in the *Camrose Canadian* reported that the city had "emerged unscathed from the annual assembly of the ASWAC." The newspaper conceded support for ASWAC's positions on pornography and child care, but expressed concern for the ability of ASWAC to "speak for all Alberta women," particularly given the organization's pro-choice stand and the perception that it was "powerfully influenced by lesbian women." Its evidence for the latter claim was that ASWAC's conference brochure stated that "the above accommodation fees are for sharing a double bed. If you would like a bed to yourself, the fee is double the above mentioned prices. To share a room with a friend, please pre-register."[17] The fear of difference expressed by the paper may have been quelled by ASWAC's reply that the organization had never claimed to represent all Alberta women and that while lesbians were certainly welcome within the organization, the proposal of shared accommodation was offered as a means to keep the conference affordable rather than as a promotion of homosexuality. The concerns expressed by Ken Rostad were less easily dismissed.[18] It would take a reminder of the importance of liberal pluralism to diffuse his attack.

To address the concerns of his constituents, the Solicitor General wrote to the minister responsible for women's issues. Rostad stated that he had received complaints from constituents who attended the conference but "had to leave in disgust and disappointment" as a result of ASWAC's "promotion of occults" as well as its support for "the formation and enhancement of lesbian groups in Edmonton." Although his initial response was that these complaints were an overreaction by a "strong-minded Christian faction," he became alarmed when "level headed people" also expressed their concern. According to these constituents, ASWAC "was thought to be destructive to the women's movement, to the family and an insult to the feminine gender. Constituents were distressed that the government would fund such an organization, let alone allow it to exist." Taking his cue from these "more moderate" people, Rostad asked the minister responsible for women's issues to inform him of the "amount we fund [ASWAC] as well as including a description of the group as we know it from their application, together with your latest intelligence on this group."[19]

Elaine McCoy's response to this query indicates the importance of liberal pluralism in defending the political legitimacy of feminist claimsmakers. After providing the requested information regarding the province's $5,000 conference grant and pointing out that the federal Secretary of State had funded ASWAC for several years, McCoy defended provincial support for ASWAC. While identifying ASWAC as "one of the more radical [women's groups] in that they address some issues which are not widely accepted" and acknowledging that "ASWAC has generated considerable controversy as a result of topics which the group has addressed," McCoy argued that "the group as a whole and the majority of its members have added, in a constructive way, to the debate on many issues facing women today."[20]

McCoy's position on ASWAC may simply have been an expression of support for pluralism as a tool for managing claimsmakers. More generously, McCoy's argument may have reflected her best effort to express personal support and political obligation to feminist claimsmakers without alienating herself from fellow cabinet members. In this regard, the observation of a New Democratic Party (NDP) representative is insightful. She stated that the women elected to the legislature in the late 1980s who were interested in placing women's concerns on the political agenda needed feminist groups, which were perceived as radical, to make their more politically constrained positions seem less extreme.[21] If the positions of elected members could be construed as a compromise between the "extremism" of feminist claimsmakers and their conservative opponents, some positive policy outcomes for women might ensue.

■ WOMEN AGAINST POVERTY

After many years of undertaking priority campaigns around one or two specific concerns, ASWAC's members wanted to embark on a project that would link issues, allow for the expression of women's experiences, provide a vehicle for grassroots organizing, and increase public awareness.[22] The Women Against Poverty (WAP) project was designed to fit these objectives. The centrepiece of the project was a series of hearings held in twelve communities throughout the province. The results of these hearings and research on the economic situation of women in Alberta were to be used as an educational resource for both the state and the community.

The work undertaken prior to the hearings, as well as the Women Against Poverty report, ensured that poverty-related issues and the government's responsibility for women's economic disadvantage became more prominent on the province's political agenda. The provincial government's decision to have a "Dialogue on Economic Equity" as the precursor to the Plan for Action for Alberta Women is one indication of a growing awareness of the impact of economic issues on the lives of women. Additionally, AACWI, while initially unmoved by ASWAC's appeal for research into the causes of women's poverty, subsequently published several studies concerning employment equity, the province's social assistance program, the economic situation of women over fifty-five, and the effects of restructuring policies on women.[23]

The WAP project had a profound impact on ASWAC as an organization. Efforts to ensure the participation of a diverse group of women required co-ordination with local community organizations, thereby building ASWAC's network of contacts as well as increasing ASWAC's profile in communities where there was a dearth of feminist organizing.[24] The preparation required for the hearings, a lengthy and difficult process associated with producing the report, and the subsequent updating of the report, released in 1996, also attest to the investment that the project represented. Moreover, while the WAP project was not the sole focus of ASWAC's work during this period, the objectives and approach to claimsmaking it honed were influential in later organizing initiatives. This influence can be seen in ASWAC's 1991 Women in Action campaign, which was, again, designed to draw on local resources and concerns in order to increase awareness of feminist issues and expand ASWAC's membership beyond the province's two major cities.[25] Additionally, this approach framed the objectives of ASWAC's long-range plan prepared for the Secretary of State Women's Program in 1992.[26]

Although the WAP project provided an important counterweight to ASWAC's introspective tendencies, it was not sufficient to restore ASWAC's position as the provincial representative of Alberta's feminists. The combination of declining resources, decreased credibility, and the presence of organizational alternatives diminished ASWAC's ability to represent a diverse group of women and advocate on a broad range of issues. As resources grew scarce, the need for a forum or organization that would serve a co-ordinating function among women's groups became imperative. However, such an organization did not emerge on a provincial scale. In Calgary, however, Women Looking Forward (WLF) was formed in 1989 to meet this need for Calgary-based women's organizations.

■ WOMEN LOOKING FORWARD

The fact that WLF was formed in Calgary rather than Edmonton is reflective of both the importance of ASWAC to feminist organizing in Edmonton and the response of women's organizations to the specific political culture of Calgary. Because ASWAC's board and staff were generally drawn from the provincial capital, women in other parts of the province perceived the organization as Edmonton-centred. Nonetheless, as ASWAC became more introspective, other feminist organizations emerged in Edmonton to both contest ASWAC's retreat from claimsmaking and to fill the void that ASWAC's inactivity had created.

For Calgary activists, this level of dissent was viewed as a luxury afforded by a local political climate in which feminists were relatively numerous and the possibility for political debate within feminist groups existed. Because Calgary is the city in which the province's dominant commodity interest is most vigorously expressed, and whose inhabitants see the Progressive Conservatives as the guarantors of that interest, residents who are critical of Conservative policies are particularly isolated. It is this sense of siege

Feminists and Family Values   87

that has contributed to the strength of the Calgary women's community.[27]

The primary vehicles established by WLF to perform its networking function included a monthly newsletter outlining events in Calgary and throughout the province and round tables held several times a year. Round-table meetings were attended by at least thirty representatives from groups including the Women's Unit of the Anglican Church, Alberta Civil Liberties Research Centre, Calgary Board of Education, Local Council of Women, Support Centre for Battered Women, Calgary Women's Health Collective, Calgary Immigrant Women's Centre, and National Action Committee on the Status of Women.[28] Of course many women were simultaneously involved in several organizations, a fact which also contributed to the integrative character of both WLF and, more generally, women's organizing in Calgary.

WLF's ability to accommodate a broad range of women's groups was a result of the organization's limited mandate. By initially insisting that the organization would not provide a lobbying function, it was possible to bring together groups whose views regarding strategy and political priorities differed substantially. At the same time, however, the fact that WLF was a focal point for disparate organizations, inscribed WLF with a representative character and public credibility. The more the media sought "the women's perspective" from WLF, the less WLF could avoid claimsmaking, not least because WLF was in a position to make public comments on women's oppression that smaller, issue-specific groups or those affiliated to religions were unwilling or unable to risk.[29] Additionally, public awareness of WLF meant that the organization was regularly called upon by community groups and government agencies to provide public education on women's issues. In the face of these demands, it became impossible to resist involvement in claimsmaking.

WLF maintained networking as its focus, and the newsletter and round tables provided important venues through which to convey the breadth of activities being undertaken by women's organizations in Calgary. However, WLF also began to organize around a few specific issues, much in the way that ASWAC had identified annual priority campaigns. In 1990, for example, WLF organized a pay- and employment-equity coalition to lobby the provincial government and to serve as a community resource on these issues.[30] Technically, it was the coalition that undertook the lobbying function, but WLF's central role in the effort could not be denied. The extent to which the lobbying phobia of WLF had been overcome is also demonstrated by the organization's 1992 year-end review in which it was reported that representatives of WLF had "met with candidates and elected politicians from different parties at their request, to advise them about our position on various policy issues such as electoral reform, child care and violence."[31]

■ RACE AND THE ALBERTA WOMEN'S MOVEMENT

The networking and co-ordinating functions of WLF, while not disposing the organization to therapeutic consciousness raising, tended to circumscribe consideration of WLF's organizational processes.[32] At a time when the issue of racism in the women's movement was topical among feminist groups in Alberta, and particularly in Calgary where the Calgary Status of Women Action Committee and the Calgary Women of Colour Collective were at the forefront of antiracist education and organizing, WLF's penchant for glossing over these concerns could not go unchallenged. To its credit, WLF did devote resources to antiracism education, participating in the development of a workshop on "unlearning racism" that was to "educate participants about understanding and overcoming internalized domination."[33] The extent to which WLF recognized the inadequacies of its own processes is, nonetheless, an open question. WLF's final report for 1992 acknowledged that "the experience of other women's groups is a clear example to us of the necessity to seriously address issues of racism in the women's movement."[34] Although WLF made several attempts to put a member of the Calgary Women of Colour Collective on its board, it apparently failed to instil inclusivity in its operation. It was reported "that in every instance that person has felt marginalized and that it is a token gesture and that women of colour are not really a priority of the organization."[35]

WLF was not alone among Alberta women's groups in attempting to address racism and falling short of the mark. ASWAC, for example, was

Feminists and Family Values   89

pressured by Calgary SWAC in 1986 to "address issues that are relevant to women of colour and to incorporate workshops on racism in next year's conference."[36] Despite several indications that the ASWAC board had had "many searching discussions on the issue of racism"[37] throughout the 1980s, a membership review conducted in 1992 indicated that ASWAC membership remained predominantly white and middle class.[38]

Additionally, in both Calgary and Edmonton women from non-European backgrounds and immigrant women were frustrated by the resistance of feminist organizations to champion their issues. Partly in response to such criticisms, ASWAC participated in the formation of Changing Together, a support group for immigrant women; the Calgary YWCA became involved in the establishment of the Immigrant Women's Centre; and the Calgary SWAC took on a more integrated relationship with the Calgary Women of Colour Collective. However, the existence of such organizations may also have tempted feminist groups dominated by women of European origin to avoid addressing the operation of racism in feminist organizing and claims-making. These groups did support efforts to address the inadequacy of the provincial government's initiatives for immigrant women and women of colour in language and job training, the government's attempt to deny sponsored women immigrants access to social services, and resistance among many cabinet members to employment-equity policies.[39] Generally, however, this support arose at the behest of immigrant women's groups or women-of-colour groups. If feminist groups were to overcome their propensity to marginalize racial and ethnic-minority women, they would have to assume some responsibility for constructing and deploying a more inclusive political analysis.[40]

In the context of a political environment in which the provincial state had an unsophisticated knowledge of feminist organizing yet felt compelled to address the concerns of women, it was possible, within limits, for feminist groups to express their political differences without jeopardizing their new-found legitimacy. Nonetheless, this legitimacy was never secure. Among its most significant challengers was the conservative women's movement.

90   STATE OF STRUGGLE

■ CONSERVATIVE WOMEN'S GROUPS

Relative tolerance for feminist claimsmaking, as well as the largely unrelated proliferation of feminist groups, was interpreted by pro-family, antifeminist groups such as AFWUF as an indication of feminism's increasing strength within the province. In response, AFWUF's executive demonstrated a shrewd appreciation for pluralist politics, intensifying efforts to undermine feminist activism by educating their members in the craft of claimsmaking. The centrepiece of this endeavour was AFWUF's organizing manual, *Good Citizens Good Government.*

Beginning from the premise that "politics and government in Canada ... is rule by pressure groups" and that Canada's recent past demonstrates that "politicians have been swayed by active and organized lobbying; and laws have been enacted reflecting the view point of the most vocal and effective lobby process," the authors of the organizing manual set out to "assist the people of Alberta to recognize their liberties, to become more politically astute and to thirst for active involvement."[41] Not all of the manual's suggestions were directed at gaining the ear of state agents, however. In a distorted echo of the importance of grassroots organizing to feminist activists, AFWUF's organizing manual suggested meeting women in their homes as a fruitful way to promote "family values." Although such encounters received no publicity, they were deemed to be effective because they provided "room for dialogue and friendship."[42] In a similar vein, the manual advised the establishment of mutual support groups and co-op play schools at which children could enjoy each other's company "without spending hours away from their mothers" and women could "support each other in their careers as wives and mothers."[43]

AFWUF did have some reservations surrounding constituency-building. While AFWUF's rhetoric celebrated the devotion of women to their families, the organizational skills, superior political access, and financial resources of their opponents meant that more aggressive claimsmaking strategies would be required if the single-income, nuclear-family model was to be preserved. As AFWUF's president in 1990 insisted,

We are up against powerful enemies....Feminist women's groups, gay rights organizations, they all receive millions of dollars in grants from the government....Individuals who belong to these groups often put their own careers first, and so are in positions of power where they can influence change to their liking.[44]

In fact, family, playgroups, and coffee klatches were not significant obstacles to the organization's access to authority. The energy devoted by AFWUF members to letter writing, radio phone-in programs, meetings with elected officials, and political constituency work, as well as the happy coincidence that at least one AFWUF board member was married to a Conservative MLA, made a substantial contribution to the organization's political legitimacy.[45]

Regardless of the evidence for AFWUF's access to decisionmakers, however, the organization operated under a sense of siege. The belief that Judeo-Christian values were under attack and that the nuclear family was in danger of extinction contributed to an organizational dynamic in which little substantive debate was apparent. With the exception of the topic of violence against women, the group's newsletters reveal little deviation from the views set out in AFWUF's founding position papers. The group's commitment to a united stance was also evident in concern surrounding the establishment of local AFWUF chapters. AFWUF's president noted: "While we cannot control everything these chapters do, *nor do we want to,* it is important to have strict policy guidelines in place for dealing with controversial subjects and the media. If an error is made it reflects on the entire provincial group [emphasis in original]."[46]

Despite the rigidity of political views within AFWUF, the emergence of new conservative women's groups in the late 1980s was not the result of philosophical differences, as was the case in the growth of feminist groups. Instead, conservative women's groups were formed to focus on a specific issue, as in the case of Kids First and its challenge to the constitutionality of child-care tax deductions for working parents, and to expand the influence of the conservative women's movement, as was the case in the takeover of the Calgary Local Council of Women (CLCW). Although the

CLCW was not an explicitly feminist organization, its membership included many groups with links to the feminist community, including the Calgary YWCA and the Calgary Birth Control Association. In the early 1990s, however, the CLCW's board was taken over by conservative women. As a result, feminist organizations withdrew their affiliations to the council while conservative women's groups filled their places.[47] From 1992 on, the minutes and resolutions of the CLCW borrow heavily from AFWUF on such subjects as birth control, the family, child care, capitalism, and cultural values.[48]

The benefit to AFWUF of the proliferation of like-minded women's groups was the opportunity to present the same set of ideas to state agents under several guises. Of course, the strategy had limited utility since bureaucrats and politicians quickly recognized the various groups as sharing the same views. If the point of a state-sponsored consultation was to gain a sense of the range of views among Alberta women, it was of little service to hear the same positions repeated several times. There was a moment of opportunity for conservative women, however, as their affiliated groups were debuting on the political scene.

The effectiveness of the conservative women's strength-in-numbers strategy was demonstrated in their successful capture of AACWI's consultation with women in southern Alberta. The consultation was not about a particular subject, yet each of the ten presentations given by individuals voiced opposition to a universal child-care strategy on the grounds that it would encourage women to engage in paid labour rather than caring for their children.[49] Of the eight presentations by organizations, Lethbridge and District Pro-Life, AFWUF, Kids First, and Teen Aid (a group advocating a sexual education curriculum emphasizing chastity) secured four spots, leaving the four remaining positions for ASWAC, the YWCA, the Lethbridge Immigrant Women's Association, and Alberta Women in Support of Agriculture.[50]

The monopolization of the meeting by conservative women did not end with their overrepresentation on the presenters' list, however. In ASWAC's account of the event, during a pause in the proceedings, pro-life advocates surrounded the few feminists in attendance and attempted to bully them into a discussion on the viability of the fetus.[51] From AFWUF's perspective, however, "everything was polite. It just happened that most of the participants were staunch believers in the importance of family life and family values."[52] The director of the Women's Secretariat, also in attendance, was less at ease with the proceedings. As she expressed it, the meeting left her with the impression that she had been "transferred to another time and place."[53]

A subsequent AACWI consultation with women in Edmonton did not fall victim to the same tactics. The *Alberta Report* noted that two women who had been allotted presentation slots as individuals were later queried about whether they held memberships in AFWUF.[54] Upon replying affirmatively, they were informed that AFWUF was already making a presentation and that the objective of the meeting was to obtain a range of views.[55]

As AACWI became a less neutral agent for the representation of women's claims to the state, conservative women became increasingly irritated with what they perceived as the incomplete representation of the range of views held by the province's women. As a response to this criticism, and consistent with Getty's personal commitment to "family values," the government established the Premier's Council in Support of Alberta Families. It was through this venue, as well as the province's increasing detachment from the public provision of social services, that AFWUF members began to realize some success in delegitimizing feminist claims-makers.

■ COMPROMISE AND PUBLIC POLICY

The period between 1986 and 1992 represented the moment of most vigorous engagement between the state and women's groups. Much of this engagement was rhetorical rather than substantive, giving credence to the argument that the inclusiveness of liberal pluralism is co-optive rather than democratic. Moreover. feminists enjoyed their greatest influence when their demands avoided economic issues and public expense.

■ REPRODUCTIVE RIGHTS

The Alberta government signalled its unwillingness to protect reproductive choice in two ways. First, the government refused to provide adequate pay to doctors performing abortions, a situation exacerbated by the termination of extra-billing in 1986.[56] Second, the hospitals minister removed coverage for sterilization and birth control counselling from the provincial health insurance program.[57]

In the case of abortion, the government's culpability for undermining access was shared by the Alberta Medical Association (AMA). Having benefited from extra-billing abortions over the previous five years, doctors were loath to accept the fee of $84.50 offered by the province.[58] Rather than accept the demise of extra-billing, physicians attempted to circumvent its prohibition by charging women $75 to obtain a referral letter to a Therapeutic Abortion Committee.[59] Since the approval of such a committee was required before an abortion could be performed, women were forced to pay the additional fee.

Even with this extra fee, however, the number of doctors willing to conduct the procedure declined. Within two weeks of the termination of extra-billing, Planned Parenthood Edmonton reported that only three of the eleven doctors who had previously accepted referrals from its office were continuing to do so.[60] Two weeks later, just one doctor remained to accept Planned Parenthood Edmonton's referrals.[61]

Although the willingness of Alberta's doctors to sacrifice women in their struggle with the province over their fee schedule was an irritation to feminist activists, the manner in which the government expressed its intransigence on the abortion question was even more galling. Rather than acknowledging that the decrease in the number of abortions being performed in Alberta, but particularly in Edmonton,[62] was the result of inadequate access stemming directly from government policy, the hospitals minister, Marvin Moore, explained the declining numbers as resulting from panic surrounding AIDS.[63] According to this logic, fewer women required abortions because they were not having sex or because they were practising safe sex. As the crisis continued, Moore augmented his argu-

Feminists and Family Values   95

ment with the claim that "people [are] looking more carefully at…using other means of birth control in advance of pregnancy."[64]

The extent to which the personal convictions of the hospitals minister informed public policy was disclosed once the Supreme Court of Canada ruled that Section 251 of the Criminal Code was unconstitutional. On the basis of this ruling, Therapeutic Abortion Committees were not required to assess the validity of a woman's desire for an abortion. Moore's immediate response, however, was that Alberta Medicare would only pay for those abortions that had garnered committee approval.[65] He later relented on this policy, only to unearth a ten-year-old law requiring a woman to consult with two doctors before terminating a pregnancy.[66] He even threatened to fine noncompliant hospitals.[67] Despite Moore's personal crusade to limit abortion access, demand and the Supreme Court's decision precipitated the establishment of an abortion clinic at the Calgary General Hospital and a Women's Health Centre at the Royal Alexandra Hospital in Edmonton. Dedicated facilities and the demise of the approval process improved the economy of providing abortions, thus diminishing the access problem, at least in the province's major cities.[68] Not surprisingly, the abortion rate in Alberta began to rise, a fact that Moore interpreted as the result of women's decreased concern with birth control in the aftermath of the Supreme Court's decision.[69] A cabinet shuffle soon relieved Moore of his responsibilities for this contentious issue, the health portfolio going to a woman to whom the feminist community was more positively inclined.

The government's efforts to de-insure sterilization and birth control counselling were also perplexing for the province's feminist community. Unlike the abortion struggle, however, this policy reform offered no opportunity for eleventh-hour intervention by the Supreme Court or the federal government. The simplicity of the issue, the clarity of the target, and the hypocrisy of the government's position, particularly in light of Moore's insistence on the need for Alberta women to seek out methods of birth control other than abortion, made the de-insurance issue a test case of the government's commitment to women's equality. The fact that women were successful in persuading the government to reverse its position on the issue was an important victory.

96 STATE OF STRUGGLE

By 1987 the worsening condition of the province's economy was nega-
tively affecting the public accounts. After years of budget surpluses, the
province began posting deficits and initiated efforts to reduce the level of
government spending. Among these efforts was the removal of "unnecessary" services from the province's medical insurance program, including
sterilization procedures and birth control counselling.

De-insurance led to the creation of the Alberta Coalition for Universal
Health Care. Its members sought to reverse the government's policy and
insisted on "public participation and consultation in the development of
provincial health care policies."[70] The assertion that the public, and not
simply government-identified stakeholders, should be consulted in the
policymaking process was poorly received by the hospitals minister. Moore
insisted that such consultation was unnecessary since he had received
opinions from the AMA and other medical groups.[71] As the leader of the
Opposition observed, however, "Women are going to find it rather amazing
that they're considered a narrower group [than the province's doctors] and
that the AMA represents them."[72]

Pressure to adopt a more inclusive approach to policymaking also came
from within the Cabinet. Elaine McCoy, then minister of consumer and
corporate affairs, pressed the minister responsible for women's issues,
Dennis Anderson, to be a stronger advocate for women and ensure that
substantive policies addressing women's concerns were implemented. In a
June 1987 memo, McCoy raised the de-insurance issue and argued that "an
effective case has been made that this government is hitting on women—
and our moves toward a 'gender free' society are nothing more than
window dressing."[73] Dissatisfied with Anderson's reply, McCoy wrote to
him again, expressing her concern with the timeline attached to his initiatives. McCoy stated:

> The impression we have managed to create is of a government that
> does not respond to concerns raised legitimately (not stridently) by
> women in all walks of life. I think it unwise to let that momentum
> build all through the summer, the fall, over Christmas and into the
> Spring of 1988.[74]

The hospitals minister was persuaded to beat a partial retreat on the issue. In June of 1987 Moore was already informing the AACWI that he would consider re-insuring sterilization procedures (de-insured on 19 May 1987). However, the minister was immovable on the issue of birth control counselling. Moore's justification was that families could meet the need and that the government would no longer support doctors who used counselling to pad their incomes.[75] The AMA's reaction was indignation. But the tarnishing of doctors' reputations was minor in comparison to the harm that Moore's decision could bring to young Albertans. In a province where the rate of teenage pregnancy was 40 per cent higher than the national average, even before de-insurance, the rationale behind further limitations to reproductive counselling could only be interpreted as ideological.[76]

Ultimately, all the blustering only enhanced the case made by women's groups for the re-insurance of both sterilization and birth control counselling. By April 1988, the combination of letter-writing campaigns instigated by women's groups, a position paper drafted by the Women's Secretariat, the recommendations of the AACWI, and the advocacy of Elaine McCoy forced the government to acknowledge that pursuing an ideological position on women's reproductive rights under the guise of cost-cutting would not be tolerated in Alberta's new political environment. Sterilization and birth control counselling were re-instated in the province's medical insurance program.

The force of conservative morality in shaping Alberta's public policy should not be discounted. It was most effective, however, when its expression was linked to an economic rationale. In the cases of abortion, sterilization, and birth control counselling, the archaic morality of the hospitals minister was unrelated to any substantive economic objective.

■ ECONOMIC EQUITY

Predictably, feminist efforts to persuade the government to further women's equality through interventions in the labour market, and through pay equity in particular, were much less successful than campaigns around moral issues such as reproductive rights. Economic recession did, temporarily, moderate the emphasis on individual responsibility so characteristic of Alberta's public policy. However, this moderation did not extend to policy initiatives that might have addressed labour-market inequities and gender-based income inequality.

In the late 1980s many feminist groups were involved in public awareness campaigns and in efforts to educate elected representatives regarding the objectives of pay-equity legislation. Both the provincial NDP and the Liberals introduced pay-equity legislation in the legislature. However, in a reprise of the Lougheed chorus, the government insisted that "pay fairness" was adequate to the task, that pay equity only represented a "quick fix,"[77] and that Albertans did not want pay equity "shoved down [their] throats."[78]

The government conceded, as per the province's human rights legislation, that people performing the same tasks should be paid the same wage. However, adjusting wages on the basis of a cross-occupational comparison of skill, responsibility, effort, and working conditions was deemed too costly and too subjective. Further, the government's imposition of such a task on employers was seen as high-handed and authoritarian.[79] More subtly, it seemed that the very phrase "pay equity" evoked the bogie of feminism. A former director of the Women's Secretariat observed, "The phrase 'pay equity' had become very much a feminist challenge to male dominated pay systems and equity systems within the labour market."[80] Indeed, the animosity towards pay equity was so intense that employees of the Women's Secretariat and Career Development and Employment were notified by their respective ministers' offices that the phrase "pay equity" was not to be used in any of the correspondence that was sent to the ministers' offices or in any briefings for committee or cabinet meetings.[81] While one could discuss equal pay for work of equal value, "pay equity" as a designation was forbidden.

Eventually, however, the government conceded that some evidence would be required to justify its position on pay equity. The absence of a rationale would only serve to keep the issue on the public agenda and expose the government to attack on the basis of its lack of commitment to fair process. Rather than conducting a public opinion poll or holding a public consultation, however, the government asked the Alberta Human

Feminists and Family Values   99

Rights Commission (AHRC) to conduct a pay-equity survey among elected representatives to determine the level of support within the legislature.

Assigning the study to the AHRC helped to ensure an outcome that was favourable to the government. Prior to the assignment, the chief commissioner of the AHRC had declared that it "would only recommend...a pay equity concept of equal pay for work of equal value which is non-gender based, but only if it can be shown that the concept would effectively eliminate wage discrimination in Alberta."[82] Moreover, ASWAC reported that, during a meeting with the commission in 1986, "comments from commissioners and commission staff included 'I think women are their own worst enemy,' 'Women will not be hired if employers are forced to increase their wages,' and 'You'll never get anywhere concentrating on gender.'"[83]

Even the strongest advocates of pay equity would concur that the standard of eliminating wage discrimination is unachievable on the basis of a pay-equity plan alone. Moreover, in arguing for a "non-gender based" initiative, the commission was attempting to "one-up" feminists by claiming that pay-equity programs should not be focused solely on women since "others" might also be paid inequitably.[84] This was a misreading of the feminist position, however, since feminist activists also supported the inclusion of race/ethnicity within pay-equity programs. Having said that, it was not clear that the commission's position was actually one of expanding the *categories* of people who should be included within a pay-equity initiative. Instead, the commission was arguing that

> the fundamental principle of equal value is the comparative measure of jobs against the relative presence of factors, such as effort, knowledge and/or skills, responsibility and working conditions, factors which are common to all jobs in themselves and which make no reference to the qualities or characteristics of the incumbents performing the jobs.[85]

Such a position describes the desired outcome of a pay-equity scheme. However, to begin the task of assessing the value of work by insisting that the attainment of equality will only occur when the qualities and characteristics of the incumbents do not matter and, therefore, that these characteristics should not matter in the implementation of the program is to stymie its success. If the commission members grasped the fundamental principle of equal value, they forgot its underlying premise—that women and racial minorities perform tasks that are undervalued by society and are systematically underpaid, that race and gender matter. Ultimately, the commission's position was simply another rehearsal of the view that human rights are synonymous with individual rights and that equality means sameness.

A study using balanced background material and fair questions might have produced results that demonstrated some support for pay equity among Alberta's elected representatives. Indeed, asking the AHRC to conduct the study indicated the Cabinet's desire to exploit assumptions about the commission's fairness and objectivity as well as its arms-length relationship to government. It was these characteristics that lent the government's efforts to study pay equity the guise of procedural fairness. The conduct of the study, however, only reinforced the conclusions already reached by the commission and the Cabinet. The instructions to study participants asked them to review background material on pay equity provided by the Fraser Institute before completing the commission's survey.[86] Given the Fraser Institute's strong opposition to pay equity, it is not surprising that this material might have contributed to the achievement of the government's desired outcome.

The Alberta government's most comprehensive effort to address both the demands of feminist claimsmakers and national obligations to improve the social and economic conditions for women, was the development of the Alberta Plan for Action for Women. The central purpose of the plan was to identify all government programs and policies pertaining to women and to place them within a framework in order "to show the comprehensive and coordinated approach the government is undertaking to address the issues of importance to Alberta women."[87] Policy initiatives and programs were to articulate principles in the areas of the family, the workplace, education and training, health, and the community.

The government had initiated a limited public consultation prior to the drafting of the plan. However, the views expressed were sufficiently disparate to render the consultation report incoherent.[88] Further, because government bureaucrats varied in their enthusiasm for crafting policies to be included in the Plan for Action, its initiatives were disparate and lacking in focus.

Employees of the Women's Secretariat, responsible for co-ordinating the plan, perceived a degree of mockery in responses to their requests for action.[89] Some of this animosity was attributed to a straightforward antipathy to feminist demands, but there were at least two other factors contributing to public servants' resistance to meeting their politically mandated obligations. First, government departments faced financial constraints as a result of the provincial government's attempts to address its growing deficit and the federal government's decision to cap the Canada Assistance Program. The expectation that new programs for women be devised at the same time program cuts were implemented was seen as unduly onerous.[90] Second, in addition to devising policies and programs for women, government departments were asked to consider the effects of their policies and programs on the family as per cabinet approval of the Family Policy Grid created by the Premier's Council in Support of Alberta Families.[91] Seen as an imposition on public servants, the Family Policy Grid was as unwelcome as the Plan for Action. Moreover, the task of devising policies and programs that would both benefit women and be sensitive to the needs of families was seen as an impossibility. Although the needs of women and of families are not antithetical to each other, there was a propensity, particularly given the emphasis of the premier's council on the "traditional" family, to understand these needs as incommensurable.[92]

The plan's most appreciable initiatives concerned child care and funding for women's shelters. The Alberta government announced that it would increase training requirements for child-care workers, expand the training capacity within the postsecondary system to improve their qualifications, and increase the day-care subsidy to low-income families.[93] This recommendation reflected day-care's prominence as a public issue as a result of the Mulroney government's intention to design a national child-care strategy and pressure from women's groups and parents. Similarly, public concern with domestic violence was reflected in increased funding to the province's existing shelters, funding for six new satellite shelters, and a new full-fledged shelter in Peace River.[94]

Among the weakest proposals were a public awareness campaign on the important roles that women play in Alberta, studies on student achievement and enrolment patterns by gender, and a review of reproductive health services.[95] These latter two initiatives were proposed without research objectives. Given the decreasing fiscal capacity of the provincial state, proposals that were unlikely to demonstrate a concrete benefit to women were ill-considered. Not only did such a decision reveal the superficiality of the government's commitment to Alberta women, it provided a justification for dismantling the Plan for Action as concern for the deficit intensified.

Despite the obstacles impeding its development, the Plan for Action for Alberta Women was sustained until the end of Getty's premiership. Its annual diminishment and narrowing focus testify to the effects of budget cuts and the rhetoric of family values. At its introduction it was touted as a "framework for the future within which government will introduce new initiatives each year" and significant expenditures were announced, among which, "20 new initiatives [would] be undertaken in 1989–90 at an estimated cost of $16 million."[96] The initiatives undertaken in 1990–92 were primarily extensions of those announced in the plan's inaugural year, while in 1992–93, the plan was to be "dedicated to the elimination of family violence and amalgamated with the initiatives being implemented under the Framework for Action on Family Violence."[97]

The Plan for Action fulfilled a symbolic function for the Alberta government, allowing provincial representatives to present evidence of action on women's equality in national forums and to the province's organized women's movement. In its substance, however, the plan fell short of claims-makers' demands. For those state agents who revelled in the symbolism but did not perceive the insufficiency of the plan, feminists' hostility was fodder for the argument that it was politically unrewarding to persist in addressing women's concerns. Indeed, the combination of mounting deficits and growing dissatisfaction with government policy among women and other social movements would contribute to a dramatic rethinking of the relationship between the state and citizens.

Feminists and Family Values   103

■ THE ALBERTA ADVISORY COUNCIL ON WOMEN'S ISSUES

Even more than the Plan for Action, the Alberta Advisory Council on Women's Issues embodied the tensions in the Alberta government's legitimation of feminists. Unlike the plan, however, the council became increasingly effective over time, thus inspiring Alberta's organized women's movement to be concerned with the council's well-being. In this case, state agents could not write off the council as suffering from a lack of interest. Its trenchant critiques of government policy, however, only fuelled the animosity of policymakers hostile to feminist demands. By June of 1992, Cabinet had rejected the recommendation of the minister responsible for women's issues regarding a new chair for the AACWI, and the council was left to wither from neglect.

Initially, the lack of familiarity with women's issues among AACWI members and the insufficiencies of the legislation under which the advisory council was created underscored the Conservative government's investment in the appearance of addressing women's concerns rather than the concerns themselves. Women's groups were impatient with both the government and the council and, hence, the inevitable missteps taken by the inexperienced and often poorly briefed council members were the subject of scrutiny and dissatisfaction.

In the first year of AACWI's operation the council was closely observed by the Social Issues Committee of the Calgary YWCA—the major impetus behind the Provincial Coalition for a Council on Women's Affairs. As anticipated, the council gave a mediocre performance. Early AACWI recommendations to government failed to set out areas of concern, suggestions to address these concerns, means by which to evaluate the government's response to the recommendations, and an articulation of the rationale supporting them. Regarding child care, for example, the council suggested that there should be minimum qualifications for child-care workers but did not set out what these should be. On the issue of violence against women, the council used language that horrified antiviolence activists, encouraging the government to "undertake an all-out attack on family violence." Its only specific recommendations on the subject were to establish a toll-free help line and undertake a public awareness campaign.[98]

The most telling example of the recommendations' shortcomings, however, was the statement that "the provincial government continue its support of native, immigrant and visible minority women's programs."[99] As the Calgary YWCA noted, "This last statement...is not a recommendation but a position statement, and, by its lack of content, speaks loudly that the council has no contribution to make toward improving provincial policy in this area....It would perhaps have been better to have said nothing at all."[100]

In response to these mildly worded recommendations, the Alberta government could represent action in areas where little action had occurred and dismiss the need for action on issues such as increasing the minimum wage as unsubstantiated by the council. The government responded to the AACWI's recommendation for improved child-care standards with the comment that it had already imposed the regulation that at least one child-care worker in each facility have first-aid certification. In response to the recommendations regarding violence against women, the council's lack of analysis allowed the government to perversely insist that a public awareness program on family violence would stress "the importance of family and caring for one another." Finally, and not surprisingly, AACWI's statement of support for government programs for Aboriginal and immigrant women and women of colour garnered positive support. All that was required was to state that "the government will continue its support of immigrant, native and visible minority women."[101]

In addition to critiquing AACWI's recommendations, the Social Issues Committee was concerned about AACWI's relationships with the Women's Secretariat and Alberta's organized women's groups. The director of the Women's Secretariat was an ex-officio member of the AACWI. Hence, interaction between the two agencies was expected. However, when the Social Issues Committee queried the director of the secretariat regarding her relationship with the council, she stated that they had infrequent communication. For the Social Issues Committee, this situation was unacceptable. As the authors of the report asked, "How [are] Alberta women's interests...served when two groups who do not communicate make recommendations to Government on our behalf?"[102]

Feminists and Family Values   105

The Social Issues Committee also expressed its concern with the "passive and ad hoc" approach adopted by the AACWI in establishing links with major women's groups. In the committee's view, the council's reliance on public forums and special meetings put the onus on groups to contact the council. AACWI's superior resources and consultative mandate meant that its members should be actively soliciting the views of women's groups. The Social Issues Committee was galled by AACWI's failure to notify women's groups regarding its recommendations to government. The Calgary YWCA had not learned of the AACWI recommendations until being asked to comment on them by the press. Further, AACWI had not made the recommendations available to groups until they were specifically requested. Members of the Social Issues Committee were further perturbed by AACWI's lack of response to an invitation to discuss the council's objectives and priorities. In a final note of caution, the report warned that, should the AACWI maintain its passive interaction with women's groups, "the council...will be successful only in alienating large blocks of the very constituents which it was formed to represent."[103]

The pressure brought to bear on AACWI by the Social Issues Committee and other Alberta women's groups soon resulted in an improvement in the council's work. Among the council's 1988 recommendations concerning immigrant women were universal access to and flexibility in English-as-a-second-language training, career counselling, employment training and encouragement to participate in nontraditional occupations, information regarding women's shelters, and the promotion of antiracist education.[104] The AACWI also recommended that the widow's pension be replaced by an income supplement for all low-income individuals between the ages of fifty-five and sixty-four, regardless of their marital status, and that the government increase funding to women's shelters.[105] The recommendations were followed by a lengthy report providing supporting arguments and demonstrating considerable research.

The minister responsible for women's issues asserted that the council's recommendations concerning Aboriginal women were focused on education, when, according to the minister, "native women have other pressing concerns." However, the attempt to discredit the council by claiming that the government had superior knowledge lacked probity.[106] Alberta's insistence that the federal government was responsible for language training and that Stepping Stones, a mentorship program for high school girls, was evidence of the Alberta government's commitment to nontraditional career paths for immigrant women revealed a truer picture of the Alberta government's commitment to women.[107]

Much of AACWI's improved advocacy can be explained by increased familiarity with women's issues. However, a complicated story of personalities and politics suggests that AACWI's willingness to challenge provincial policy can also be read as a strategy to boost the reputation of the council's chair, Margaret Leahey, while discrediting the minister responsible for women's issues. It was in the context of the growing prominence of the family in the province's political discourse and the province's superficial policy responses to feminist claimsmakers that Elaine McCoy attempted to address what she perceived as Leahey's mismanagement of the AACWI. Leahey allegedly responded to the minister's concern by playing to the skepticism of Alberta's organized women's groups regarding the government's commitment to women's equality. As a consequence, a crisis was fuelled regarding government interference with the advisory council and, indeed, the fate of the council itself.

When Elaine McCoy was named the minister responsible for women's issues in 1987, she discovered that many AACWI members were considering resigning because of their disillusionment with Leahey.[108] Because a mass resignation would have been a terrible embarrassment to the government, McCoy set out to address the concerns of the individual council members.[109] Part of this initiative included crediting AACWI for government policy initiatives, notably the decision to re-insure sterilization and birth control procedures. In the re-insurance announcement, the government's press release noted, "The Alberta Advisory Council on Women's Issues was instrumental in bringing forward recommendations which reflected the views and concerns of Alberta women."[110] McCoy also defended AACWI against the criticisms of the Social Issues Committee, stating that the general terms in which the recommendations were framed were, in fact, desirable since bureaucrats were to work out the policy details.

Feminists and Family Values 107

As McCoy addressed the disquiet of AACWI members, however, Leahey charged the minister with interfering in the council and attempting to restrict its mandate.[111] When it became apparent that McCoy would not renew her contract, Leahey intensified her critique of the government. She argued, for example, that "'women were tired of begging for money' from the Getty government," that the government was eliminating or under-funding services essential to women, including shelters and social assistance payments, and that women were suffering while the provincial government was bailing out ski operators in Kananaskis and promoting free trade.[112] The veracity of these charges, and the expectation, on the part of progressive women's groups, that AACWI would publicize inadequate government policies helped to deflect attention from the personal motivations behind Leahey's actions.

Anxiety around interference with the advisory council was also heightened by the government's failure to appoint replacements to the council. Delays were explained as the result of a large number of nominations and the provincial election. However, many observers wondered whether this neglect of the council signalled its impending demise.[113] The government's pre-election Throne Speech added to the concern. The combination of vacancies on the AACWI and emphasis on "the family" in the Throne Speech led Leahey to speculate on the possibility of the government collapsing the AACWI into the newly announced Premier's Council in Support of Alberta Families.[114]

Even if rumours of the council's demise were exaggerated, progressive women's groups were alarmed by the minister's apparent refusal to address the concerns of AACWI's newly vocal chair. Discussions with the minister regarding the appointment process and the research capacity of the council had been unproductive. McCoy had informed ASWAC that she "would not recommend that Cabinet expand the council's role to include research."[115] The minister also stated that she would not consider an independent appointment process for the council, arguing that "if it's government-funded, it's government-appointed."[116] Further, McCoy had informed two activists, in a private meeting, that "only Tory women would qualify for appointments to the council, to ensure that Tory policy would be followed."[117]

Alberta women had every indication that AACWI's new-found critical voice would be silenced.

In the heat of the crisis, Leahey announced her resignation from the council. Her term had nearly expired and McCoy had made it clear that she would not be reappointed. Nonetheless, Leahey's resignation was interpreted by women's groups and by the press as another indication of the government's contempt for the advisory council. This interpretation was fuelled by the subsequent resignations of two council members who charged that the government's treatment of the council "had been terrible,"[118] that the new chair would be ineffective,[119] that the remaining council members were "a bunch of duds who won't do anything," and that the council lacked autonomy, adequate funding, and a proper appointment process.[120]

In fact, the appointment of Elva Mertick as chair of the AACWI did merit some concern. Mertick's connections to the Progressive Conservatives were strong. She had served as an executive member of Dennis Anderson's riding association and had been appointed to the council when Anderson was the minister responsible for women's issues.[121] Although it was conceded that she had a sound knowledge of women's issues, her party affiliation suggested that she would be unlikely to challenge the government.[122] Indeed, Mertick announced her support for McCoy, stating that she found the minister "approachable, open, and supportive" and asserted that she did not feel it was "advantageous for us to take on an adversarial role with government."[123]

The brouhaha surrounding the AACWI was finally resolved in the aftermath of the spring election of 1989. However disingenuous and self-serving Margaret Leahey's critique of the provincial government might have been, she had, nonetheless, inspired a groundswell of support for the advisory council. This support, as well as the dissatisfaction with the government expressed in the provincial election, resulted in the vacancies on the council being filled by highly qualified individuals. As an editorial in the *Calgary Herald* observed:

What a difference an election makes....Alberta Tories couldn't have cared less who sat on the Alberta Advisory Council on Women's

Issues six months ago...[but] the eight new appointments to the advisory council announced last week indicate that the Tories have acquired a heretofore undiscovered respect for women's issues. The Calgary women [three of the eight] joining the council are long experienced in non-partisan organizations working for women and can be counted on to protest loudly and effectively if they are ignored in the same shabby manner as their predecessors.[124]

Moreover, despite Mertick's conciliatory comments, she, too, asserted that "if the government responds in an appropriate and timely fashion to council concerns 'we won't rattle them. If they don't, they'll hear about it very loudly.'"[125]

As it turned out, Mertick maintained a friendly relationship with both McCoy, who maintained her position as minister responsible for women's issues in the new Cabinet, and with the province's progressive women's organizations. Unfortunately, however, as the AACWI finally came into its own, the significance of women's concerns on the political agenda was diminishing. Despite the positive indications of increased responsiveness to women emanating from the 1989 election results, traditionalist, rural-based politicians and fiscal conservatives were reclaiming ground within Cabinet. Since the social policy reforms and developments demanded by feminists and other women's groups were associated with both increased spending and a rethinking of the social order, feminists found themselves increasingly delegitimized.

Key initiatives undertaken by the AACWI that contributed to its reclaimed integrity among the province's women's groups were its strong pro-choice stand and opposition to the federal government's attempt to recriminalize abortion.[126] The council also became active in supporting women's groups that felt they had been excluded from the Lieutenant Governor's Conference on the Family. The AACWI, in conjunction with several women's organizations, issued a news release that challenged the narrow view of the family being considered at the conference. The release stated that

single parent families, refugee and immigrant families, native families, families headed by teenage parents and families on limited incomes are all common forms of families in Alberta. These families are under-represented at this conference and we are concerned that their views are not being heard.[127]

Not surprisingly, these views did not endear the advisory council to conservative women's groups.

The more thoughtful and competent the advisory council became, the more inaudible was the government's response to their reports and recommendations. When queried about the character of the relationship between the council and the government in the early 1990s, one council member stated that this "was the huge grey zone. It was like the X-file."[128] McCoy and Mertick maintained a good relationship and council members respected the minister, but the declining importance and even hostility towards women's issues among other government members reduced AACWI's significance as an agent of legislative and policy change. Even the minister conceded that the government was unresponsive to the recommendations of the council.[129]

The tumultuous year of 1989 marked the high point of both the AACWI's influence on government and the Alberta state's commitment to addressing women's inequality. By the end of Mertick's term in 1992, the AACWI had established itself among feminist claimsmakers as a respected advocate. This was an important accomplishment given the skepticism that had prevailed among the province's women's groups in the aftermath of AACWI's founding and during the crisis surrounding Leahey's resignation and Mertick's appointment. Still, in the context of the decreasing legitimacy of feminist claimsmakers, AACWI's respect among progressive women's groups did not translate into enhanced influence on state policy. While the minister remained committed to the council, nominating a seasoned feminist activist to replace Mertick, the Cabinet had, by that point, lost interest in legitimizing feminist claimsmakers. McCoy's nominee was rejected by Cabinet and the AACWI was left without a chair for the remainder of Getty's term as premier.[130]

Feminists and Family Values

■ THE FAMILY

Feminists, particularly at the provincial level, had long encountered unsympathetic politicians and bureaucrats. Nonetheless, in the 1980s, as women secured greater legitimacy, the political imperative of appearing to hear all sides of a debate and of taking gender-equity issues seriously meant that explicitly invoking patriarchal norms of social organization was politically hazardous. However, attention to women's struggles for equality invoked fear from both constituents and elected officials and pressure to acknowledge these fears intensified. The political strategy was not, however, to dismantle state agencies and rewrite policy that reflected feminist demands but, instead, to add state agencies and policies that legitimized the pro-family movement. In this way the force of feminist arguments for equality was diluted.

Although the rhetoric of "family values" was ominous and unnerving for feminists, it was also true that the Getty government's commitment to the family was extremely thin. The family, nostalgically understood, was a logical site at which to download and privatize state responsibilities, though this outcome was not realized by the Getty government. Even if one concedes that the government was genuinely concerned about reinforcing the virtues of the traditional family, elected officials demonstrated little appreciation of the resources required to realize their rhetorical devotion to strengthening Alberta families.

Throughout the late 1980s and early 1990s, much was said regarding the family as a site of strength and support while alternative configurations of some families as places of violence, instability, and distrust were either ignored or explained as the product of deviation from the traditional family form. The chair of the Premier's Council in Support of Alberta Families, Stockwell Day, provided an excellent example of this approach to the family when he announced that statistics showed that the children of divorced parents are more likely than the children of parents who are not divorced to have emotional and psychological problems that lead to drug abuse, crime, and suicide. "These statistics are the reality of what may happen to your kids should you choose divorce," said Day.[131]

In another case, the province announced that $100 million, drawn from lottery funds, would be used for leisure facilities on the basis that "people who 'work together, play together and enjoy themselves together' tend 'to hold the community together and families together.'"[132] When asked why this money was not being spent on social services, the minister responsible, Jim Dinning, replied, "Why not think of the 1.2 million married Albertans? If we can help them to stay strong then I think we're taking the right approach."[133]

These comments cast a negative moral judgement on families other than those of the two-parent, and doubtless heterosexual variety, and subsequently deny such families access to state resources. Day did not offer a policy strategy that addressed the alleged risks faced by children of divorced parents and ignored the various economic and social pressures that contribute to marital breakdown. Instead, he offered the low-cost policy solution of maintaining marriages. Similarly, Dinning's comments reveal his view that the community was a place of support for the middle class, that social assistance recipients were unmarried parents, and that they had already received their fair share from the state. If the province was going to spend money, its programs should benefit taxpayers and voters.

Perhaps the most revealing illustration of the government's thin commitment to the family was the premier's 1989 election call. At the news conference following the announcement that the campaign would focus on the family, drug abuse, and federal issues, a reporter remarked on a recent news story asserting that Getty regularly disregarded the province's seat-belt legislation and called Getty a seat-belt abuser. Getty objected to the charge, saying, "I maybe whacked my kids, beat my wife, but I've never abused a seat-belt in my life."[134] A retraction and acknowledgement of the seriousness of domestic violence was issued within several hours, but the premier's gaff underscored the instrumentalism of his nostalgic invocations of the family.

The Getty administration's most substantive contribution to the reclamation of the traditional family was the establishment of the Premier's Council in Support of Alberta Families. The council was chaired by a member of the Conservative caucus, with members appointed by the Cabinet, and supported by social groups that were much less suspicious of the provincial government and the Alberta state than the feminist groups to which AACWI was to cater. The council asserted that its agenda was the product of a broadly representative consultative process in which 3,000 Albertans expressed their concerns about families. The council declared that it was "guided in its mandate by the belief that the family has always been and remains the best environment in which the skills and values vital to a strong, democratic environment are acquired,"[135] and that "the family is the single greatest influence on our lives, shaping who we are, how we feel about ourselves and how we approach the challenges of life."[136] The list of participants suggests that more critical insights regarding the family and the character of citizenship were put forward, but these insights were not considered in the consultation summary or in the council's subsequent publications.

Virtually all of the premier's council's publications began with the claim that the government needs to recognize the diversity of Alberta families. Such a claim suggests that the council deployed a broad definition of the family. In truth, however, the council's only definitional effort was the statement that "two or more persons related by birth, marriage, or adoption" was the most frequently cited definition in their public consultations.[137] The documents do acknowledge that broader definitions exist, but there are many indications that "the best" family is the heterosexual, two-parent, nuclear model in which "traditional" gender roles are the norm.

Evidence for the premier's council's support for the nuclear family ranges from the absence of any reference to same-sex couples to the claim that "a strong partnership between spouses is...important in modeling and teaching caring and loving behaviour to family members."[138] In an appendix listing the issues identified through the consultative process, the roles and responsibilities of family members are categorized as nurturer, provider, and contributor. Issues relating to the nurturer role include providing greater support, recognition, and respect for stay-at-home mothers. In order to enhance the capacity of the provider role, the report suggests increasing the ability of a single income to meet basic family needs. As for contributors, that is, women employed in paid labour, the council observes:

> While many households require two earners…some families become two income households by choice rather than necessity. Some argue that this has chipped away at the family foundation by reducing family time and by placing an emphasis on accumulating possessions and material wealth to achieve happiness or success.[139]

Given that, by the late 1980s, sixty-five to eighty hours of work per week were required to sustain a family, as opposed to forty-five hours per week in the 1970s, the suggestion that women work simply to provide the family with luxury items was worthy of challenge.[140] A council less enamoured with the nuclear family might have offered more critical engagement with this perception.

Of course, the premier's council was neither an institution with much power, nor could the council itself exercise any influence on the way people lived their lives. Its purpose seemed to be to provide empirical support for the government's rhetorical position. However, the more deeply the council investigated the stresses impacting families, the less useful the council would become to the government. If the provincial state was truly invested in maintaining the single-income nuclear family, resources would have to be directed to augmenting family income so that families could actually afford to have only one participant in the paid labour force. If marriages were to be based on strong partnerships, women would have to be sufficiently financially independent and emotionally autonomous that they could demand their partners' respect. If the family was to foster an environment in which children could learn to be good citizens, educational and community resources would have to be widely available. A meaningful family policy initiative would require the investment of more rather than less resources, and women and children would be its primary beneficiaries.[141]

OVER ALBERTA'S SIH-YEAR crisis of the welfare state, the province's organized women's groups reached the height of their claimsmaking capacity. The serious economic crisis faced by the province as the result of decreased oil revenues, a legislative Opposition that viewed women's issues as a vulnerability for the government, the appointment of a sympathetic minister responsible for women's issues, the prominence of women's issues at the federal level, and a regular calling to account of the government by a growing array of women's groups, ensured women's issues a place on the province's political agenda.

Political legitimacy, however, was never secure. Feminists were frequently confronted by attempts to circumscribe their achievements, as with the de-insurance of sterilization and birth control counselling, the struggle over access to abortion, and the rhetoric of family values invoked by antifeminist organizations and some elected representatives. Even those government initiatives designed to address gender inequity were fraught with contradictions and marked by inadequacy. The shortcomings of the Plan for Action for Alberta Women and the unwillingness of its sponsoring minister to consider pay equity highlights the government's unwillingness to address the social conditions that perpetuate women's marginalization. Additionally, the approach to the AACWI, beginning with the appointment of an unqualified chair, limiting appointments to Conservative Party members, and disregarding the council's work, also indicated the superficiality of the government's commitment to women's issues and the extent to which women had to remain vigilant if their legitimacy was to be preserved.

As for feminist activists themselves, the late 1980s was a time of increasing concern for organizational practices and inclusiveness, as well as the efficacy of state-focused claimsmaking. ASWAC's centrality to the Alberta feminist movement diminished as a series of boards refocused the organization's energies on feminist spirituality and consciousness raising at the expense of claimsmaking. To some degree, ASWAC's Women Against Poverty initiative represented another realignment, this time towards claimsmaking on feminist terms. But the public funding required for the initiative meant that the state, though particularly the federal state, continued to play a role in shaping ASWAC's claimsmaking strategies. Disagreements with ASWAC's shift in focus and the project-based funding structure of the Secretary of State Women's Program led to the development of many smaller, issue-specific, feminist organizations. The knowledge of specific social policy issues that these groups acquired meant that state actions regularly faced challenge and criticism. The growth of these groups contributed significantly to the maintenance of women's issues on the provincial government's agenda. However, women's increased political strength also inspired a strongly negative reaction from those who interpreted the social upheaval that accompanied the province's economic crisis as resulting from an unstable moral foundation to which feminists were a major contributor.

The resort to "family values" represented the most coherent and sustained attempt by the state and pro-family organizations to contain feminist claimsmakers in the late 1980s and early 1990s. Although conservative values were never absent from the policies of the Alberta state in the 1980s, their explicit articulation in the celebration of the traditional nuclear family with a male breadwinner and a stay-at-home mother represented a departure from the earlier insistence on formal equality and, subsequently, the legitimation of feminist claimsmaking marked by the adoption of liberal pluralism. Even here, however, inconstancy and incongruity were prominent features. The fact that "the family" was regularly deployed in response to demands for increased social spending suggested that the province's devotion to family matters was motivated more by fiscal crisis than an authentic concern for the well-being of the family unit.

In the context of the fiscal crisis of the welfare state, the inadequacies of liberal pluralism as a strategy to manage growing demands on the state became increasingly apparent. The disparate character of the groups to which the state distributed resources lent a profound inconsistency to the normative underpinnings of Alberta's public policy. Moreover, acknowledging the political legitimacy of these groups, however tenuous, meant that both feminists and antifeminists could lay claim to state resources. Several years of deficit budgets and an economy in recession, however, meant that there were fewer resources available. It did not help that the provincial government had also participated in a series of public investment failures, including Novatel, Alberta Pacific Terminals, Gainers, and MagCan, totalling more than one billion dollars in forfeited tax dollars. By the end of Getty's premiership, many Albertans were disgusted by the condition of governance in the province. Conditions were ripe for an overhaul of the politics of claimsmaking.

Learning Neoliberalism

IN AUGUST OF 1992, Don Getty resigned as Alberta's premier. The damage he had inflicted upon the credibility of the Conservative Party meant that his successor would have to distinguish him/herself from the cavalier approach to fiscal management that had become associated with the Getty government. It was not then clear that this process of distancing the Conservative Party from its penchant for private-sector bailouts would entail a full-blown transformation of state form. Only four months later, however, Albertans had embarked upon a thoroughgoing effort to rethink and reshape the complex relationships among society, the state, and the market.

For Alberta's progressive women's organizations, Getty's resignation and the ensuing leadership race offered, ironically, some cause for rejoicing. The front runners for the Conservative Party leadership, Nancy Betkowski (now MacBeth) and Ralph Klein, had been relatively supportive of progressive causes throughout their political careers. The fact that Betkowski was a woman even inspired some Alberta feminists to take out memberships in the Conservative Party to support her candidacy.[1] As it turned out, however, Ralph Klein's successful leadership bid and his subsequent remaking of the provincial state dealt a series of mortal blows to women's organizing in Alberta. Dramatic and far-reaching reductions in social spending, wholesale rejection of the legitimacy of claimsmaking by groups not associated with the business sector, and increased demands on the unpaid labour of women served to undermine feminist organizing in a manner unparalleled by the resort to formal equality deployed during the 1970s or the use of liberal pluralism in the 1980s.

Although women's groups have been involved in a variety of initiatives since Klein reorganized the provincial state, most of these were time-limited, single-focus projects, often involving broad-based coalitions and not identifiably feminist in their approach or their demands. The notable exception has been the women's shelter movement. The explanation for this weakening of explicitly feminist claimsmaking is multi-faceted, and includes organizational changes within women's groups, a broadening analysis of the sources and objects of oppression, decreased funding on the part of the federal and provincial governments, and a political climate of hostility towards demands for equality. Central to all of these changes, however, has been the shift from a welfare to a neoliberal form of the state.

Klein's transformation of provincial governance so that market emula-tion became the singular focus of public policy achieved two important strategic objectives for the Conservative government and the provincial state. At the time of the 1993 provincial election, the expression of neolib-eralism through deficit elimination and fiscal prudence helped to distance the Conservative Party from its previous incarnation, thus enhancing the party's credibility. At a more sustained level, the government's refusal to accept the political legitimacy of any constituency outside of the business community meant that politically contentious issues surrounding the means to improve the well-being of Albertans and the content of that well-being were largely absent from the political agenda. This lack of debate concerning issues of "the good" was sustainable as long as the deficit-elim-ination strategy could be maintained. However, the speed with which budget surpluses were achieved complicated this approach. In September 1993 Alberta's treasurer announced that the province's deficit was $310 million greater than anticipated.[2] In 1994–95, however, the province posted a budget surplus of $958 million.[3] Still, the government persisted with its dire economic forecasts, predicting a budget deficit in 1995–96 of $506 million.[4] In fact, oil and gas revenues boosted the province's surplus that year to $1.1 billion.[5]

Interestingly, the constituency most optimistic about expanding the political agenda in the wake of the province's improved economic fortunes was not that of welfare-state defenders but rather, moral conservatives. This constituency supported the Klein government because of its fiscal conservatism, but hoped that they would be rewarded for their support through the adoption of social legislation espousing their "traditional" vision of an orderly society. The overt articulation of conservative morality has not, however, been a central feature of the Klein government, despite the presence of several caucus and cabinet sympathizers, and has created discontent among these constituents. Social progressives, while also discontented, have resisted efforts to bend market logic to their own ends, pointing, instead, to the duplicity in the Klein government's claims that the achievement of economic growth through the free market is without moral content. Public outcry surrounding private hospital legislation is only the most obvious effort to challenge the alleged amorality of the government's support for market solutions to issues of collective goods provision.

The relationship between both feminist and conservative women's groups and the Alberta state over the period of the Klein administration is a microcosm of the tensions inherent in the consolidation of neoliberal governance. The reconstitution of the relationship between the state and civil society is a central feature of this new state form. However, despite the desire of neoliberal adherents to absent the state from acrimonious social policy debate, political contestation remains a key feature of the neoliberal state. The means through which this contestation is expressed, however, have undergone some important alterations because of the dynamics of neoliberalism. This chapter examines the unsuccessful struggles of both ASWAC and AFWUF to adapt to the new regime, and contrasts their short-comings in negotiating the neoliberal terrain with the success of the Alberta Council of Women's Shelters (ACWS). In addition to these organi-zations, temporarily constituted groups and coalitions have also had some

Learning Neoliberalism

success in both resisting and advancing social policy reform, particularly in the areas of abortion, kindergarten, health, and human rights. Although it might be presumed that the provincial state agencies designed to address women's issues would have been rapidly and unceremoniously abandoned by the Klein government, the process of their dismantling was not straight-forward. The fate of the AACWI and the Women's Secretariat and the persistence of a minister responsible for women's issues demonstrate the complexities of imposing neoliberal governance.

■ WOMEN'S GROUPS AND THE NEW REGIME

The zeal with which the Klein government pursued its deficit-elimination agenda overwhelmed Alberta women's groups. The announcements of spending reductions and program cuts in the areas of health, education, and social services came with such rapidity that women's organizations, along with other social justice groups, were incapable of mounting a sustained counter-attack.[6] These spending reductions were not confined to undermining the capacity for advocacy, however. They also increased the demand on women's groups to provide services that the provincial government had cut back or abandoned as part of its deficit-elimination strategy. Moreover, women's groups increasingly found that their access to funding, whether from the province, the federal government, or other granting agencies, was dependent on service provision or the development of specific projects.[7] Funding was largely unavailable for explicitly political activity and those groups, such as ASWAC, that had pursued advocacy, feared that they were primary targets for "punishment" via funding reductions.[8] In addition to the increased demand for service provision and reduced funding, women's groups were also constrained by diminishing numbers of activists and volunteers as the demand for volunteer labour increased within the education, social services, and health sectors.[9]

All of these factors took their toll on ASWAC. While ASWAC staff certainly served as referral agents to the many women who contacted its offices seeking help, this service function was derivative of its advocacy work. ASWAC did attempt to publicize the effects of the Klein govern-ment's policies on women, particularly through continued work on poverty, and also encouraged women to participate in the electoral process through the production of a voter's guide, the circulation of an election question-naire to all candidates, and the organization of a women's lobby day at the provincial legislature.[10] However, regular struggles with the federal govern-ment's Secretary of State Women's Program surrounding funding, diminished energy within the organization, and a drawn-out legal battle over allega-tions of unemployment insurance fraud foundered the organization. ASWAC closed its doors in 1997, leaving its resources to the provincial archives.

Although AFWUF has avoided a similar fate, the neoliberal regime of the Klein government has not proved to be the godsend some of its members had hoped for. Certainly the group attempted to put the best face on the consequences of social-spending reductions, arguing that the shift from institutionalized health care to home-based care could "again make us into a caring, enriching, life-enhancing, family and community oriented society."[11] Further, while they acknowledged that the burden of care would fall on women "this [did] not have to be a problem, because women are naturally inclined to be nurturing and caring."[12] However, the deficit-elimi-nation agenda did not spare "pro-family" government initiatives. In fact, the Premier's Council in Support of Alberta Families was disbanded well before the AACWI. Further, the unwillingness of many members of the Conservative caucus, including the premier, to support morally conserva-tive issues was often confounding to AFWUF members. A particularly irksome example for AFWUF was Klein's decision to extend provincial support for the UN Convention on the Rights of the Child despite his inability to ensure that the Convention would not override parents' rights.[13] AFWUF proved its adaptability to the new regime, however, in the repackaging of its policy prescriptions for abortion and gay rights. The demand for the abolition of abortion was reconstituted in an appeal to end "tax-funded abortions" while AFWUF's condemnation of homosexuality was expressed in resistance to the extension of human rights protection to gays and lesbians on the grounds that such recognition would constitute "special rights."

The greatest bulwark against the advance of conservative women, however, was the justice system. The campaign against the inclusion of gays and lesbians within Alberta's human rights legislation and the prevention of adoptions to same-sex couples have been the central preoccupations of AFWUF during Klein's tenure. In each case, however, its efforts have been thwarted by the Supreme Court of Canada and by the Alberta government's unwillingness to invoke the notwithstanding clause to override the Court's decision on the inclusion of sexual orientation within the equality provisions of the Charter of Rights and Freedoms. Although the Alberta government and AFWUF both argued against the inclusion of gays and lesbians within the province's human rights legislation at the Supreme Court, the Court's ruling in support of inclusion forced the province to acknowledge that further resistance would be futile. The provincial government did promise that it would review existing legislation to prevent further encroachments on heterosexuality in the areas of marriage, benefits, and sex education curriculum, but this promise has proven to be empty.[14] When two lesbian couples from Calgary launched a suit challenging the heterosexual exclusiveness of the province's adoption legislation, the province, while initially defending the existing legislation in court, ultimately opted to withdraw from the case before a decision had been rendered, and rewrote the legislation in order to accommodate same-sex parents. AFWUF struggled to maintain the province's initial legal challenge by applying to serve as *amicus curiae*, or "friend of the court" on the case, but the requirement that such an intervention be made by a neutral party and the clear absence of neutrality in AFWUF's position effectively terminated its capacity for involvement. Moreover, the province's legislative reform initiative left AFWUF without a case to defend.[15] One exception to this dismal record for the advance of conservative policy was the passage of a private member's bill outlawing same-sex marriages. This legislation was remarkable in that it represented the first time that Alberta successfully included the notwithstanding clause within the content of legislation.[16] Here too, however, the initiative may be thwarted by the Court on grounds outside the purview of section 33, as the fact that the province does not have constitutional jurisdiction over marriage is likely to eliminate the bill's legal effect.[17]

The revival of the abortion debate under the ruse of fiscal austerity draws together the various dynamics informing the interactions among moral conservatives, the neoliberal state, and feminist activism. The renewal of the abortion debate was instigated in February 1995 by a group calling itself the Committee to End Tax Funded Abortions and was strongly supported by AFWUF. Connected to several pro-life MLAs and the media voice of the *Alberta Report,* the committee was well equipped to establish a place for the abortion issue on Alberta's political agenda.[18] Arguing that it was "impossible to beat the pro-abortionists with the argument that the fetus is a person," pro-life supporters adopted the position that taxpayers should not be required to fund abortions and that withdrawing state funding for abortions would represent a substantial savings to the health-care budget.[19] Although this argument required the pro-life camp to accept abortions that were paid for by patients themselves, this sacrifice of moral principle was deemed necessary to re-open the abortion debate. Moreover, by positioning their argument at the level of deficit reduction, pro-life proponents hoped to gain the support of people who would otherwise consider themselves pro-choice.[20]

In addition to the strategic acquisition of neoliberal discourse for the framing of the abortion debate, the committee took advantage of the political opportunity provided by the elimination of the deficit. Although the premier was not a supporter of the pro-life position and was well aware of the political liabilities associated with opening the abortion debate, it was also true that he had benefited from the support of his more morally conservative caucus members throughout the period of deficit reduction. The announcement of a budget surplus meant that the need for a unified front to achieve the government's primary objective had dissipated. If Klein was to avoid dissension within the ranks, some concessions would need to be granted to the moral right of the party.[21] Klein's decision to consider the question of abortion did not happen immediately, however. Despite the committee's concerted efforts to lobby Conservative caucus and party members, a motion to end tax-funded abortions was narrowly defeated at the Conservative Party convention in April 1995, after Klein announced that he would not take action to de-insure abortion even if the motion was carried.[22] The premier was not alone in his reluctance to place the abortion issue on the Conservative Party agenda. One caucus member argued that "the Tories were elected on Ralph's coattails and not on issues like abortion and eliminating funding for the arts or gay rights," while another asserted that he "didn't think it [was] the government's job to address the social issues."[23] It was not until the Community Services Committee of the legislature had held hearings into the issue and formally proposed to the Conservative caucus that the government eliminate public funding for all abortions, except those in which a woman's life was in danger, that the premier finally relented, agreeing to hold a closed-door, free vote within caucus.[24]

For its part, the pro-choice opposition, embodied primarily by Planned Parenthood Alberta and the Calgary-based Pro-Choice Coalition, developed a two-pronged response to the committee's efforts. One avenue of response was to remind the provincial government of the legal precedents supporting a woman's right to abortion and the unlikelihood that the province could successfully abrogate that right.[25] The second avenue of response involved pushing the debate beyond the narrow constraints of the Conservative Party and into the public sphere. Large ads in which over 500 Albertans expressed their support for the continued inclusion of abortion as a provincially insured medical service were run in the city newspapers of Calgary, Grande Prairie, Lethbridge, and Red Deer.[26] Additionally, pro-choice advocates engaged committee members in public debate as a means to expose the committee's tax argument as a cover for its antichoice position. In a CBC radio debate a pro-choice supporter queried a spokesperson for the committee on her position that women who had been raped should not be eligible for a publicly funded abortion. The committee representative replied that the stress of the abortion would only intensify the trauma experienced by victims of sexual assault.[27] It was clear from this statement that the committee's expressed concern for the hapless spending of taxpayers' money was a fresh cover for an old debate. Indeed, the coherency of the fiscal austerity argument fell apart in the face of evidence that bringing a fetus to term cost taxpayers more than an abortion.[28] Moreover, in the face of a budget surplus of $958 million and a health department budget of $3.5 billion, the $4 million that the committee claimed represented the annual cost of abortions was an insignificant sum.[29]

Ultimately, the compromise brokered between the neoliberals and the moral conservatives within the party was to provide funding only for those abortions that were deemed medically necessary. In fact, the medical necessity argument was a creative political manoeuvre designed to displace the controversy away from the political arena and onto the "scientifically objective" assessment of the province's doctors. The Alberta Medical Association, however, argued that the existing definition of medical necessity did not require revision and, as a result, all abortions performed in Alberta would continue to be funded under the province's medical insurance program.[30] Thus, the moral controversy surrounding abortion had its airing and the government cleverly negotiated the political minefield that abortion politics inevitably presents.

The dynamics of organizing opposition to the Committee to End Tax Funded abortions were rife with the strains placed on progressive organizations as a result of neoliberalism. Although Planned Parenthood Alberta and the Calgary Pro-Choice Coalition responded quickly to the Committee to End Tax Funded Abortions, there were many pro-choice activists, particularly in Edmonton, who were initially unmoved by the committee's efforts. In a moment when activists were particularly concerned about making the best use of their diminishing resources, these people felt that the weight of judicial precedent undermined the credibility of the threat to women's reproductive choice posed by the committee, and, hence, that the matter would resolve itself.[31] In fact, the Edmonton Planned Parenthood office actually chastised the provincial office for addressing the financial arguments of the Committee to End Tax Funded Abortions.[32] The Edmonton office failed to appreciate that while the majority of Canadians supported women's reproductive autonomy, financing this autonomy with public funds was a point of vulnerability in an era when fiscal austerity and individual responsibility were central to the generation of electoral enthusiasm for social spending reductions. Given the strong linkages between the committee and several Conservative MLAs, this reticence to oppose the pro-life forces and unwillingness to attack the foundation of their argument was ill-considered. Indeed, the executive director of Planned Parenthood Alberta argued that if pro-choice forces had not demonstrated their objec-

Learning Neoliberalism   127

tions to the committee, the position of the premier and other pro-choice caucus members in opposing the de-insurance of abortions would have been dangerously weakened.[33]

In contrast to the thwarted initiatives of moral conservatives and feminist advocacy organizations, the issue of violence against women has been remarkably resilient to the onslaught of neoliberal governance. Several factors account for the continued presence of this issue on the political agenda. Unlike other parts of Canada, the shelter movement in Alberta was not the product of grassroots feminist activism, but rather of the work of the wives of wealthy oilmen and more traditional women's groups, including the Catholic Women's League and the Business and Professional Women's Association.[34] The shelters that emerged and their provincial umbrella organization, ACWS, concerned themselves solely with operating shelters. In fact, the shelter movement did not undertake any feminist advocacy until after Klein's election.[35] These conservative roots and history of apoliticism contributed to the shelter movement's strength under neoliberalism in two important respects. First, avoiding the link between feminism and violence against women meant that the shelter movement subsequently escaped the full wrath of deficit cutting that was visited upon "special interests." However, the latent feminism retained by the issue contributed to its potential reconfiguration as a feminist champion when many other groups disbanded. Second, the shelter movement was able to use its apoliticism to achieve charitable status, thus making financial contributions to these organizations tax deductible. The capacity to issue tax receipts to donors makes shelters more compelling organizations to support than advocacy groups, whose politics disqualify them from charitable status, and also increases the probability that some financial resources will be available even when public monies are not.

Women's shelters have become an accepted component of provincial social service provision, receiving approximately 50 per cent of their operating budgets from the provincial government.[36] Hence, the fact that women's shelters have been integrated into the work of government also contributes to the persistence of violence against women on the political agenda. This is not to say that the shelter movement has not endured threats to its continued operation. Indeed, the increasing advocacy work of the ACWS inspired the minister of community development to threaten to withdraw his ministry's portion of funding for the organization's administrative work. After the ACWS said it would call a press conference to publicize his threat to the provision of services for abused women and their children, the minister rethought his position.[37] Still, like other social services, shelters have had to endure budget cuts and have been distanced from the levers of power through their submersion under an additional layer of bureaucracy provided by the creation of Regional Authorities for Child and Family Welfare. Nonetheless, the salience of the issue has been integral to the continued strength of the shelter movement.

At the deepest explanatory level for the success of the shelter movement, however, is the unarticulated, "common sense" understanding of femininity on which it rests. According to this view, women are presumed to be physically weak, emotionally vulnerable, and in need of protection. Women subjected to physical and psychological violence meted out by their intimate partners thus justifiably invoke responses of sympathy and compassion. The fact that male partners would use their physical advantage to insist on their authority is reasonably interpreted as an act of cowardice. But the solution to this power imbalance does not lie in the stopgap measure of providing temporary shelter. Rather, it lies in overturning social, psychological, and political structures that perpetuate women's subordination in the home and in the workplace. It is this far-reaching project of enabling women to gain the tools and resources for autonomy and hence, the capacity to resist domination, that has, broadly speaking, been the focus of the feminist movement. It is also the source of feminism's threat to existing structures of power.

Advocating for a reconceptualization of the gender order, however, is a difficult program to pitch, both within an organization that has succeeded on the basis of traditional understandings of men and women, and to a neoliberal state disinterested in issues of equity. To its credit, the ACWS has made some important advances in this direction. A critical analysis of Alberta's social assistance program as a temporary income support for women leaving abusive domestic situations is one such initiative.[38] Ironically, the organization may achieve some success in its feminist advocacy efforts by simultaneously challenging and relying on traditional understandings of heterosexuality, masculinity, and femininity.

Compassion in the face of injustice has been integral in the success of two additional campaigns of progressive activism against the neoliberal state—the struggle for the reinstatement of full public funding for kindergarten and resistance to the privatization of hospital laundry services in Calgary. In the case of kindergarten, deficit elimination provided a weak justification for reducing early childhood education by 50 per cent. Children represented a particularly cruel target for the government's restructuring agenda. Moreover, the women who organized around the issue were experienced advocates who made excellent use of their middle-class privilege to resist the neoliberal encroachment on this universal benefit. Successful resistance of the privatization of laundry facilities and the subsequent job loss for laundry workers was less predictable, given the pervasiveness of a popular discourse of disdain for organized labour and a well-entrenched faith in the market. However, a fortuitous combination of circumstances helped to illuminate the indignity of the government's policy in this area.

■ KINDERGARTEN

Resistance to the Alberta government's funding cuts to kindergarten was mounted throughout the province, with a union-led and community-supported coalition, the Common Front, spearheading the initiative in Calgary, while a small group of women from the affluent community of Glenora took up the struggle in Edmonton. Some co-ordination among the groups occurred in the compilation of a 22,000-name petition opposing the cuts, but for the most part, resistance was mounted by disparate groups in disparate communities.[39] The Edmonton group, the Glenora Parent Teacher Association, was largely composed of veteran feminist activists. This group's struggle provides the focus of this discussion.

The decision to reduce funding for kindergarten from 400 to 200 hours a year was announced in early 1994 and was to take effect in September of that year, as part of an overhaul of the provincial education system. Support for charter schools, home schooling, and greater private sector involvement in the provision of education were central features of the Klein government's educational reforms.[40] The heavy-handedness with which the government imposed its education initiatives elicited strong condemnation from teachers, students, and parents. It was in this context that the kindergarten funding decision was announced. The government's formal justification for its decision was that children could be prepared for formal learning with less time in the classroom.[41] The group opposing the kindergarten cuts argued that the Ministry of Education had no basis for this claim, as the government had undertaken "no research or study into the implications of the cut."[42] The *Calgary Herald* reported that many parents believed that the government had chosen to target kindergarten funding because it was not a mandated educational program and because of a perception that parents had not, historically, been overtly supportive of provincial funding for kindergarten.[43] From the perspective of community organizers, however, the government's plans for kindergarten were a blatant and poorly calculated attack on young children that only served to underscore the ruthlessness of the Klein government.[44]

The issue of equity was the central concern of the struggle surrounding kindergarten funding. Although the provincial government had made it clear that it would not provide funding beyond 200 hours of instruction, the regionalization of educational programming meant that the various school boards and private kindergarten operators could respond differently to the cuts. The Edmonton Public School Board, for example, reallocated resources from other programs to ensure that all kindergarten-aged children within its jurisdiction would be able to attend classes without charging parents an additional fee.[45] The Calgary Public School Board, by contrast, required parents to pay $466 for the provision of 400 hours of instruction.[46] Calgary children whose parents were unable to afford the fee would enter kindergarten without cost beginning in February.[47] As the Glenora Parent Teacher Association argued, the effects of this flexibility in the provision of kindergarten risked the creation of a patchwork of arrangements that would subsequently pose difficulties for grade-one classrooms, as children would be at widely divergent levels of preparation for schooling.[48]

Further, the implication that a child's class background would limit her access to a basic education was also challenged by opponents of the kindergarten cutbacks.

The Klein administration's approach to the reduction in kindergarten funding presumed that parents, particularly mothers, would reorganize their lives in order to care for their children themselves or pay for the care of their children for at least the extra 200 hours that children would no longer spend in kindergarten. Additionally, the fact that 99 per cent of kindergarten teachers are women and that many either lost their jobs or had their hours significantly reduced as a result of the government's funding changes also reflected the disproportionate effect of the new policy on women.[49] Revealingly, however, the gender dimension of the kindergarten issue was not taken up as a central argument of opposition. Instead, the strategy was to focus on the harm caused to young children rather than risk delegitimation by being associated with "special interests" or partisan politics.[50]

Although the opposition to kindergarten funding cuts was widely perceived as a grassroots endeavour, the initiative undertaken by the Glenora Parent Teacher Association suggests that the skills and access to resources that are the stock-in-trade of the upper middle class had an important impact on the attainment of concessions and the eventual reinstatement of full funding to kindergarten programs. The women behind the Glenora initiative drew on long-standing ties to the Conservative Party establishment and government connections built up over years of political activism and employment in the public sector to facilitate their access to decisionmakers.[51] Their high levels of educational achievement and relative familiarity with the process of claimsmaking, though not necessarily with the issue of early childhood education, were important assets as they confronted government hostility. They were also aided by the fact that the provincial treasurer was the representative for the Glenora riding and was a neighbour of one of the group's most active members.[52] The opportunity to make the argument for the reinstatement of kindergarten funding to the treasurer as he waxed his car on a sunny afternoon was certainly not one that was available to most community activists.[53]

After a year of marshalling arguments, presenting briefs, and cajoling government representatives, the Alberta government announced, in December 1994, that it was prepared to increase government funding for kindergarten for an additional thirty-two hours.[54] Not surprisingly, the response of community organizations was that it was too little, too late.[55] Once it became clear that the coffers of the provincial treasury were being substantially enriched by high oil and gas prices, the government's stinginess regarding kindergarten funding could no longer be maintained. Finally, in late 1996, the Alberta government reinstated full funding for kindergarten.[56]

■ LAUNDRY WORKERS

One of the most impressive and spontaneous acts of resistance to the imposition of the neoliberal state in Alberta was instigated by a group of 120 hospital laundry workers in Calgary. Their position as low-paid workers performing a necessary but unglamorous service to the health-care industry and the subsequent callousness with which they were informed of impending job losses, galvanized Albertans against the Klein government's health-care restructuring initiatives. The struggle of the laundry workers and the ensuing labour crisis within the health-care sector was a profound testament to citizens' expectations that the Alberta state was obliged to resist the collapse of the public interest in the service of private gain.

The decentralization of the health ministry's responsibilities to seventeen regional health authorities (RHAs) was central to the Klein government's restructuring of health care. RHAs were seen as necessary mechanisms to "take politics out of health decisions at the provincial government level and have government focus on setting policy and standards, [make] global budget decisions, [ensure] equity and [monitor] outcomes."[57] Each of the authorities was given responsibility for the governance and management of health care, thus allowing them to reorganize health-care provision within their jurisdictions.[58] If the result was an inability to provide some medical services, an arrangement might be made with a neighbouring health authority.[59] If cost-savings could be achieved through salary reduc-

Learning Neoliberalism 133

tions, or by contracting out various support and medical services, the health authorities were at liberty to do this as well.[60]

As a consequence of the ensuing privatization initiatives, unionized laundry workers at two Calgary hospitals, most of whom were immigrant women, were informed that their jobs would disappear. In the effort to realize cost-savings, the Calgary Regional Health Authority announced that it had awarded a contract for the cleaning of the city's hospital laundry to K–Bro; a private, Edmonton-based firm. The workers, in an attempt to save their jobs, had agreed to pay cuts averaging 28 per cent of their meagre salaries. With the announcement of the K–Bro deal, they were told that regardless of their wage concessions, they were out of work. A small sum of money for retraining would be available to them, but they would receive no severance pay.[61] A cost-savings of $2 million over five years would accrue to the health authority as a result of the elimination of the laundry workers' jobs.[62] As the president of K–Bro later stated, "It's a question of priorities. Do you want to spend money subsidizing a laundry worker or getting your grandmother's hip replaced?"[63]

The laundry workers had anticipated the privatization of the laundry facilities. In fact, they had been involved, through the Canadian Union of Public Employees (CUPE) and the Alberta Union of Public Employees (AUPE) in advancing their own bids to run the laundry.[64] What was surprising to the laundry workers and to Calgarians generally, however, was that shipping hospital laundry from Calgary to Edmonton and back again would be more efficient than simply cleaning the laundry in Calgary. In fact, the Calgary Health Authority effectively ruled out the viability of all of the Calgary bids by insisting that the recently improved laundry facilities of the Bow Valley Centre (formerly the Calgary General) would not be available. The health authority was unwilling to accept the risks and liabilities of maintaining this public facility and the costs of constructing a new laundry facility were too high.[65]

The efficiency justification became increasingly dubious when it was revealed that the chair of the Calgary Regional Health Authority had only recently resigned as a board member of Vencap, a provincially funded, venture capital investment firm, that owned 60 per cent of K–Bro.[66]

Although the province's Auditor General cleared the health authority of conflict of interest in awarding the contract to K–Bro, the public relations damage had been done.[67]

A further contribution to the sense of injustice being visited upon the laundry workers was the premier's entanglement in a conflict of interest investigation resulting from his wife's participation in a sweetheart stock purchase. Under the terms of this deal, Mrs. Klein was permitted to forego the purchase price of Multicorp stocks until they were sold.[68] Although the premier was cleared of wrong-doing in this incident, his "just plain folks" image was tarnished. A columnist for the Globe and Mail reported that a caller to a Calgary phone-in show "landed the ultimate insult against the man he had voted for: 'Ralph,' he said, 'you're becoming Mr. Klein.'"[69] As David Bercuson observed, "There is nothing more pathetic than a man walking around in a tux saying, 'I, too, have cowshit on my boots.'"[70]

For the laundry workers and their supporters, however, the machinations of power were of secondary importance to the impending job losses. On 14 November 1995, after hearing the announcement that their jobs would be eliminated, sixty laundry workers at the Bow Valley Centre told their employer that they were too ill to work and walked off the job.[71] They met that evening to formulate a plan and formed a picket line at 5:30 a.m. the next morning.[72] Although many workers were concerned about the repercussions of undertaking an illegal job action, as well as the implications for their families, particularly so close to the Christmas season, they decided they had little to lose.[73] The following morning laundry workers at the Foothills Hospital staged a wildcat strike. On November 16 the Alberta Labour Relations Board ordered the laundry workers back to work. Over this two day period, however, an enormous amount of worker and public support was generated and the laundry workers decided to ignore the back-to-work order. As the strike went on, 2,500 CUPE and AUPE health-care workers joined the laundry workers on the picket line. Calgary members of the United Nurses of Alberta and170 cleaners in Edmonton voted to work to rule, while 2,000 AUPE organized health workers endorsed a wildcat strike and 200 members of the Health Sciences Association of Alberta walked out, despite a narrow vote against joining the strike.[74] By the time

Learning Neoliberalism   135

the laundry workers returned to work on 25 November 1995, Alberta was on the brink of a province-wide health-care walkout.[75]

The government's initial response to the growing crisis was that the issue should be resolved by the Calgary Health Authority.[76] Albertans, however, would not accept that the health authority was solely responsible for its decisions when it was clear that the provincial government's budget cuts and commitment to privatization severely constrained the decision-making process. Regardless of the government's conception of where accountability lay, Albertans insisted that health care remained an essential component of the public trust, and hence that the government was responsible for the efficacy of its administration.

The rising level of public support for the laundry workers and the growing sense of scandal led to a softening of the planned cuts. Only one week after the laundry workers at the Bow Valley Centre set up their picket line, the minister of health announced that $53 million of the $123 million in cuts planned for the following fiscal year would not proceed.[77] Having built a reputation as the "guy who didn't blink," the premier suddenly became responsive to discontent, claiming, "I've said before if we reach a roadblock and we have to make a detour, we will do that....We're getting the feeling people are impacted by the overall health care restructuring."[78] In fact, by the time the writ was dropped for the provincial election in 1997, virtually all of the money that had been cut from the health-care budget had been restored.[79]

So impressive was the laundry worker's fight that the National Action Committee on the Status of Women awarded them the "Women of Courage Award" at their 1996 annual meeting. As with the kindergarten struggle, however, the issue of gender was not a prominent feature of the laundry workers' strike. While it was apparent that the laundry workers were women, and predominantly immigrant women, the momentum of the strike was built on widespread dissatisfaction with the Klein government's approach to health-care restructuring rather than its peculiarly gendered dimensions. As it turned out, public disillusionment with health-care restructuring was not immediately transferable to other sites of discontent, although its capacity to galvanize opposition to the provincial government was demonstrated again in the spring of 2000 when the Alberta government passed legislation allowing for overnight stays in private hospitals.

In a sad irony, the people whose courage forced the Alberta government's retreat and inspired activists across the province obtained only a qualified success in securing their immediate objective—their continued employment. The settlement reached by the laundry workers only ensured that their jobs would not be contracted out for one year, though it did entitle workers to severance pay.[80] While the Calgary Health Authority eventually decided to maintain the laundry facilities at the Bow Valley Centre, it awarded the hospital laundry contract to K–Bro and another private firm, both of which were not unionized. Approximately fifty of the original laundry workers availed themselves of retraining opportunities while another twenty workers were hired by the private firms.[81]

The complex dynamics of women's organizing and resistance under the neoliberal state reveal the importance of several factors in achieving success. The demise of ASWAC and the success of ACWS, and the kindergarten and laundry workers' struggles illuminate the importance of access to resources. The provision of a valuable service or a clarity of focus are also imperative for an organization to maintain interest and support. Further, organizing initiatives are most likely to garner public support when radicality is deployed strategically rather than universally. Government attempts to renege on commitments to social justice could, as was the case for the abortion issue, also be successfully challenged by judicial precedent.

These precursors for successful organizing initiatives are laden with the weight of the neoliberal political environment from which they emerged. There are few opportunities, within these requirements, for participants to challenge the democratic shortcomings of their organizations or, indeed, of the state they seek to influence. Among the hallmarks of women's organizing during the 1980s was the development of an appreciation for the many sites of oppression and privilege that conflate in the formation of individual and political identities. The advance of neoliberal governance, however, has stymied this analysis and, in turn, narrowed the range of policy options under debate in both provincial and national political forums. It is not that all progressive initiatives are doomed, but rather that the possible range of legitimate political action is increasingly circumscribed.

Learning Neoliberalism   137

■ IDENTIFYING THE REMAINS OF WOMEN IN THE STATE

Resolving the welfare state's "crisis of ungovernability" by undermining the political legitimacy of interests articulated outside of the conventional party system has been a defining activity of neoliberal governance. Even in Alberta, however, this process has been undertaken with caution. Public consultations in virtually every government sector were carefully orchestrated to ensure the generation of support for restructuring initiatives. AACWI and the AHRC were similarly addressed, although in at least the case of the AHRC the outcome was not what the government had anticipated. In fact, the Alberta government felt compelled to retain the vestiges of its links to community organizations through the establishment of the Human Rights and Citizenship Branch within the Ministry of Community Development. In its neoliberal formulation, however, the community has become a central component in the provision of public services. Under the terms of this new relationship, the state conveys its agenda to citizens through community organizations, while the community finds it increasingly difficult to articulate its ideas and concerns to the state.[82] The appearance of openness that public consultations and links to community groups afforded is readily critiqued as a façade, but the fact that the consultations and links existed at all is a testament to the government's grudging appreciation of their political benefits. Democracy could be seen to be done, even if critics of the government felt that the consultations produced predetermined outcomes and that dissenting views were ignored.

With regard to the incorporation of women's concerns within Alberta's public policy, the hypocrisy of inclusiveness is particularly apparent. Although there continues to be a minister responsible for women's issues, falling within the broader responsibilities of the Ministry of Community Development, the portfolio has hardly been acknowledged since AACWI's closure in 1996. Indeed, after the Cabinet was shuffled in 1999, the responsibility was no longer included on the minister's website. It was mentioned in documentation from the Human Rights and Citizenship Branch but the ministry's annual reports have not included any activities undertaken under this portfolio.[83] Indeed, the Liberal Opposition's critic for women's issues was unaware that the portfolio existed.[84] One government employee undertakes the work formerly performed by the Women's Secretariat, although her activities are defined as providing "the Alberta Multiculturalism Commission with administrative support and [serving] as a catalyst within government to ensure that women's perspectives are considered."[85]

Outside of the Community Development Ministry, there has been even less regard for gender issues. Claims that the government's policies adversely and disproportionately affected women have been met with denial and hostility. When asked about the gendered effects of spending reductions in the area of social assistance, a spokesperson for the Department of Family and Social Services told the Alberta Advisory Council on Women's Issues (AACWI), "We don't track by gender. We don't care if it's a man or a woman, the head of the household is the one making the decisions. It makes no difference to our programs."[86] The last chair of the AACWI observed that, in drafting reports for the government "the feeling was very much 'don't use the word "woman," use the word "Albertan"' which means white middle class men. It put me in a difficult position to be the chair of AACWI and not be able to speak of women."[87] In legislative debates concerning the continued efficacy of the AACWI and the Women's Secretariat, several Conservative members asserted that it was inappropriate for the provincial state to fund these offices when other women's groups, notably AFWUF, raised their own money to lobby government.[88] To his credit, however, the minister responsible defended these offices, insisting that the meagre budgets of the secretariat ($669,000) and the AACWI ($338,000) were well invested[89] and that, at thirteen cents per Albertan, the AACWI, in particular, delivered excellent value for money.[90]

The tensions within the Klein government's attempt to undermine the legitimacy of women and other organized groups while also appearing to take their concerns seriously, is well illustrated in the dismantling of the AACWI, the public consultation surrounding the AHRC, and subsequent amendments to the Individual Rights Protection Act. Although it might be argued that the sunset clause attached to the advisory council sealed its fate, it is also apparent that the council's historically precarious relationship to its constituency and women's organizations' diminished resources contributed to a lack of defenders. By contrast, the government-led attack

Learning Neoliberalism   139

on the AHRC inspired an overwhelming response. Although women and the commission also had a difficult relationship, the commission could draw support from a broader constituency and from the prestige afforded to human rights. Moreover, the vehemence of the attack on sexual orientation that served as the centre point for the debate concerning the commission's continued existence also inspired concerted resistance.

■ THE DEMISE OF AACWI

In the early days of the Klein government, the fate of the AACWI seemed precarious indeed. The reporting structure through which the council conveyed its recommendations was transferred from the executive council to the minister of community development. At that time, the minister, Dianne Mirosh, was a woman whose disdain for pay equity and for feminism generally, as well as her undisguised homophobia, earned her the accolades of AFWUF.[91] In addition to this foreboding signal, the council also faced rumours of amalgamation with some combination of the Alberta Human Rights Commission, the Seniors' Secretariat, and the Premier's Council on the Status of People with Disabilities.[92] Further, the government had neglected appointments to the council, leaving it with ten vacancies and no chair.

Although the council avoided amalgamation and, in fact, did receive a new chair, Catharine Arthurs, her appointment was widely interpreted as part of a plan to dismantle AACWI. Arthurs did have some experience with women's issues, having served as the director of the Women's Bureau in the 1970s. But the Women's Bureau had never been a strong advocate for gender equality and, as far as the feminist community was concerned, Arthurs' years of faithful service to the Conservative Party appeared to be the real justification for her appointment.[93] The political climate of fiscal restraint, the discourse of "special interests" arrayed against "ordinary Albertans," and the various attempts to weaken the council that had preceded Arthurs' appointment did not portend a bright and vigorous future for the AACWI. Interestingly, however, Arthurs' integrity trumped her political allegiances. During her tenure as chair, she rejected the unstated agenda of the Klein government to dismantle the council, and

140   STATE OF STRUGGLE

worked diligently to save AACWI.[94] Her frustration with the government's duplicity towards her and towards women's issues eventually became so intense that she resigned from the position in disgust.[95]

Arthurs' unwillingness to eliminate the AACWI left the minister as a target for both women supporters of the Conservative Party, who were livid about the government's treatment of the AACWI, and several Conservative MLAs who continued to voice their loathing for the council.[96] Cleverly negotiating this minefield, the government re-equipped the council with a new chair selected through an open competition and the appointment of ten new members, but insisted that the ten-year sunset clause would be enforced.[97]

In the two years remaining in its mandate, the AACWI extensively investigated the economic situation of women over fifty-five, the usefulness of risk-assessment techniques for women in potentially abusive relationships, and the gendered effects of the Klein government's restructuring initiatives.[98] The council's reports were strongly critical of the government's policy initiatives and contained well-supported policy recommendations to address the inequities arising from the restructuring process. Indeed, these initiatives were a testament to the potential efficacy of an advisory council.

In addition to the council's research undertakings, the AACWI, at the request of the community development minister, conducted a public consultation soliciting women's views on the responsiveness of government and ideas for mechanisms through which Alberta women could access elected officials and policymakers. The council met with over 400 women drawn from a range of class, cultural, and educational backgrounds and geographic regions.[99] According to the consultation report, women's experiences in communicating with government elicited the greatest level of frustration among participants: "Many women were unsure if their activities had any impact on government. Some women expressed feelings of helplessness and hopelessness, believing that none of the strategies they had used had yielded positive results. There were very few success stories."[100]

Proposals for future consultative mechanisms included the extension of AACWI's mandate and alterations to its structure and processes, the creation of a new council, the creation of a provincial coalition of existing

Learning Neoliberalism   141

women's groups, the development of a regionalized Alberta women's consortium with local advisory circles, and allowing women to devise their own means of communicating with the provincial state.[101] One woman wryly suggested that a new agency could be funded through the proceeds from a video lottery terminal.[102] The government, however, had no intention of maintaining an advisory agency in any form. Despite the weight of participants' support for some form of consultative structure, the government argued that "times have changed, women's groups have multiplied and grown in strength, and they can and want to speak for themselves to government without a publicly funded intermediary."[103] The public consultation process amounted to nothing more than palliative care.

AACWI's last publication was a review of its activities over the course of its mandate. As part of the review process, eight council members, three council staff, and six government representatives were asked to share their views on AACWI's performance. Although council members felt that their research initiatives had been valuable, their frustration with the government's inaccessibility appeared to undermine their sense of accomplishment.[104] Indeed, the review noted that only seven of eighty-six recommendations made since 1987 had received a positive response from the Alberta government.[105] Staff members also voiced frustration with government but felt that council members had been overly cautious in their relationships with MLAs and in their reticence to approach the media.[106] The views of government officials were more divergent. One government representative stated:

> The women on the Council were spectacular. They modelled tolerance, understanding and valuing of each other's opinions. They've always done the hard thing. As a group, they've always welcomed diverse opinions. If that model of valuing diversity could be bottled or injected into other agencies, it would be great.[107]

By contrast, another government representative asserted:

> We don't need AACWI. Women are already active individually and in groups. They need to also become involved in a political party; talk

142　STATE OF STRUGGLE

to MLAs; talk to their husbands; get onto boards and committees; and research organizations such as churches which have influenced change and emulate them.[108]

Created as a means to placate Alberta women in a moment of precarious political fortunes and economic recession, the advisory council revealed all of the weaknesses of the welfare state's deployment of liberal pluralism as a means to quell the rising demands of extraparliamentary groups. The more relevant the advisory council became to its constituency, however, the less desirable it was to the state. Without some responsiveness on the part of policymakers, the advisory council was unable to maintain a distinctive position within the Alberta women's movement, becoming, in practice, just one more women's advocacy group. As neoliberal governance took hold and the relationship between the state and virtually every social justice organization came under scrutiny, the advisory council's elimination was predictable. Indeed, the biggest surprise was that the Klein government exercised so much caution in closing it down. The women's community viewed the council's demise with sadness, but its contribution to improving the lives of Alberta women had not been sufficiently significant to generate much resistance. By contrast, the government's challenge to the AHRC and to the necessity of human rights legislation was viewed with much stronger concern.

■ HUMAN RIGHTS

In the period between Don Getty's resignation as leader of the Conservative Party and the selection of Ralph Klein as his successor, the AHRC, in conjunction with three gay and lesbian advocacy groups, asked Albertans who believed they had experienced discrimination on the basis of their sexual orientation to report their complaints to the commission. As a result of this study, considerable public support, and an Ontario Court of Appeal ruling that sexual orientation was implicitly included in the Charter, the commission announced, in December 1992, that the investigation of complaints based on sexual orientation would be included as a regular feature of the commission's work.[109] When Klein became premier and appointed Dianne Mirosh as the new minister responsible for the AHRC, however, she immediately vetoed the commission's decision, instructing commission staff not to investigate sexual orientation complaints.[110] The minister subsequently launched a legal review of the commission's action and publicly advocated the commission's abolition.[111] It had been many years since the provincial government had displayed such disregard for the arms-length relationship between itself and the AHRC.

Mirosh's actions and public statements set off a storm of controversy to which the government responded by establishing a review of the AHRC and replacing the minister. Initially, the outcome of these actions appeared contradictory. Jack O'Neill's appointment to the chair of the AHRC and the review process was viewed with skepticism since he was thought to be a conservative patsy who opposed the inclusion of sexual orientation in the Act.[112] At the same time, however, the new minister, Gary Mar, was supportive of a strong human rights commission. His appointments to the review panel included Conservatives but other partisan commitments were also represented, as well as people who had been active in the disabled, Aboriginal, immigrant, multicultural, and women's communities.[113]

For women's groups it was clear that the Klein government's efforts to shut down the AHRC would have to be opposed, despite their history of grievances with the commission and the legislation it enforced. Although the review process appeared to offer an opportunity to express these long-standing misgivings and offer suggestions for improvement, feminist activists were also aware that pointed criticism could serve as a justification for closure of the AHRC. Many groups voiced similar concerns, but ultimately chose to participate. By the time the review panel had completed its six months' of hearings, its members had received more than 1,700 submissions.[114]

The Calgary group Women Looking Forward was particularly instrumental in co-ordinating women's groups' demands and presentations in order to maximize resources. Common concerns were underscored and specific issues were extensively researched. Most progressive organizations recommended that the commission have more independence and resources, a more open appointment process, an enhanced education function, and the power to initiate investigations, and that sexual orientation be included as a proscribed ground within the Act. Women's groups, Aboriginal peoples, and immigrant service organizations also emphasized the need to include systemic discrimination within the Act and to improve the accessibility of the commission to non-English speakers and people whose knowledge and/or experience of quasijudicial bodies was one of intimidation.[115] Women's groups also recommended the inclusion of a clause permitting affirmative-action programs, a strengthening of the pay-equity provisions to include equal pay for work of equal value, the inclusion of domestic and farm workers within the terms of the Act, and protection for people with HIV or other infectious diseases.[116] Antipoverty groups recommended that Albertans should have the right to an adequate income and should not be discriminated against on the basis of source of income.[117] Edmonton Working Women offered a pointed critique of the commission's approach to addressing sexual harassment complaints.[118]

Opposition to the commission was also well organized. For the most part, opponents of the AHRC focused on previous commissions' support for sexual orientation and argued that human rights represented the conferral of "special rights" for the groups enumerated in the Act. As AFWUF argued, "Individuals or groups who are granted special rights by being singled out in legislation diminish the rights of the non-mentioned."[119] But the logic of this argument was weak, as demonstrated in the position of a Conservative MLA who asserted that homosexuals were advocating protection of a specific sexual lifestyle that did not constitute "normal" behaviour and that homosexuality was a reflection of a person's character and morality.[120] Rather than conferring a *special* right, the conservatives' objection to the inclusion of sexual orientation lay in allowing the morally repugnant to enjoy the *same* rights as the morally virtuous. As an article in an AFWUF newsletter noted: "The proposed amendment could lead to the eventual legalization of homosexual and lesbian marriages and child adoption."[121] Further, "Homeowners could lose all freedom in deciding whether or not to rent to homosexuals or lesbians, [and] employers would lose the right to refuse employment to homosexuals."[122]

In addition to the "special rights" argument, the presentations of opponents of the inclusion of sexual orientation also involved testimonials by "reformed" homosexuals and graphic, licentious, and hateful accounts of the sexual activities of gay men and lesbians.[123] This attack against homosexuals was sufficiently vicious to persuade the panel's chair to reverse his stand on the inclusion of sexual orientation.[124] In fact, by the end of the hearings, all of the panel members agreed that the need for human rights protection in Alberta was far more serious than they had realized.[125] Still, panel members struggled over whether their report should be written to ensure that the government would accept it, or to reflect the recommendations and concerns of the majority of presenters. In the end, the panel chose the latter course, presuming that the government would reject much of the report but that it would serve as an important organizing and educational tool for the community.[126]

Although the review panel's recommendations were warmly received by supporters of a strengthened human rights regime, women were disappointed by the report's treatment of the pay-equity issue. Arguing that pay equity was outside the scope of the review because of its "enormous ramifications" and its complexity, the panel avoided the issues of job ghettoization and the wage gap.[127] Nonetheless, the panel did recommend that the government adopt an employment-equity policy and that the AHRC take an active educational role in this area.[128]

Albertans and government members who had assumed that the review panel would recommend the commission's eradication suffered the most substantive disappointment with the review panel's report, however. Although Minister of Community Development Gary Mar later stated that he was personally prepared to support all of the panel's recommendations, most government members were not so inclined.[129] It was clear that more money for the commission would not be forthcoming, that the commission would not enjoy greater independence, and sexual orientation would certainly not be included in any revised human rights legislation.[130] Importantly though, abolishing the commission was no longer a consideration. Public opposition was sufficiently well organized and widespread to convince the government to evade the potential political fallout of shutting down the AHRC.

The government's new-found appreciation of the public's attachment to the AHRC was illustrated in its published response to the human rights review. In this document the government made the claim that it had accepted 70 per cent of the panel's recommendations, and asserted that "human rights protection is a vital part of the Alberta Advantage."[131] But this was a dubious claim. In accepting the recommendation that the commission administer provincial human rights legislation without interference from a government department, the government asserted that this was the current practice: "The fact that staff of the Commission are employees of the Department of Community Development does not affect the operation of the commission and it will continue without interference."[132] As was clear from the experience with sexual orientation, however, the association between the employees of the commission and the ministry had grave consequences for the independence of the commission. A similarly dubious response was offered regarding human rights protection for carriers of infectious agents as well as farm and domestic workers. The government argued that the Act already provided such protection—either under physical disability or by the repeal of the section excluding farm and domestic workers from protection. This assertion was then contradicted by the qualification that "Section 11.1 of the IRPA allows for discrimination where that discrimination is reasonable and justifiable."[133] Hence, those people concerned about hiring, employing, or renting accommodation to someone with HIV or who felt that abusing the rights of their domestic or farm workers was justifiable under the circumstances did not have to be overly concerned with these inclusions in the Act.

In addition to this formal response to the review panel's report, the Alberta government drafted a series of amendments to the province's human rights legislation. Weaknesses in the proposed amendments became the impetus for extending the initial organizing initiative, and involved the development of a strategic alliance of groups representing disparate interests that were nonetheless united in supporting human rights and opposing the government's proposals. The group with the greatest political credibility, at least from the perspective of the Conservative government, was the Dignity Foundation. This group was established by Conservative Senator Ron Ghitter, former AHRC chair Fil Fraser, and law professor Kathleen Mahoney in response to the attack on the AHRC launched by Mirosh.[134]

Learning Neoliberalism 147

Over the course of the review panel's hearings both the Dignity Foundation and community groups had attempted but failed to form a coalition. Members of the Dignity Foundation were unaccustomed to the attention to democratic process that featured centrally in community organizing and were wary of compromising their credibility by associating with more radical members of the community.[135] Similarly, community groups were critical of Dignity's penchant for control and were concerned that they might be "sold out" by its more "establishment" members.[136] Once the provincial government proposed Bill 24, the Individual Rights Protection Amendment Act, however, both Dignity and the community groups agreed to set aside their suspicions and pool their resources. The result was a predominantly Calgary-based, 102-member coalition.

Using the resources of Senator Ghitter's office and the Oxfam Human Rights Initiative, the coalition was able to ensure that its critique of the proposed amendments and their alternatives received substantial publicity and that considerable pressure was brought to bear on the government.[137] The fact that Senator Ghitter had served as a provincial cabinet minister, had a history of involvement with human rights and was now a vocal opponent of the Klein government's vision of human rights, made for a compelling news story.[138] The coalition was more than happy to take advantage of the situation.

On the government's part, a number of strategies were deployed to defuse the intensifying criticism of Bill 24. Klein offered to meet with Ghitter and a few members of the coalition, but Ghitter insisted that if the premier wanted to meet with him, he would have to meet with all coalition members.[139] Klein rejected the idea, stating that an encounter with the entire coalition would not be a meeting but a demonstration.[140] Subsequently, Klein attempted to dismiss concerns regarding Bill 24, claiming that the proposed legislation was "not an issue."[141] In his estimation, the only negative feedback he was receiving on Bill 24 came from "groups who might have a special interest in this matter, but from normal Albertans, people from throughout this province, I can assure the (Liberal) member that I am not getting a lot of cards and letters."[142]

Despite Klein's hesitations and denials, the coalition's significance eventually precipitated a meeting between its members and the Calgary caucus

148 STATE OF STRUGGLE

of the Conservative Party. In addition to reiterating their support for the recommendations made by the review panel, coalition members were concerned that there was no mechanism to control or limit interference by the minister and that appointments to the commission would not be made on the basis of merit and open competitions.[143] They were also displeased with the addition of a clause prohibiting "frivolous or vexatious complaints," particularly since it did not state who would make such determinations or what the penalties would be.[144] Additionally, Bill 24 removed a clause that made the AHRC subject to the Ombudsman Act, and did not provide protection on the basis of source of income, political belief, sexual orientation, and pardoned criminal convictions.[145]

As a result of this meeting, the government agreed to include source of income as a protected ground of discrimination and to extend the period for launching a complaint from six months to one year. Additionally, since Bill 24 was to serve as the statutory basis for the amalgamation of the Human Rights Commission with the Multicultural Commission, the government agreed to add a commitment to multiculturalism in the preamble of the Act and to include "Multiculturalism" in its title—the Human Rights, Citizenship, and Multiculturalism Act.[146] Having made these changes, the government then invoked closure, doubtless hoping that it had had the last word on the issue.[147]

The revised Act fell well short of the demands of the coalition and of the recommendations of the human rights review panel. Moreover, homophobic conservatives managed to ensure a temporary victory in the moral battle surrounding sexual orientation. Nonetheless, given the original political motivation to entirely abolish the commission, supporters of human rights secured a qualified win.

As activists are at pains to point out to political analysts, defining the achievements of claimsmaking solely on the basis of policy and legislative changes provides an incomplete representation of the work of community organizing. For people involved in advocacy and education around human rights issues in Alberta, the struggle around Bill 24 was important because it created connections among organizations and raised the level of awareness surrounding human rights issues throughout the province.[148] A level of politicization was generated that ensured continued vigilance over the actions of the commission and the province with regard to human rights. Indeed, the Vriend decision, which forced the Alberta government to include sexual orientation within its human rights legislation, public outcry surrounding the government's attempt to impose the notwithstanding clause in legislation limiting financial compensation to victims of forced sterilization, and the legislation permitting homosexual adoption are, in many respects, a product of this struggle.

■

ALBERTA'S NEOLIBERAL STATE has developed an impressive arsenal of techniques and strategies to displace politics from the provincial state, but as the activities discussed in this chapter reveal, the imposition of neoliberal policies and techniques of governance are also subject to contestation and negotiation. The delegitimation of claims-makers has been paralyzing for many advocacy organizations and has had grave consequences for the practice of democracy in Alberta. However, it is also true that the attempt to implement neoliberalism has revealed significant weaknesses in its efficacy as a mode of public administration. Indeed, despite its intentions, the provincial government has regularly been forced to maintain a role for the state in protecting the extra-economic well-being of its citizens.

Of course, the lines of contestation are not drawn simply between proponents of a minimalist state and their equity-seeking critics. Moral conservatives have also shaped the political debate, ironically creating opportunities for progressive claimsmakers where a more narrowly defined political landscape may have foreclosed them. In the face of polarized demands, the neoliberal state's preferred response has been to dissociate itself from contestation, in effect taking on a kind of neutrality through evacuation. As this discussion has revealed, however, such a position is impossible to maintain. Alberta's neoliberal state has not evacuated politics from the state.

The contrast between the relatively low level of organizing undertaken by women under the strictures of the neoliberal state and the dynamism of

150   STATE OF STRUGGLE

feminist claimsmaking in the two previous decades testifies to the debilitating effects of neoliberal policies on women. It is not simply that the state is no longer receptive to the demands of women, but that social policy has been reconfigured in such a way that the demands on women's labour have intensified. Still, although the disappearance of some women's groups can be seen as a failure to come to terms with neoliberalism, those that remain have devised new strategies to achieve social change. The retreat from advocacy and the adoption of a service orientation, participation in coalitions and coalition building, and the strategic deployment of resources for limited, goal-focused activities are among these strategies of adaptation. While it is undeniable that the advent of neoliberalism has represented a profound transformation in the politics of feminist claimsmaking, it is also true that the central task of organizing remains the fostering of a social climate in which the struggle for equity remains central. The struggle is irresolvable, but if neoliberalism has taught women anything it is that the struggle must continue.

6

Oil, Sex, and Power

THE PREVIOUS STORIES of women's encounters with the Alberta state have been organized around two central objectives. The first objective was to demonstrate the interconnections among the form of the state, the political economic context in which feminist claimsmaking has been undertaken, and the strategies and dynamics of feminist organizations as they interpret and reinterpret relations of power within these changing circumstances. Broadly speaking, these interconnections are denoted by the consolidation and crisis of Alberta's peculiar rendering of the welfare state and its transformation to a neoliberal form; the boom and bust of the oil and gas sector that accompanied that process and the reinforcement of the capitalist market in response to the ensuing fiscal crisis; and feminists' adoption and disillusionment with state-centred claimsmaking; the emergence of antifeminism and the simultaneous fragmentation of feminist organizations; and the temporary paralysis and subsequent initiation of new strategies of claimsmaking as neoliberal techniques of governance and economic practices have developed.

The second, more subtle objective of this study, was to disrupt the stereotypical conceptions of the province that are common both in Alberta and in the rest of Canada. Political analysts are frequently called upon to explain Albertans' seemingly extraordinarily unified support for one-party government at the provincial level and one-party sweeps of the province in federal elections. It would appear that the province's politicians and policymakers would have little need to broker interests and assuage discontent within the electorate. But, as this focus on women's organizing has revealed, outward appearances can be deceiving. Even in moments of robust economic health, the province has faced discontent. In moments of economic and political crisis, that discontent has intensified.

The 1970s in Alberta was notable for the unprecedented wealth flowing into provincial state coffers from the booming oil and gas industry's resource rents. Public investment arising from this windfall was directed at facilitating the continued expansion of the industry through joint, public-private investment schemes, infrastructure projects (including the purchase of an airline), and in the public goods of health and education. The strength of the social consensus surrounding the province's industrial policy was sufficient to impede efforts by marginalized Albertans, particularly women, to demonstrate the considerable economic, social, and political inequities arising from the Conservative government's myopic policy agenda. Nonetheless, the momentum of feminism's second wave and the support of the federal government helped to establish and sustain a variety of women's organizations in Alberta.

Once the price of oil began its rapid and steady decline in the early 1980s, the provincial state's capacity to depoliticize claimsmakers by maintaining a strong social consensus began to break down. However, a delayed realization of the altered political landscape among politicians and policymakers and the lack of responsiveness to feminist claimsmaking that had pervaded the previous decade contributed to feminists' growing disillusionment with state-centred initiatives. Further, the development of feminist theory and practice contributed to a radical rethinking of the objectives and strategies of claimsmaking, most notably the class and racial exclusivity that had marked the movement throughout the 1970s. In turn, this rethinking fostered a trend towards fragmentation, as groups of women attempted to focus on issues of specific concern, be they personal or political, rather than broad programs of social change. This trend would be particularly marked by the end of the 1980s. In the first part of the decade, however, some of the enthusiasm for single-minded, state-centred claims-making was still present, as evidenced by the campaign of the Provincial Coalition for a Council on Women's Affairs.

Paradoxically, as this trend towards fragmentation and disillusionment intensified among feminist claimsmakers, the provincial state finally began to acknowledge women's political legitimacy. In part, this acknowledgement became possible because the federal government ceased to serve as the province's primary target of antipathy. Additionally, the emergence of the Alberta Federation of Women United for Families helped to foster the development of liberal pluralism as a technique for managing Alberta's increasingly fractious political environment. Although one of the primary benefits of liberal pluralism for state actors is the capacity to recast public policy as a neutral compromise among vested interests, the disconnection between AFWUF's prescriptions for social organization and the everyday challenges of women's lives shifted the balance of policymaking initiatives for women in the direction of feminist, rather than antifeminist demands. Between 1981 and 1986 the premier ended the practice of rotating responsibility for women's issues among cabinet ministers, assigning the portfolio to a single minister, and established cabinet and interdepartmental committees on women's issues, the Women's Secretariat, and the Alberta Advisory Council on Women's Issues. However, despite the best intentions of some of their personnel, the work of these agencies and committees was constrained by the Alberta government's lack of commitment to women as well as the barrier that liberal pluralism posed for those feminists whose changemaking strategies remained focused on the state.

In the latter half of the 1980s, the fragmentation of feminist groups intensified at the same time that women attained the height of their political legitimacy vis-à-vis the provincial state. The intensification of Alberta's political crisis offers the most persuasive explanation for this incongruity. The bottoming out of oil prices at $10 a barrel in 1986, from a high of $44 a barrel only five years before, and the political liabilities of imposing fiscal restraint when the demand for state services was most intense contributed

Oil, Sex, and Power 155

to a political environment in which the process of governance and the management of public resources were regularly subject to stinging critique. Certainly, the increased ranks of the legislative opposition helped sustain popular discontent with the provincial government, this discontent becoming an increasingly significant feature of political life in Alberta. Moreover, the fact that criticism of the government's long-standing neglect and thinly veiled contempt for feminist claimsmakers was central to the Opposition's strategy for challenging the government also contributed to the relative increase in attentiveness regarding issues of concern to women. The provincial state's acknowledgement of women's political legitimacy could thus be understood in terms of raw political calculation—as a means to offset some popular criticism and, perhaps, court political constituencies that had not previously been identified with the Conservative Party.

Having made this claim, however, it is also true that the contradictory character of the provincial state's approach to women persisted in the late 1980s. Examples of the Alberta state's recalcitrance to acknowledge the veracity of women's experiences of inequality are numerous. Among the most notable were the temporary removal of sterilization and birth control counselling from the provincial health insurance scheme; the resistance to pay and employment equity; and the evocation of the traditional, nuclear family as a solution to violence against women, inadequate child care, and as a means to contain feminist demands. At the same time, however, feminist claimsmakers were largely successful at convincing the government of the need to provide adequate funding to women's shelters and improve child-care standards. Moreover, although the early work of the advisory council was a disappointment to the feminist community, the appointment of a new chair in 1989 helped to revitalize the council and improve its stature among the province's progressive women. The appointment of a minister responsible for women's issues who had some sympathy for the demands of feminist claimsmakers also marked an important, if largely symbolic, gain for women, as did the province's drafting of a Plan for Action for Alberta Women.

To a significant degree, these contradictory responses towards women resulted from the expansion of women-focused programs among several state agencies. The particular biases of individuals and departmental structures contributed to a variety of idiosyncratic approaches to women's issues. This expansion of state agencies and programs targeted at women can be viewed as indicative of the welfare state's capacity to contain insurgent movements by absorbing them within the purview of state policymaking, often through the deployment of liberal pluralism. This strategy could only be successful, however, as long as state agents were committed to the welfare state's inherent promises of equity, inclusiveness, and social justice. The desirability of and capacity to realize these promises began to be challenged, however, when the fragility of containment and liberal pluralism as governing techniques became apparent. The conflation of a series of expensive private-sector bail-out initiatives, the contradictions of public policy, and a general climate of political discontent within the province resulted in diminished confidence in the management capacities of the provincial government. But the situation could no longer be resolved through technical adjustments and renewed commitments to old promises. Instead, the form of the state itself was called into question.

The attempt to reshape the provincial state into a neoliberal form has had a devastating impact on Alberta's feminist organizations and progressive organizations in general. The reconfiguration of the state through the strategic deployment of a deficit and debt elimination program has resulted in the jettisoning of social justice principles. The Alberta government asserts that both the accumulation and legitimation functions of the state can be realized by maximizing market freedom. While public consultations may occur, the agenda is constrained and the outcome often predetermined. More frequently, political decisions are taken by way of stealth.[1]

The consequences of this new governance regime for feminist groups have included reduced access to state funding, though this was a greater factor at the level of the federal rather than provincial government, and increased expectations for community organizations and the volunteer labour of women to fill the gap left by budget cuts and the withdrawal of the state from a variety of social, health, and educational services. These demands on the time and financial resources of women have imposed substantial structural barriers to the advocacy capacity of feminist organizations. Further, the effectiveness of feminist mobilizing has also been diminished by the provincial government's insistence that equality is achieved by treating everyone the same way. Groups and individuals who do not conform to a particular model of the Alberta citizen and who dare to challenge the assumption that all provincial residents are equally well served by provincial policies are labelled "special interests" and "left-wing nuts."

Not surprisingly, the combination of these techniques of delegitimation and depoliticization has been to seriously undermine the efficacy of feminist organizing and to cast a pallor of despair across women's organizations generally. A number of organizations have closed down, most notably the Alberta Status of Women Action Committee, while others have curtailed their advocacy work in the interests of service provision and continued access to the few public dollars that remain available to them. Despite the bleakness of the situation, however, there have been several instances of relatively successful resistance to the imposition of the neoliberal state. In large measure, this success was derived from a combination of co-operative efforts among quite disparate organizations and serendipity. Moreover, even in the case of the Alberta Advisory Council on Women's Issues, the closure of which was deemed inevitable by the Klein government and women's groups alike, there was some indication of the government's concern to avoid attracting the animosity of Alberta women in the care with which the council was shut down. Further, the intensity of popular discontent surrounding the government's alterations to the provision of the public goods of health and education, in particular, demonstrates that the imposition of neoliberalism is a matter of political contestation and calculation rather than an unstoppable wave of reform in the interests of capitalist market function.

In addition to the political dynamics created as a result of neoliberal state restructuring and popular resistance, the contemporary terrain of politics in Alberta continues to be marked by a significant incidence of moral conservatism. Although this particular ideological persuasion does not always reside peaceably with the neoliberal political agenda, proponents of these views have recognized the political opportunities presented to them as a result of a policy program centred on the withdrawal of public funding. The case of abortion is indicative of this opportunism. Rather than persist with the argument for fetal rights, pro-life advocates in Alberta recast their position under the guise of ending public financial support for abortions. Although they ultimately failed in this attempt to restrict women's reproductive choice, their arguments did gain them some supporters among people who were pro-choice but were supportive of government efforts to reduce public expenditures. It is these kinds of strategic alliances that give pause to progressive activists and underscore the importance of reclaiming the discourse surrounding state function.

Having expressed this reservation, however, the most recent engagement of the abortion debate demonstrates a recurring phenomenon in the history of feminist claimsmaking with the Alberta state. Feminist claimsmakers are most successful when their demands are directed at challenging issues of morality rather than reforming the market to achieve some level of social and gender equity. Since the early 1970s, pay- and employment-equity programs, increases to the minimum wage, and the establishment of training programs for women on social assistance that do not reinforce the gendered division of labour have been almost uniformly rejected by the Alberta government. This rejection has been made on the basis that individuals have responsibility for their own well-being and that the opportunities exist for women to realize equality within the labour market. By contrast, women's struggles surrounding sexuality and reproductive rights, while having met substantial resistance from both state agents and social movements, have also largely succeeded in their objectives. The notable exception to this trend has been the province's concerted resistance to the recognition of sexual orientation as a protected ground under the province's human rights legislation. Even here, however, judicial decisions in various provincial and federal jurisdictions have forced the province's hand such that sexual orientation has now been included within the provincial human rights code, gay and lesbian couples have been permitted to adopt children, and homosexual couples have obtained the status of spouses.

■ THE VIEW FROM HERE

The recent history of women's organizing in Alberta demonstrates that the exercise of meaningful citizenship involves a commitment to activism on the part of both individuals and state agencies and an insistence on the state's responsibility for articulating the public interest. Although the activist community has despaired at the Alberta state's adoption of neoliberal governance, some acts of resistance have succeeded in tempering its harshest consequences. Regular elections and especially, budget surpluses do, in the end, enforce some level of responsiveness on the part of elected officials. Moreover, those progressive organizations and social causes that have withstood the transformation to the neoliberal state have been strengthened by the experience. Their strategizing has been successful and they have convinced the broader community of the value of their principles and their work. They may enjoy greater autonomy due to access to private sources of financial support, and because the justice of their causes has been supported by the courts.

In the midst of the crisis of the welfare state, progressive organizations and particularly feminists became increasingly sensitive to the social categories defining human subjectivity. The political and social meanings of gender, sexuality, race, class, ethnicity, and ability were acknowledged, sometimes reluctantly, as intersecting structures that worked together to shape the individual's experience of the social world, her identification of the issues that should be addressed, and the policies needed to achieve social change. This increasingly complex analysis of the dynamics of power and oppression radically altered the meaning of feminism and feminist struggle. Public policy, however, failed to keep pace. Having inadequately incorporated even feminists' initial demands for the acknowledgement of difference within public policy, decisionmakers, faced with an intensifying economic crisis, rejected calls for increased inclusivity. Instead, neoliberal governance was adopted as a means to quash these growing demands by asserting the allegedly amoral understanding of human subjects as rational economic actors. Difference would be accommodated in the marketplace and those groups that insisted on the state's obligation to guarantee meaningful citizenship would be dismissed as "special interests" seeking "special treatment" and "special rights."

Thus, the recent accomplishments of social activists are both remarkable and fragile. Public discourse and public policy only grudgingly admit of a few categories of citizenship that are worthy of public support, while a broadly shared moral obligation to ensure the well-being of all citizens regardless of their differences is dismissed as untenable, anticapitalist, and authoritarian. This is not an environment in which the meanings of social categories are readily interrogated and debated with the objective of lessening the oppression of people whose humanity is circumscribed by the rigidity of those categories. Instead, the flow of public debate travels in the opposite direction, forcing feminists, antiracists, antipoverty, and human rights activists to defend their accomplishments against either moral conservatives seeking to reinvigorate an allegedly organic, hierarchical social order in which privilege and power are a natural and uncontestable right or neoliberals who would bestow power and privilege through the mechanism of success in the market.

In the face of these rebukes and in the context of diminished resources and heightened need for services, there is a temptation for progressive organizations to adopt the simplistic understanding of citizenship that the neoliberal state is advancing. The debates surrounding the incorporation of difference within progressive organizations were difficult for those who found their power contested, just as they were for those with social and economic power in the broader society. The onset of neoliberalism has thus provided a rationale for progressive activists to discount the issue of difference as a distraction from the serious work of resistance to the diminishment of social justice. The reinforcement of exclusiveness that such an approach implies, however, is dangerous for the efficacy of a democratic project that is attempting to distinguish itself from neoliberalism. The severity of neoliberal policies on the lives of citizens and the practice of democracy requires creative, far-reaching, and inclusive strategies rather than anxious and ill-considered reactions.

The task that lies ahead for Alberta's feminist claimsmakers and progressive activists generally, is the development of a political program

Oil, Sex, and Power   161

that does not succumb to the discursive force of neoliberalism—that does not adopt its universalizing and economistic interpretations of the organization of social life. This program requires a commitment to the public interest, to equity, collective responsibility for social well-being, an insistence on the interdependence of citizens, and an assertion of the primacy of citizens rather than the economy in state policymaking. Rather than rejecting the state as an historical anomaly in an era of global capital, a progressive democratic project requires a rethinking of the state as a site through which to articulate, debate, and act on our visions of how best to create opportunities for citizens to live good lives, whatever they democratically determine those to be. This state need not squelch innovation or bind us in bureaucracy. In the need to rethink the state and its relationship to civil society, at least, neoliberalism has made a valid point. Its assertion that the organization of social life is a private rather than a public responsibility and that only those who share this view should be entitled to political legitimacy, however, is both dangerous and undemocratic.

Even as neoliberals celebrate the increased freedom they claim accompanies the down-sizing of the public sector, increasing numbers of people are paralyzed by the diminishment of their life chances in the absence of public investment and oversight. For these people, the coerciveness of public policy has only intensified as the neoliberal state insists that citizens' failings are individual rather than structural and offers little respite for those who cannot succeed in the private sector. The state, in its apparent absence, has become increasingly present, increasingly disciplinary, increasingly unaccountable.

The experience of feminist claimsmaking in Alberta over the previous three decades highlights the creativity, dedication, and resiliency of women in facing the considerable challenges posed to them in their struggles for equality. It is from them that this book has drawn its inspiration and to whom it offers hope for the possibility of a democratic future. As one activist asserted, "Success is the dream and the vision but it's also the best journey there is. And what is the alternative? Hedonism?"[2]

Notes

1   Sites of Engagement

1. *Alberta Women's Newsletter* 1 (spring 1974): 4.

2. Hugh Horner, "An Address by Hon. Dr. Hugh M. Horner, Deputy Premier and Minister of Transportation, Government of Alberta to Alberta Status of Women Action Committee," 29 October 1976. Alberta Status of Women Action Committee (ASWAC) Resource Library, Edmonton.

3. Julie Anne Le Gras, "Council on Women's Affairs, Background Paper," 15 January 1983, ASWAC Resource Library, Edmonton, 2.

4. Monica Blais, "Feminist Politics in Alberta in the 1980s," MA thesis (University of Alberta, 1990), 65.

5. ASWAC, newsletter, May 1986, ASWAC Collection, Provincial Archives of Alberta, Edmonton.

6. Nanci Langford, interview with author, tape recording, 12 December 1996; Boynton, interview.

7. Government of Alberta, *Debates*, 8 June 1988, 1577.

8. Janine Brodie, "Meso-Discourses, State Forms and the Gendering of Liberal-Democratic Citizenship," 1 *Citizenship Studies* 2 (1997): 226.

9. Philip Corrigan and Derek Sayer, *The Great Arch: English State Formation as Cultural Revolution* (Oxford: Basil Blackwell, 1985), 8.

10. Nancy Fraser, "Struggle Over Needs: Outline of a Socialist-Feminist Critical Theory of Late-Capitalist Political Culture," in Linda Gordon, ed., *Women, the State and Welfare* (Madison: University of Wisconsin Press, 1990), 209.

11. Donna Haraway, *Simians, Cyborgs and Women: The Reinvention of Nature* (New York: Routledge, 1991). This concept has also been discussed by Janine Brodie in "Meso-Discourses"; Isabella Bakker in "Introduction: The Gendered Foundations of Restructuring in Canada" in Isabella Bakker, ed., *Rethinking Restructuring: Gender and Change in Canada* (Toronto: University of Toronto Press, 1996); and in Judy Fudge and Brenda Cossman, "Introduction: Privatization, Law and the Challenge to Feminism," Fudge and Cossman, eds., *Privatization, Law and the Challenge to Feminism* (Toronto: University of Toronto Press, 2002).

12. Janine Brodie, "The Women's Movement Outside Quebec: Shifting Relations with the Canadian State," in Kenneth McRoberts, ed., *Beyond Quebec: Taking Stock of Canada*, (Montreal and Kingston: McGill-Queen's University Press, 1995), 340.

13. Ibid., 339–40.

14. See Iris Marion Young, *Justice and the Politics of Difference,* for an extended discussion of liberal pluralism and distributive justice.

15. Ibid., 72.

16. A variety of terms are used throughout this text to denote specific agents of claimsmaking. The terms "feminist claimsmaking" and "feminist organiza- tions" pertain specifically to those groups that self-identified as feminist. "Progressive women's organizations" refers to groups whose work was guided by the principle of women's equality. While some of these groups were femi- nist in their orientation, others eschewed the label as radical and alienating—particularly in terms of gaining social and political legitimacy. This term is generally invoked to include a wide spectrum of organizations including both feminist and more mainstream women's groups. The term "conservative women's organization" refers to those groups whose organizing initiatives were explicitly antifeminist and directed towards maintaining a "traditional" gender order in which the appropriate functions of men and women are determined by their "essential" natures as breadwinners and nurturers respectively.

17. Sue Findlay, "Facing the State: The Politics of the Women's Movement Reconsidered," in *Feminism and Political Economy: Women's Work, Women's Struggles* (Toronto: Methuen, 1987), 33, cited in Brodie, "The Women's Movement Outside Quebec," 339.

18. Michelle Barrett and Mary McIntosh, *The Anti-Social Family,* 2nd ed. (London: Verso, 1991), 21.

19. Mimi Abramovitz, *Regulating the Lives of Women: Social Welfare Policy from Colonial Times to the Present* (Boston: South End Press, 1989), 9.

20. Jean Cohen and Andrew Arato, *Civil Society and Political Theory* (Cambridge, Mass.: MIT Press, 1992), 15.

21. Anna Yeatman, *Postmodern Revisionings of the Political* (London: Routledge, 1994), 106.

22. "Ralph's World," *Ottawa Citizen*, 14 March 2001, A14.

2   The Big Boom and a "Resounding Thud of Nothingness"

1. "In Calgary, the report is just 'ho hum'," *Calgary Herald*, 8 December 1970: 61.

2. Ernest Watkins, *The Golden Province: A Political History of Alberta* (Calgary: Sandstone Publishing, 1980), 207.

3. See Watkins; John Richards, and Larry Pratt, *Prairie Capitalism: Power and Influence in the New West* (Toronto: McClelland & Stewart, 1979), 149; Larry Pratt, "The Political Economy of Province Building: Alberta's Development Strategy, 1971–81," in David Leadbeater, ed., *Essays on the Political Economy of Alberta* (Toronto: New Hogtown Press, 1984) and Howard Palmer and Tamara Palmer, *Alberta: A New History* (Edmonton: Hurtig Publishers, 1990).

4. Linda Trimble, "The Politics of Gender in Modern Alberta," in Allan Tupper and Roger Gibbins, eds., *Government and Politics in Alberta* (Edmonton: University of Alberta Press, 1992), 224 and 233.

5. In commenting on this period in Alberta's politics, Roger Gibbins argued that "to criticize the stand taken by the provincial government is frequently portrayed, particularly by the party in power, as tantamount to treason against the provincial interest. Thus to criticize or oppose the provincial government in such matters is potentially suicidal, while either not to act or to support the provincial government reduces the opposition to a state of irrelevance." Roger Gibbins, "Western Alienation and the Alberta Political Culture," in Carlo Caldarola, ed., *Society and Politics in Alberta* (Toronto: Methuen, 1979), 161

6. Richards and Pratt, 328.

7. Palmer and Palmer, 336.

8. Ibid.

9. Helen Hunley to all Preventive Social Service Board chairmen, 16 March 1976, Calgary Birth Control Association Collection, Glenbow Archives, Calgary. The Preventive Social Services (PSS) program was a cost-shared innovation in which municipal governments vetted funding applications from local service organizations. The municipality would pay 20 per cent of the grant with the province contributing 30 per cent and the remaining 50 per cent provided by the federal government. Couched in terms of allowing communities to deter-

mine their own needs, innovations like the PSS program kept the inadequacy of at least some aspects of social service provision at a distance from the provincial legislature.

10. Summary of the activities of the Calgary Status of Women Action Committee (CSWAC), accession file to the CSWAC Papers, Glenbow Archives, Calgary.

11. Review of CSWAC 1976–77 (ca. fall 1977), CSWAC Papers 1974–78, Glenbow Archives, Calgary.

12. CSWAC, board meeting minutes, 18 January 1978, CSWAC Papers 1974–78, Glenbow Archives, Calgary.

13. CSWAC, board meeting minutes, 20 January 1977, CSWAC Papers 1974–78, Glenbow Archives, Calgary.

14. Surprisingly, there is no evidence in CSWAC's early papers of any debate surrounding the efficacy or morality of using funds raised from gambling to facilitate claimsmaking. The need for adequate resources to sustain the *Calgary Women's Newspaper* was the primary concern. See CSWAC Collection 1974–78, Glenbow Archives, Calgary.

15. CSWAC, board meeting minutes, 17 May 1979, CSWAC Papers 1974–78, Glenbow Archives, Calgary.

16. "'Everyday woman' sought by city group," *Calgary Herald*, 6 April 1978: B4.

17. CSWAC, board meeting minutes, 8 January 1979, CSWAC, July 1980, CSWAC Papers 1974–78, Glenbow Archives, Calgary.

18. Suzanne Zwarun, "Feminist group explores its future, raison d'etre," *Calgary Herald*, 28 February 1973: B4.

19. Edmonton Options for Women (OFW) Council, Societies Act (ca. 1974), OFW Collection, Provincial Archives of Alberta, Edmonton.

20. OFW, minutes of founding meeting, 13 October 1973, OFW Collection, Provincial Archives of Alberta, Edmonton.

21. Ibid.

22. Edmonton Social Planning Council, "Where Did These Laws Come From?" 15 March 1976, OFW Collection, Provincial Archives of Alberta, Edmonton.

23. Edmonton Social Planning Council for OFW, "Maternity Leave in Alberta," 10 May 1975, OFW Collection, Provincial Archives of Alberta, Edmonton.

24. Edmonton Social Planning Council, "Where Did These Laws Come From?"

25. OFW to Neil Crawford (Minister of Social Services), 22 December 1975, OFW Collection, Provincial Archives of Alberta, Edmonton.

26. Alberta Women's Bureau, *Alberta Labour Legislation of Interest to Women in the Paid Workforce*, July 1977, 9.

27. OFW Coordinating Committee, minutes, 18 December 1975, OFW Collection, Provincial Archives of Alberta, Edmonton; University Women's Club of

Calgary, "Brief on Maternity Leave," 26 April 1976, University Women's Club of Calgary Collection, Glenbow Archives, Calgary.

28. OFW, "Information for Women" (ca. 1975), OFW Collection, Provincial Archives of Alberta, Edmonton.

29. Minutes of the inaugural meeting of the ASWAC, 27 September 1975, CSWAC Papers 1974–78, Glenbow Archives, Calgary.

30. ASWAC, *Joint Initiatives: A Goal for Women and Government in Alberta* (Edmonton: Alberta Status of Women Action Committee, 1976), 3.

31. Ibid., 4–5.

32. Ibid., 46.

33. Edmonton OFW, minutes, general meeting, 7 October 1976, OFW Collection, Provincial Archives of Alberta, Edmonton.

34. Hugh Horner, "An Address by Hon. Dr. Hugh M. Horner, Deputy Premier and Minister of Transportation, Government of Alberta to Alberta Status of Women Action Committee," 29 October 1976.

35. Pauline Bélanger and Laverne Booth, "ASWAC: The History of a Women's Organization 1976–1980," (course paper, University of Alberta, 1981), ASWAC Resource Library, Edmonton, 10; Patricia Stansfield, margin note on "An Address by Hon. Dr. Hugh M. Horner, Deputy Premier and Minister of Transportation, Government of Alberta to Alberta Status of Women Action Committee," Patricia Stansfield Collection, Glenbow Archives, Calgary. Bélanger and Booth noted that Horner addressed several women as "my dear" while Stansfield described the meeting as a disaster and added that Horner addressed the chair of the meeting by her first name. Stansfield recalled, "This so incensed me I got up and addressed Dr. Horner as 'Hugh, my dear.' The whole room burst out laughing and Hugh went white with rage."

36. Ann Hall to Lou Hyndman, 22 February 1977, Women's Secretariat Documents, Provincial Archives of Alberta, Edmonton.

37. Lou Hyndman to Ann Hall, 3 March 1977, Women's Secretariat Documents, Provincial Archives of Alberta, Edmonton.

38. Ibid.

39. Ruth Simken to Lou Hyndman, 6 December 1977, CSWAC Papers 1974–78, Glenbow Archives, Calgary.

40. Ibid.

41. ASWAC, Annual Report 1977–78, OFW Collection, Provincial Archives of Alberta, Edmonton.

42. Cathy Bray, "Government and the Women's Movement: The ASWAC Example" (course paper, University of Alberta, 1983), ASWAC Resource Library, Edmonton, 6.

43. Harry Hobbs, Deputy Minister Executive Council, to L. Hyndman, N. Crawford, J. Horsman, B. Bogle, and L. Young, 18 May 1979, Women's Secretariat Documents, Provincial Archives of Alberta, Edmonton.

44. Alberta Legislative Assembly, *Debates*, 12 May 1983. This frustration was noted by Dick Johnston on the occasion of his assuming a more permanent position as minister responsible for women's issues.

45. See especially, "Submissions to the Provincial Cabinet by Women of Unifarm," 1973–78, Legislative Library, Alberta Legislature, Edmonton; Calgary Local Council of Women, "Resolution on the Division of Property Between Spouses" (ca. 1974), Calgary Local Council of Women Collection, Glenbow Archives, Calgary; University Women's Club of Calgary, "Brief on Reform to Matrimonial Property Legislation," October 1974, University Women's Club of Calgary Collection, Glenbow Archives, Calgary.

46. Pat Wright, speech at press conference on matrimonial property, 17 October 1977, Women's Secretariat Collection, Provincial Archives of Alberta, Edmonton.

47. CSWAC to Jim Foster, Attorney General of Alberta, 13 February 1978, CSWAC Papers, Glenbow Archives, Calgary.

48. Edmonton Women's Place, newsletter, January 1976, OFW Collection, Provincial Archives of Alberta, Edmonton.

49. Ibid.

50. Jim Foster, Attorney General, to OFW, 26 May 1977, OFW Collection, Provincial Archives of Alberta, Edmonton.

51. Halyna Freeland, *Matrimonial Property: The New Legislation*, 5.

52. Pat Wright, speech at press conference on matrimonial property.

53. Halyna Freeland, interview; OFW, newsletter, February 1978, OFW Collection, Provincial Archives of Alberta, Edmonton.

54. Mair Smith, interview by Sheila Dunphy, 15 July 1989, Northern Alberta Women's Archive Project, Provincial Archives of Alberta, Edmonton.

55. Al "Boomer" Adair to CSWAC, 13 December 1977, CSWAC Collection, Glenbow Archives, Calgary. In the context of the rapidly accumulating wealth of the men employed by the burgeoning oil and gas sector, one is tempted to speculate that Adair's comments about the "wife of the millionaire" are suggestive of part of the motivation behind the government's unwillingness to consider implementing a system of deferred sharing.

56. Ibid.

57. Ibid.

58. In 1974, the provinces of British Columbia, Alberta, and Saskatchewan each had a Women's Bureau while Ontario had established an office of Women's Programs in the Ministry of Labour. By 1979, the provinces of Quebec, Prince

Edward Island, New Brunswick, and Nova Scotia and the federal government had established advisory councils, while each of the remaining provinces had either established a Women's Bureau or offices for women's programs through their Departments of Labour, or in the case of Newfoundland, the Department of Justice. By the time Alberta finally established the Alberta Advisory Council on Women's Issues in 1986, British Columbia was the only remaining Canadian province not to have established such a council. *Canadian Almanac and Directory 1974* (Toronto: Copp Clark Publishing, 1974) and *Canadian Almanac and Directory 1979* (Toronto: Copp Clark Publishing, 1979).

59. John Tompkins, "Women move closer to equality in work," *Edmonton Journal,* 9 November 1972: 18.

60. Chairman, Alberta Human Rights Commission, "Introductory Remarks," news conference, February 1980, Alberta Human Rights Commission (AHRC) Collection, Provincial Archives of Alberta, Edmonton, 5.

61. AHRC, Annual Report 1974–75, 14.

62. One of the more notable cases of the AHRC's ruling against a "special" program involved a complaint made by a non-Aboriginal woman who was refused admission to a business course offered through the University of Calgary on the Hobbema Indian Reserve. The woman was turned down because the course was intended for Aboriginal students. The AHRC's board of inquiry found that because the course gave special preference to Aboriginal people, it was in violation of the IRPA. As a result, the University of Calgary cancelled the course. ASWAC, "Equal Pay for Work of Equal Value: Prospects for Alberta," 19 March 1980, ASWAC Resource Library, Edmonton.

63. AHRC, April public agenda, 3 April 1979, CSWAC Collection, Glenbow Archives, Calgary.

64. Chairman, AHRC, "Introductory Remarks," news conference, 5 February 1980.

65. AHRC, press release, 11 May 1978, CSWAC Collection, Glenbow Archives, Calgary.

66. AHRC, April public agenda, 3 April 1979.

67. AHRC, "Summary of a Report Submitted to the AHRC on Occupational Segregation and its Effects. A Study of Women in the Alberta Public Service," (ca. 1980) 4, AHRC Collection, Provincial Archives of Alberta, Edmonton.

68. Greg Stevens to Peter Lougheed, 22 August 1979, AHRC Collection, Provincial Archives of Alberta, Edmonton.

69. AHRC, press release, 15 October 1979, AHRC Collection, Provincial Archives of Alberta, Edmonton.

70. Ibid.

71. ASWAC, "Equal Pay for Work of Equal Value: Prospects for Alberta," a brief presented to the Canadian Human Rights Commission by the ASWAC, 19 March 1980, ASWAC Resource Library, Edmonton, 3–4.

72. Ibid., 4. These comments were reportedly made at a meeting between the AHRC and representatives of a number of women's groups.

73. CSWAC, board meeting minutes, 18 January 1978, CSWAC Collection, Glenbow Archives, Calgary.

74. CSWAC, *Proceedings: Women in a Violent Society Conference April 21–23, 1978* (Calgary: CSWAC, 1978), CSWAC Collection, Glenbow Archives, Calgary, 167.

75. *Alberta Human Rights Journal* 2 (fall 1984): 4. In no other instance of discrimination adjudicated by the AHRC was the complainant required to demonstrate that the act of discrimination had been unwanted.

76. ASWAC, newsletter, May 1980, ASWAC, correspondence and issues files, Provincial Archives of Alberta, Edmonton.

77. Marilyn Moysa, "Alberta women's council urged," *Edmonton Journal*, 27 April 1981: B2.

78. "3rd rights staffer quits; stays mum," *Edmonton Journal*, 19 July 1980: B1.

3   Disparate Strategies and Expedient Responses

1. Palmer and Palmer, *Alberta: A New History*, 355.

2. Ibid., 354.

3. Ken McRoberts, "Federal Structures and the Policy Process," in Michael Atkinson, ed., *Governing Canada: Institutions and Public Policy* (Toronto: Harcourt Brace, 1993), 166–67.

4. Dick Johnston to Peter Lougheed, 26 September 1984, AHRC Collection, Provincial Archives of Alberta, Edmonton.

5. ASWAC, Annual Report 1981–82, ASWAC, correspondence and issues files, Provincial Archives of Alberta, Edmonton.

6. The provincial committee was also known as the Provincial Coalition for a Council on Women's Affairs, and will be referred to throughout the chapter as either the provincial committee, the coalition, or the committee when these short forms make clear reference to the Provincial Committee for a Council on Women's Affairs.

7. Julie Anne Le Gras, *Pushing the Limits: Reflections on Alberta Women's Strategies for Action* (Edmonton: Unique Publishing Association, 1984), 3–4.

8. Renate Shearer, "Review of Alberta Status of Women Action Committee and Women's Programme, Secretary of State, Alberta," 15 April 1986, ASWAC, correspondence and issues files, Provincial Archives of Alberta, Edmonton, 36.

9. Francis Adams, interview with Sheila Dunphy, 15 August 1989; Julie Anne Le Gras, interview with Sheila Dunphy, 26 July 1989: Northern Alberta Women's Archive Project, Provincial Archives of Alberta, Edmonton.

10. ASWAC, newsletter, May 1984, Women's Secretariat Collection, Provincial Archives of Alberta, Edmonton.

11. Sheila Wynn to Dick Johnston, 26 February 1985, Women's Secretariat documents, Provincial Archives of Alberta, Edmonton.

12. Flores Langeslag to potential contributors, February 1985, Women's Secretariat documents, Provincial Archives of Alberta, Edmonton.

13. Sheila Wynn to Dick Johnston, 26 February 1985.

14. "Women's groups winning," *Edmonton Journal*, 22 October 1984: B1.

15. ASWAC, newsletter, August 1985 and January 1986, ASWAC Collection, Provincial Archives of Alberta, Edmonton.

16. ASWAC, newsletter, January 1986.

17. ASWAC, newsletter, August 1985.

18. ASWAC to Myrna Coombs (Social Development Officer, Secretary of State), 5 January 1982, ASWAC Resource Library, Edmonton.

19. ASWAC, "Documentation and Clarification" (re: interactions between ASWAC and pro-life organizations), (ca. December 1981), ASWAC Resource Library, Edmonton, 5.

20. Ibid.

21. I have relied on ASWAC's account as it is the most consistent across sources.

22. Campaign Life, press release, 16 November 1981, Women's Secretariat Collection, Provincial Archives of Alberta, Edmonton.

23. Alberta Federation of Women United for Families (AFWUF), *The AFWUF Voice*, December 1982, personal papers of Julie Anne Le Gras, Provincial Archives of Alberta, Edmonton.

24. AFWUF, "What Humanism can do to your Child," pamphlet, n.d., ASWAC, Resource Library, Edmonton.

25. AFWUF, *The AFWUF Voice*, December 1982.

26. In correspondence with the minister responsible for women's issues, the AFWUF president thanked the minister for a $5,000 grant but asserted: "We are finding it difficult to keep up with photocopying expenses etc. ... However we are more than happy to have our budget trimmed from $9000 to $5000 if ONLY an equal amount was awarded to other women's groups such as ASWAC. If, however, they receive more, we would like to request your consideration in giving us an equal amount." Pat Thompson to Dick Johnston, 3 December 1984, Women's Secretariat documents, Provincial Archives of Alberta, Edmonton.

27. Sheila Wynn (Senior Intergovernmental Officer, Social and Cultural Affairs Division, Department of Federal and Intergovernmental Affairs) to Richard Dalon (Executive Director, Social and Cultural Affairs Division), 22 February 1982. Women's Secretariat Collection, Provincial Archives of Alberta, Edmonton.

28. Ibid.

29. Al Kennedy to Les Young, 25 March 1982, Women's Secretariat Collection, Provincial Archives of Alberta, Edmonton.

30. Ibid.

31. AFWUF, *The AFWUF Voice,* winter 1987, Julie Anne Le Gras, personal papers, Provincial Archives of Alberta, Edmonton.

32. See Kim McLeod, "Balance views, Real Women told," *Edmonton Journal,* 28 November 1987: B5.

33. Calgary Committee for the Proposed Council on Women's Affairs, minutes, 15 November 1983, Calgary Committee for a Council on Women's Affairs Collection, Glenbow Archives, Calgary.

34. Calgary YWCA to women's groups, 10 November 1981, Women's Secretariat Collection, Provincial Archives of Alberta, Edmonton.

35. Julie Anne Le Gras, "Council on Women's Affairs, Background Paper," 15 January 1983, ASWAC Resource Library, Edmonton, 2.

36. Les Young to Pat Cooper, Mary Collins, and Monica Sloan, 21 August 1981, Calgary Committee for a Council on Women's Affairs Collection, Glenbow Archives, Calgary.

37. Monica Blais, "Feminist Politics in Alberta in the 1980s," MA thesis (University of Alberta, 1990), 44.

38. Julie Anne Le Gras, "Council on Women's Affairs, Background Paper," 4.

39. Lorraine Locherty, "Time's up, women tell Tories," *Edmonton Journal,* 3 July 1985: B1.

40. Ed Oman (Chair of Calgary Progressive Conservative Caucus) to Doreen Blitz, 8 September 1982, Women's Secretariat Documents, Provincial Archives of Alberta, Edmonton.

41. Susan Braungart, "40,000 women back campaign," *Calgary Herald,* 14 March 1983: B6.

42. Provincial Committee for a Council on Women's Affairs, minutes, 7 May 1983.

43. Margaret Ethier (President, United Nurses of Alberta) to Norma Farquharson, 12 December 1983, personal papers of Sylvia McKinley, Edmonton.

44. Kathleen Higgins (President, AFWUF) to Maureen Towns (Co-chair, Provincial Committee for a Council on Women's Affairs), 3 May 1983, Women's Secretariat documents, Provincial Archives of Alberta, Edmonton.

45. Ibid.

46. Kathleen Higgins to Peter Lougheed, 22 February 1983, Women's Secretariat documents, Provincial Archives of Alberta, Edmonton.

47. Edmonton Committee of the Provincial Committee for a Council on Women's Affairs, minutes, 7 May 1984, Women's Secretariat documents, Provincial Archives of Alberta, Edmonton.

48. Ibid.

49. Robert Walker, "Membership claim challenged," *Calgary Herald*, 28 February 1985: B4.

50. Ibid.

51. Provincial Coalition for a Council on Women's Affairs, newsletter, 22 February 1985, Provincial Coalition for a Council on Women's Affairs Collection, Glenbow Archives, Calgary.

52. Cheryl Cohen, "Women's issues to get boost," *Edmonton Journal*, 19 October 1983: A15.

53. Ibid.

54. Ibid.

55. Alberta Legislative Assembly, *Debates*, 25 March 1983, 299. Sheila Wynn, the first director of the Women's Secretariat noted Johnston's reluctance to estab- lish an advisory council. According to Wynn, Johnston regularly asked his fellow ministers responsible for women's issues at national meetings about their experiences with advisory councils. She recalled that Johnston came away from these meetings opposed to the idea of an advisory council in Alberta. In his view, it made no sense to pay people to criticize public policy and act as a thorn in the side of government. Ultimately, however, the concerted efforts of the provincial coalition persuaded Johnston to change his mind. Sheila Wynn, interview with author, tape recording, 19 December 1996, Victoria, BC.

56. Roman Cooney, "MLA promises change for women," *Calgary Herald*, 13 September 1983: B1.

57. Government of Alberta, press release, 28 February 1984.

58. Interdepartmental Committee on Women's Issues, minutes, 29 October 1984, Women's Bureau Collection, Provincial Archives of Alberta, Edmonton.

59. Phyllis Ellis to Mary LeMessurier, 20 June 1983, Women's Secretariat Collection, Provincial Archives of Alberta, Edmonton.

60. Janet Koper to Norma Farquharson, 28 February 1984, personal collection of Sylvia McKinley, Edmonton.

61. Dick Johnston to Norma Farquharson (ca. April 1984), Women's Secretariat Collection, Provincial Archives of Alberta, Edmonton.

62. Phyllis Ellis, "Summary of Second Annual Meeting of the Provincial Committee for a Council on Women's Affairs," 9 November 1984, Women's Secretariat Collection, Provincial Archives of Alberta, Edmonton.

63. Ibid.

64. Norma Farquharson to Dick Johnston, 23 October 1984, Women's Secretariat Collection, Provincial Archives of Alberta, Edmonton.

65. See Alberta Legislative Assembly, *Debates*, 17 April 1984, 523–35.

66. Ibid., 523.

67. Alberta Legislative Assembly, *Debates*, 1 November 1984, 1333.

68. Ibid., 1326.

69. Ibid., 1328.

70. Ibid.

71. Phyllis Ellis, "Summary of Second Annual Meeting of the Provincial Committee for a Council on Women's Affairs."

72. Maureen Towns (Chairperson, Provincial Committee for a Council on Women's Affairs) to coalition members, 22 February 1985, personal papers of Sylvia McKinley, Edmonton.

73. Nanci Langford, personal communication, 3 January 1996, Edmonton.

74. Ibid.

75. See Calgary Committee for an Alberta Council on Women's Affairs, newsletter, fall 1984, Provincial Coalition for a Council on Women's Affairs Collection, Glenbow Archives, Calgary.

76. Lorraine Locherty, "Koziak and Getty camps anger women," *Edmonton Journal*, 24 August 1985: B1.

77. Sheila Pratt, "Ghitter draws fire on advisory council plan," *Calgary Herald*, 6 October 1985: A3. In addition to the sense of ambiguity surrounding an advisory council evoked by Ghitter's comments during the Conservative leadership race, Ghitter's views on activism and consultation are of historical interest here since he would become chair of the Dignity Foundation, an independent human rights watchdog in Alberta in the mid-1990s.

78. Kathy Kerr and Sheila Pratt, "Women annoyed only Ghitter will attend forum," *Calgary Herald*, 3 October 1985: A9.

79. Monica Blais, "Feminist Politics in Alberta in the 1980s," 65.

80. Linda Goyette, "Zeroing in on the real enemy," *Edmonton Journal*, 16 June 1986: A7.

81. Richard Helm, "Boycott women's advisory body, prospective members told," *Edmonton Journal*, 7 May 1986: B1.

82. AFWUF, *The AFWUF Voice*, spring 1986, personal collection of Julie Anne Le Gras, Provincial Archives of Alberta, Edmonton.

83. Sheila Pratt, "Women's council bill favoured," *Calgary Herald,* 2 August 1986: A7.

84. Lorraine Locherty, "Critics tell women's council to prove its worth," *Calgary Herald,* 17 November 1986: A9.

85. Sylvia McKinley and Norma Farquharson to Dennis Anderson (Minister Responsible for Women's Issues), 14 November 1986, personal papers of Sylvia McKinley, Edmonton.

86. Nanci Langford, personal communication.

87. Sylvia McKinley and Norma Farquharson to Dennis Anderson, 14 November 1986.

88. AHRC, press release, 24 July 1984, AHRC Collection, Provincial Archives of Alberta, Edmonton; Marlene Antonio (Chairman, AHRC) to Les Young (Minister of Labour), 22 June 1984, Department of Labour Collection, Provincial Archives of Alberta, Edmonton. The Alberta court was bound in its decision on *Vivian Wong vs. Hughes Petroleum* by the Supreme Court of Canada's ruling in the *Bliss* case.

89. Marlene Antonio to Les Young, 22 June 1984; Albert Kennedy (Assistant Deputy Minister, Ministry of Labour) to Les Young, 11 September 1984, AHRC Collection, Provincial Archives of Alberta, Edmonton.

90. Alberta Women's Secretariat, "Brief on Protection Against Discrimination on the Basis of Pregnancy," August 1984, Ministry of Labour Collection, Provincial Archives of Alberta, Edmonton, 4.

91. Ibid.

92. Albert Kennedy to Les Young, 11 September 1984.

93. Government of Alberta, press release, 15 April 1985, Women's Bureau Collection, Provincial Archives of Alberta, Edmonton.

94. Alberta Women's Secretariat, "Brief on Protection Against Discrimination on the Basis of Pregnancy," August 1984, 5.

95. Marlene Antonio to Les Young, 22 June 1984.

96. *Alberta Human Rights Journal* 2 (fall 1984), 2.

97. AHRC, "Background Paper on the Inclusion of Sexual Orientation as a Prohibited Grounds for Discrimination," 25 April 1984, AHRC Collection, Provincial Archives of Alberta, Edmonton.

98. Ibid.

99. Sharon White (Senior Employee Relations Officer, Personnel Administration) to Albert Kennedy, 11 September 1984, Department of Labour Collection, Provincial Archives of Alberta, Edmonton.

100. AHRC, "Background Paper on the Inclusion of Sexual Orientation as a Prohibited Grounds for Discrimination." The assistant deputy minister's initials are hand-written at the top of this copy.

101. Ibid.

102. The letter to ASWAC was reprinted in the organization's newsletter, June 1985, ASWAC, correspondence and issues files, Provincial Archives of Alberta, Edmonton.

103. *Alberta Human Rights Journal* 1 (spring 1983), 7.

104. *Alberta Human Rights Journal* 3 (June 1985), 2.

105. Ibid.

106. See Alberta Legislative Assembly, *Debates*, 1 November 1984, 1328.

107. Les Young, "Potential Opening Remarks Re: Affirmative Action," meeting of Ministers Responsible for Human Rights, 8–9 September 1983, Women's Bureau Collection, Provincial Archives of Alberta, Edmonton.

108. Ibid.

109. Ibid.

110. Ibid.

111. Government of Alberta, press release, 15 April 1985.

112. Ibid.

113. Donna Jackson to Peter Lougheed, 22 January 1985, Women's Bureau Documents, Provincial Archives of Alberta, Edmonton. At the time of the announcement of the two committees it was not clear whether both of them would receive representations from women's groups or only the interdepartmental committee. Dick Johnston had written to the provincial committee in May of 1984, that the cabinet committee would be interested in meeting in the fall (Dick Johnston to Norma Farquharson, 25 May 1984, personal papers of Sylvia McKinley, Edmonton.) The premier's notorious disdain for women's issues, however, likely ensured that representations by women's groups would be limited to the interdepartmental committee. In the 14 January 1983 edition of the *Calgary Herald*, Suzanne Zwarun wrote that "a pulse in the premier's temple is supposed to be set to throbbing by the mere mention, in cabinet, of women's programs." Suzanne Zwarun, "Blitz continues quest for provincial women's council," *Calgary Herald*, 14 January 1983: B5.

114. Alberta Women's Secretariat, "Summary of AFWUF's Presentation to the Interdepartmental Committee on Women's Issues," 27 March 1985, Women's Bureau Collection, Provincial Archives of Alberta, Edmonton.

115. Ibid.

116. Sheila Wynn to Janina Vanderpost, 27 March 1985, Women's Bureau Collection, Provincial Archives of Alberta, Edmonton.

117. Sheila Wynn to Janina Vanderpost, 20 March 1985, Women's Bureau Collection, Provincial Archives of Alberta, Edmonton.

118. Lorna Lagrange to Jim Horsman, 2 April 1985, Women's Bureau Collection, Provincial Archives of Alberta, Edmonton.

119. Ibid.

120. Sheila Wynn to Lorna Lagrange, 24 April 1985, Women's Bureau Collection, Provincial Archives of Alberta, Edmonton.

121. Ibid.

122. Sheila Wynn to Dick Johnston, 4 October 1985, Women's Bureau Collection, Provincial Archives of Alberta, Edmonton.

123. Ibid.

124. Sheila Wynn to members of the Interdepartmental Committee on Women's Issues, 7 January 1986, Women's Bureau Collection, Provincial Archives of Alberta, Edmonton.

4   Feminists and Family Values

1. Palmer and Palmer, *Alberta: A New History*, 355.

2. *The Other Alberta Report*, 19 October–14 November 1986.

3. See Allan Tupper, Larry Pratt, and Ian Urquhart, "The Role of Government," in Allan Tupper and Roger Gibbins, eds., *Government and Politics in Alberta* (Edmonton: University of Alberta Press, 1992), 33, and Howard Palmer and Tamara Palmer, *Alberta: A New History* (Edmonton: Hurtig Publishers, 1990), 357–60. The collapse of the Principal Group, a family-run investment firm, was a central event from which evidence for the seriousness of the government's mismanagement was garnered. The inquiry into the collapse of the firm revealed the close relationship between the management of the firm and the provincial Cabinet. Investors received some compensation, and the government of Alberta saw losses of $100 million, as well as a considerable loss of public confidence. Mark Lisac, *The Klein Revolution* (Edmonton: NeWest Press, 1995), 31.

4. Tupper, Pratt, and Urquhart, "The Role of Government," in Allan Tupper and Roger Gibbins eds., *Government and Politics in Alberta* (Edmonton: University of Alberta Press, 1992), 42–45.

5. Linda Trimble, "The Politics of Gender in Modern Alberta," in Allan Tupper and Roger Gibbins, eds., *Government and Politics in Alberta* (Edmonton: University of Alberta Press, 1992), 233.

6. See ASWAC newsletters, January 1986–December 1989. Julie Anne Le Gras, interview with author, tape recording, 19 December 1996, Vancouver.

7. ASWAC, newsletter, March 1988.

8. See particularly, Northern Alberta Women's Archives Project, interviews with Sheryl Ackerman, Mair Smith, Julie Anne Le Gras, and Trudy Richardson, Provincial Archives of Alberta, Edmonton.

9. ASWAC, newsletter, May 1986.

10. ASWAC, newsletter, March 1986, August 1987, and *The Other Alberta Report,* 29 December 1986–18 February 1987.

11. Francis Adams, interview with Sheila Dunphy, 15 August 1989, Northern Alberta Women's Archives Project, Provincial Archives of Alberta, Edmonton.

12. ASWAC, newsletter, March, 1990; Halyna Freeland, interview with Sheila Dunphy, 28 June 1989; Mair Smith, interview with Sheila Dunphy, 15 July 1989. Northern Alberta Women's Archives Project, Provincial Archives of Alberta, Edmonton.

13. ASWAC, newsletter, May, 1990.

14. ASWAC, conference program, November, 1987. ASWAC Resource Library, Edmonton.

15. ASWAC, newsletter, January, 1988.

16. Linda Olson to Ken Rostad, 15 November 1987, Women's Secretariat Collection, Provincial Archives of Alberta, Edmonton.

17. *Camrose Canadian,* editorial, 18 November 1987, Women's Secretariat Collection, Provincial Archives of Alberta, Edmonton.

18. Luanne Armstrong to the Editor, *Camrose Canadian,* November 1987, Women's Secretariat Collection, Provincial Archives of Alberta, Edmonton.

19. Ken Rostad to Elaine McCoy, 18 November 1987, Women's Secretariat Collection, Provincial Archives of Alberta, Edmonton.

20. Elaine McCoy to Ken Rostad, 17 December 1987, Women's Secretariat Collection, Provincial Archives of Alberta, Edmonton.

21. Marie Laing, interview with author, tape recording, 8 January 1997, Edmonton.

22. ASWAC, *Women Against Poverty,* 1992.

23. ASWAC, newsletter, July/August 1988. The newsletter reported that members of ASWAC had made a presentation to the AACWI on issues relating to women and poverty but found AACWI members were not interested.

24. Anne McGrath, interview with author, tape recording, 10 January 1997, Calgary.

25. ASWAC, newsletter, June 1991, ASWAC Collection, Provincial Archives of Alberta, Edmonton.

26. ASWAC, "Organizational Review Update: Report to the Secretary of State Women's Program," June 1992, ASWAC Resource Library, Edmonton.

27. McGrath, interview.

28. See Women Looking Forward, minutes of the round table, various dates, Office of Women Looking Forward, Calgary.

29. Women Looking Forward, "Final Report, Annual General Meeting," 1993, Office of Women Looking Forward, Calgary.

30. Women Looking Forward, "Activity Report 1989–90" and minutes of round table and annual general meeting, 1991, Office of Women Looking Forward, Calgary.

31. Women Looking Forward, "Final Report, Annual General Meeting," 1992, Office of Women Looking Forward, Calgary.

32. Anne McGrath made this observation at the general level of women's organizing in Calgary. McGrath, interview.

33. Women Looking Forward, "Final Report, Annual General Meeting," 1992, Office of Women Looking Forward, Calgary.

34. Ibid.

35. Pam Krause, interview with author, tape recording, 10 January 1997, Calgary.

36. ASWAC, newsletter, December 1986, ASWAC Collection, Provincial Archives of Alberta, Edmonton.

37. ASWAC, newsletter, October 1987. See also newsletter, September 1987; ASWAC to Elaine McCoy, 6 March 1989, ASWAC Collection, Provincial Archives of Alberta, Edmonton.

38. ASWAC, "Organizational Review Update: Report to the Secretary of State Women's Program", March 1992, ASWAC Resource Library, Edmonton.

39. ASWAC to Elaine McCoy, 6 March 1989, ASWAC Collection, Provincial Archives of Alberta, Edmonton.

40. Amal Umar, one of the founders of the Calgary Immigrant Women's Centre, made this point in relation to her experience as a member of the Alberta Advisory Council on Women's Issues. Amal Umar, interview with author, tape recording, 10 January 1997, Calgary.

41. AFWUF, *Good Citizens, Good Government*, 1.

42. Ibid., 4.

43. Ibid.

44. Bernadette Lougheed, "Message from the President," in AFWUF, *The AFWUF Voice*, November 1990, Women's Secretariat Resource Library.

45. In 1989 Valerie Day became an AFWUF board member. Her husband, Stockwell Day, was the first chair of the Premier's Council in Support of Alberta Families, served as Alberta's Treasurer, and later became the leader of the Alliance Party. AFWUF, *The AFWUF Voice*, April/May, 1989.

46. AFWUF, *The AFWUF Voice*, December, 1987.

47. See Calgary Local Council of Women, minutes of executive meeting," 14 April 1992 and 1 September 1992, Calgary Local Council of Women Collection, Glenbow Archives, Calgary.

48. See Calgary Local Council of Women Collection, Glenbow Archives, Calgary.

49. ASWAC, newsletter, March, 1988, ASWAC, Provincial Archives of Alberta, Edmonton.

50. Alberta Advisory Council on Women's Issues, "Summary of Public Input, Lethbridge Public Meeting," 25 February 1988, Alberta Advisory Council on Women's Issues Collection, Provincial Archives of Alberta, Edmonton.

51. ASWAC, newsletter, March, 1988, ASWAC, Provincial Archives of Alberta, Edmonton.

52. *Alberta Report,* 2 May 1988, 44.

53. Boynton, interview.

54. *Alberta Report,* 2 May 1988, 45.

55. Ibid., 44.

56. *The Other Alberta Report,* 7 September–18 October 1986.

57. ASWAC, newsletter, June, 1987.

58. ASWAC, newsletter, December, 1986.

59. Ibid. Interestingly, while the Alberta Medical Association (AMA) supported the additional fee for the referral letter, the College of Physicians and Surgeons argued that medical-legal letters were a component of the therapeutic abortion process and, hence, that doctors could not charge for them. *The Other Alberta Report,* 15 November–28 December 1986.

60. *The Other Alberta Report,* 19 October–14 November 1986.

61. *The Other Alberta Report,* 15 November–28 December 1986.

62. Planned Parenthood reported to the Alberta Women's Secretariat, in January of 1987, that the number of therapeutic abortions performed in Alberta had decreased by 9.5 per cent in the last quarter of 1986 over the last quarter of 1985. However, the number of abortions performed in Edmonton had decreased by 40 per cent in the same period. Calgary doctors were taking up some of the slack, as abortions actually increased in that city by 23 per cent ("Notes," 20 January 1987, Alberta Women's Secretariat, Provincial Archives of Alberta, Edmonton). However, shortly after Planned Parenthood discussed this issue with the Women's Secretariat, five Calgary doctors served notice that they would not take on any new abortion cases after one of the doctors was "rebuked by the government for charging $75 to provide a legal-medical letter" (*The Other Alberta Report,* 29 December 1986–18 February 1987). In response, the Hospitals Minister said he would leave the matter of disciplinary action in the hands of the College of Physicians and Surgeons, while the AMA insisted that doctors cannot be compelled to perform any service unless it is an emergency and, moreover, that abortions were rarely emergencies. (Ibid.)

63. *The Other Alberta Report,* 29 December 1986–18 February 1987.

64. *The Other Alberta Report,* 16 July–11 September 1987.

65. *The Other Alberta Report,* 1 January–14 February 1988.

66. *The Other Alberta Report* February 16–March 31, 1988.

67. ASWAC, newsletter, March 1988.

68. Although the clinics in Calgary and Edmonton helped to accommodate the demand for abortion, access remained inadequate. The situation improved

after Henry Morgentaler established a clinic in Edmonton in 1991 and in Calgary in 1992.

69. *The Other Alberta Report*, 1 July–15 August 1988.

70. ASWAC, newsletter, June 1987.

71. *The Other Alberta Report*, 1 June–15 July 1987.

72. Ibid.

73. Elaine McCoy to Dennis Anderson, 4 June 1987, Women's Bureau Collection, Provincial Archives of Alberta, Edmonton.

74. Elaine McCoy to Dennis Anderson, 2 July 1987, Women's Bureau Collection, Provincial Archives of Alberta, Edmonton.

75. *The Other Alberta Report*, 3 April–31 May 1987.

76. Ibid.

77. Government of Alberta, "Cabinet Response to the Recommendations of the Alberta Advisory Council on Women's Issues," 1987, Library of the Alberta Legislature Library, Edmonton.

78. Ashley Geddes, "McCoy will push help for women," *Calgary Herald*, 19 January 1989: A1+.

79. *The Other Alberta Report*, 6 November–31 December 1987.

80. Pat Boynton, interview with author, tape recording, 14 January 1997.

81. Nancy Langford, interview with author, tape recording, 12 December 1996; Boynton, interview.

82. *Alberta Human Rights Journal* 5 (November 1987): 1.

83. ASWAC, newsletter, May 1986.

84. Ibid., 2.

85. Ibid.

86. Laing, interview. See also Julie Anne Le Gras, "Pay Equity: Valuing Women's Work," backgrounder and briefing notes, prepared for the New Democratic Party Caucus, 1989, private papers of Julie Anne Le Gras, Vancouver, BC.

87. Government of Alberta, "Alberta Plan for Action for Women: A Proud History, A Bright Future," July 1989.

88. See Alberta Women's Secretariat, "Person to Person: An Alberta Dialogue on Economic Equity for Women," 1989, Edmonton.

89. Boynton, interview.

90. Ibid.

91. Ibid. It should be noted that the Family Policy Grid was not imposed on the bureaucracy until 1991.

92. Ibid.

93. Government of Alberta, press release, 1 August 1989.

94. Government of Alberta, "Update! Alberta Plan for Action for Women," April 1990.

95. Ibid.

96. Government of Alberta, press release, 1 August 1989.

97. Government of Alberta, "Working Together to Prevent Family Violence," 1992.

98. Alberta Advisory Council on Women's Issues, Annual Report, 1 April 1987–31 March 1988.

99. Alberta Advisory Council on Women's Issues, press release, 13 October 1987.

100. Social Issues Committee, YWCA of Calgary, "Report Concerning Recommendations and Activities of the Alberta Advisory Council on Women's Issues," March 1988, Alberta Advisory Council on Women's Issues Collection, Provincial Archives of Alberta, 9.

101. "Cabinet Response to the 1987 Recommendations of the Alberta Advisory Council on Women's Issues," 1987, Library of the Alberta Legislature, Edmonton.

102. Social Issues Committee, YWCA of Calgary, "Report Concerning Recommendations and Activities of the Alberta Advisory Council on Women's Issues," March 1988, Alberta Advisory Council on Women's Issues Collection, Provincial Archives of Alberta, 9.

103. Ibid.

104. Alberta Advisory Council on Women's Issues, "Recommendations to the Government of Alberta," June 1988, Library of the Alberta Legislature, Edmonton, 23–29.

105. Ibid., 34 and 29.

106. Elaine McCoy to Margaret Leahey, 15 December 1988, Alberta Advisory Council on Women's Issues Collection, Provincial Archives of Alberta, Edmonton.

107. Government of Alberta, "Response to Alberta Advisory Council on Women's Issues June 1988 Recommendations," 1988, Library of the Alberta Legislature, Edmonton.

108. Elaine McCoy, interview with author, tape recording, 16 December 1996, Calgary.

109. Ibid.

110. Government of Alberta, press release, 7 April 1988, Alberta Advisory Council on Women's Issues Collection, Provincial Archives of Alberta, Edmonton.

111. Barb Livingstone, "McCoy under attack over advisory role," *Calgary Herald*, 20 February 1988: C1.

112. Marilyn Moysa, "Leahey leaves war-weary but wiser," *Edmonton Journal*, 2 April 1989: B1.

113. "Minister says women's group won't get axe," *Calgary Herald*, 29 March 1989: A1.

114. Lasha Morningstar and Duncan Thorne, "Future of women's council in doubt," *Edmonton Journal*, 9 March 1989: B1.

115. Kim McLeod, "Women seek answers from Getty," *Edmonton Journal*, 21 February 1989: B4.

116. "Minister says women's group won't get axe."

117. Julie Anne Le Gras to the Editor, *Edmonton Journal*, 1 May 1989: A7.

118. "Minister says women's group won't get axe."

119. Marilyn Moysa, "Council 'not working' for women in Alberta," *Edmonton Journal*, 5 June 1989: F5.

120. Ashley Geddes, "Women's council interim head named," *Calgary Herald*, 4 April 1989: B3.

121. Marilyn Moysa, "Feminists slam new women's council chairman," *Edmonton Journal*, 21 April 1989: B1.

122. Ibid.

123. "Women's council interim head named."

124. "Women's council strong," editorial, *Calgary Herald*, 20 June 1989.

125. Vicki Barnett, "Women's council head vows she will be heard," *Calgary Herald*, 21 April 1989: B2.

126. Alberta Advisory Council on Women's Issues, Annual Report 1989–90, private papers of Linda Trimble, Edmonton.

127. Alberta Advisory Council on Women's Issues et al., press release, 20 February 1990, ASWAC Resource Library, Edmonton.

128. Umar, interview.

129. McCoy, interview.

130. Women Looking Forward, minutes of round table," 24 September 1992, Office of Women Looking Forward, Calgary.

131. Ted Byfield, "'Family values' do count for something," *Financial Post Daily*, 15 June 1992: S3.

132. *The Other Alberta Report*, 1 October–13 November 1988.

133. Ibid.

134. *The Other Alberta Report*, 15 February–31 March 1989.

135. Premier's Council in Support of Alberta Families, *Directions for the Future* (Edmonton: Government of Alberta, 1992), 3.

136. Premier's Council in Support of Alberta Families, *Family Policy Grid* (Edmonton: Government of Alberta, 1992), 6.

137. Premier's Council in Support of Alberta Families, *Albertans Speak Out About Families* (Edmonton: Government of Alberta, 1992), 6.

138. Premier's Council in Support of Alberta Families, *Perspectives on Family Well-Being* (Edmonton, Government of Alberta, 1993), 2.

139. *Albertans Speak Out About Families*, 10.

Notes 183

140. Judy Fudge, "Fragmentation and Feminization: The Challenge of Equity for Labour Relations Policy," in Janine Brodie, ed., *Women and Canadian Public Policy* (Toronto: Harcourt Brace, 1996), 67.

141. Langford, interview.

5   Learning Neoliberalism

1. The leadership selection process undertaken by the Alberta Conservatives in 1992 departed from previous practices in that all party members, regardless of how long they had held their memberships, were entitled to vote. Two ballots were held a week apart and memberships could continue to be purchased between ballots. Although Nancy Betkowski led the race by a single vote on the first ballot and obtained the support of those candidates who did not proceed to the second ballot, Ralph Klein's supporters aggressively pursued membership sales and, as a result, Klein won by a substantial margin on the second ballot.

2. *Canadian News Facts*, 1–15 September 1993, 4804.

3. Alberta Treasury, Treasury Annual Report for the fiscal year ended 31 March 1997, 9.

4. Ibid.

5. Ibid.

6. Marilyn Fleger, the last chair of AACWI, noted that many of the women consulted over the course of AACWI's meetings with Alberta women noted the chaos that had accompanied the provincial government's deficit-reduction strategy and their subsequent difficulty in strategizing a response. There were so many concerns that needed to be raised that it became difficult to find a focus for action. Marilyn Fleger, interview with author, tape recording, 13 December 1996, Edmonton.

7. Women Looking Forward, "Calendar," January 1996.

8. Evidence for this fear was articulated with regard to ASWAC's participation in the federal government's social security review. A member of the Political Action Committee noted, "We don't want to make ourselves a target, because then we could get our funding cut." The committee recommended that ASWAC's board direct women participating in townhall meetings to "speak only if you feel it is safe to." Political Action Committee meeting minutes, 16 October 1994, ASWAC Collection, Provincial Archives of Alberta, Edmonton.

9. McGrath, interview.

10. ASWAC Plan of Action 1994–95; press release, 14 May 1993, ASWAC Collection, Provincial Archives of Alberta, Edmonton.

11. AFWUF, *The AFWUF Voice*, May/June/July 1994, 4.

12. Ibid.

13. Hermina Dykxhoorn, "President's Message," *The AFWUF Voice*, spring 1999.

14. Larry Johnsrude, "Gov't looks at building 'fences' to limit fallout from court ruling," *Edmonton Journal*, 10 April 1998: A5.

15. Hermina Dykxhoorn, "President's Message," *The AFWUF Voice*, spring 1999.

16. Patrick Nugent, "Marriage bill not proper use of notwithstanding clause," *Edmonton Journal*, 27 March 2000: A11.

17. Kelly Harris, "New law to ban same-sex marriage," *Calgary Herald*, 16 March 2000: A1.

18. The chief spokesperson for the Committee to End Tax Funded Abortions was Joanne Hatton, the wife of Link Byfield, the editor of *Alberta Report*.

19. AFWUF, *The AFWUF Voice*, September–October 1993.

20. Melanie Anderson, interview with author, tape recording, 10 January 1997, Calgary.

21. "Alberta may stop funding abortions: intense debate likely in caucus," *Globe and Mail*, 20 July 1995, A1+.

22. "Klein's stock soaring, party gets thin skin," *Globe and Mail*, 3 April 1995: A1+. The motion was defeated by a narrow margin.

23. Brian Laghi, "Right turn for the Tories?" *Edmonton Journal*, 9 September 1995: A1.

24. "Alberta may stop funding abortions."

25. Marie Gordon, interview with author, tape recording, 13 January 1997, Edmonton.

26. In response to these ads, an editorial in the *Alberta Report* suggested that Revenue Canada should investigate Planned Parenthood on the premise that the cost of the ads would have exceeded 10 per cent of its budget and thus, as a charitable organization, Planned Parenthood would have exceeded its spending limit on lobbying activities. In fact, this investigation did take place, but the organization was found to be well within the limit. The majority of the funds for the ads had, In fact, come from the member organizations of the Pro-Choice Coalition. Anderson, interview.

27. Gordon, interview.

28. Anderson, interview.

29. "Alberta PCs face tough test," *Globe and Mail*, 7 March 1996: A7. Women accessing abortions at private clinics, however, were still expected to pay the clinic facility fee—an amount ranging between $300 and $800. The Klein government has been a strong proponent of the establishment of private clinics at which provincial medical insurance contributes to the cost of proce-dures and clinic owners make their profit through additional charges, including facility fees. The federal government, however, has adamantly

opposed this practice and levied fines against the province in the amount of $442,000 per month. Despite the commitment to deficit reduction, the government paid the fine for ten months before reconsidering its position. In July of 1996 the province began paying the costs of facility fees. It seems that at least some of the pressure brought to bear on Alberta by the federal government regarding this matter stemmed from the federal government's concern regarding women's access to abortion. Anderson, interview.

30. "Alberta PCs face tough test."

31. Anderson, interview.

32. Ibid.

33. Ibid.

34. Fleger, interview.

35. Arlene Chapman, Executive Director, Alberta Council of Women's Shelters, interview with author, 28 June 2000, Edmonton.

36. Ibid. The government's official formula for shelters splits the funding at 80 per cent for the province and 20 per cent for private fundraising but, according to Chapman, the actual split is fifty-fifty.

37. Ibid.

38. Patricia Lawrence, *Supports for Independence and the Cost of Living in Alberta: Regional Differences* (Edmonton: Alberta Council of Women's Shelters, 2000).

39. Glenora Parent-Teacher Association, "Submission of the Glenora PTA to the Edmonton Public School Board," 16 May 1994, private papers of Sheila Greckol, Edmonton.

40. Charter schools are publicly funded but are autonomous from local school boards. Students are provided with a specialized curriculum addressing particular educational needs and talents. Critics of the charter school concept argue that these schools serve privileged children at public expense and may foster a racially homogeneous student body despite Canadian society's racial and ethnic diversity. Moreover, at least in Alberta, while teachers in charter schools must be certified they do not have to be members of the Alberta Teachers' Association. As Heather-Jane Robertson and Maude Barlow point out, this circumvention of the teachers' union means that charter schools do not have to pay teachers according to provincial pay scales or provide them with negotiated benefits. Heather-Jane Robertson and Maude Barlow, "Restructuring from the Right: School Reform in Alberta" in Trevor Harrison and Gordon Laxer, eds., *The Trojan Horse: Alberta and the Future of Canada* (Montreal: Black Rose Books, 1995), 204.

41. Roberston and Barlow, 195.

42. Glenora Parent-Teacher Association, "Submission to the Edmonton Public School Board," 1994, private papers of Sheila Greckol, Edmonton.

43. Lisa Dempster, "Halls of Learning: Teachers, students facing a strange new world," *Calgary Herald*, 30 June 1994: A5.

44. McGrath, interview.

45. Glenora Parent-Teacher Association, "Submission of the Glenora PTA to the Edmonton Public School Board," 16 May 1994.

46. Dempster, A5.

47. Trevor Harrison and Gordon Laxer, "Introduction," in Harrison and Laxer, 11.

48. Glenora Parent-Teacher Association, "Submission to the Edmonton Public School Board," 1994.

49. Alberta Advisory Council on Women's Issues, *Differential Impact and the Alberta Advantage*, October 1995.

50. Sheila Greckol, interview with author, 6 January 1996, Edmonton.

51. Ibid.

52. Ibid.

53. Ibid.

54. Glenora Parent-Teacher Association, "Fact Sheet on Kindergarten," 1996, private papers of Sheila Greckol, Edmonton.

55. Ibid.

56. Larry Johnsrude, "A little relief on the way: Klein to spend some of that $570 million surplus," *Edmonton Journal*, 30 January 1996: A1.

57. Alberta Health, *Getting Started: An Orientation for RHAs* (Calgary: Health Plan Coordination Project, 1994), 7.

58. Ibid., 16.

59. Ibid., 26.

60. Ibid., 13.

61. Dave Pommer, "Labor board orders laundry staff to end illegal walkout," *Calgary Herald*, 17 November 1995: B2; Dave Pommer, "Dirty laundry helps to define labor history," *Calgary Herald*, 26 November 1995: A3.

62. Robert Walker, "Authority backed on laundry," *Calgary Herald*, 12 December 1995: B1.

63. Kim Lunman, "City firm fighting for hospital laundry deal," *Edmonton Journal*, 11 January 1996: A1.

64. McGrath, interview.

65. Walker, B1.

66. Pommer, "Labor board orders laundry staff to end illegal walkout," B2.

67. Walker, B1.

68. Mark Lisac, "Multi-Corp caper leaves troubling trail," *Calgary Herald*, 17 November 1995: A14.

69. Alanna Mitchell, "Loss of jobs doesn't wash with populace," *Globe and Mail*, 24 November 1995: A2.

70. Ibid.
71. Anne McGrath and Dean Neu, "Washing our blues away," *Our Times*, 15 (March/April, 1996): 26.
72. Ibid., 34.
73. Ibid., 26.
74. Gordon Kent and Graham Thomson, "Healthcare workers set to strike," *Edmonton Journal*, 22 November 1995: A1.; Pommer, "Dirty laundry," A3.
75. Pommer, "Dirty laundry," A3.
76. Pommer, "Labor Board orders laundry staff to end illegal walkout," B2.
77. Pommer, "Dirty laundry," A3.
78. Kent and Thomson, A1.
79. "Health-care coffers refilled by Klein: election not a factor, Tories say," *Globe and Mail*, 26 November 1996: A1+.
80. Pommer, "Dirty laundry," A3.
81. Mark Scharf, Senior Materiel Manager, Calgary Regional Health Authority, telephone interview, 11 May 1998. In February 1998, the City of Calgary approved a ten-year lease on the Bow Valley laundry facility, enabling K–Bro to establish its operations in Calgary. Calgary Regional Health Authority, "Laundry: where are we at?" 20 February 1998 (accessed on-line at www.crha-health.ab.ca/publicaffairs/news/laundry.htm on 31 July 2000).
82. Jane Jenson and Susan Phillips, "Regime Shift: New Citizenship Practices in Canada," *International Journal of Canadian Studies* 14 (fall 1996): 129.
83. On-line at www.gov.ab.ca/mcd.
84. Laurie Blakeman, interview with author, 22 June 2000, Edmonton.
85. Alberta Community Development, Annual Report, 1996.
86. Alberta Advisory Council on Women's Issues, *Differential Impact and the Alberta Advantage*, October 1995, 37.
87. Fleger.
88. Alberta Legislative Assembly, *Debates*, 28 September 1993, 525.
89. Ibid.
90. Alberta Legislative Assembly, *Debates*, 30 September 1993, 611.
91. AFWUF, *The AFWUF Voice*, summer 1993, 13. The newsletter cited Mirosh's views on pay equity as follows: "She also celebrated the rejection of a leading cause of the political left. 'Well isn't that wonderful,' she enthused when hearing of the New Democrat's demise. 'Pay equity is dead. That was the NDP's issue and there's none of them anywhere, so that should be settled.'"
92. Calgary YWCA to Ralph Klein, 6 April 1993, private papers of Dale Hensley, Calgary.
93. Amal Umar, interview with author, tape recording, 10 January 1997, Calgary.
94. Umar, interview.

95. Ibid.

96. Blakeman, interview.

97. Fleger, interview.

98. See Alberta Advisory Council on Women's Issues, *The Economic Situation of Women Over 55, Present and Projected,* June 1994; *Desperately Seeking Certainty: Assessing and Reducing the Risk of Harm for Women Who Are Abused,* October 1995; *Differential Impact and the Alberta Advantage,* October 1995.

99. Alberta Advisory Council on Women's Issues, *Breadmakers and Breadwinners ... The Voices of Alberta Women,* February 1996, 1.

100. Ibid., 10.

101. Ibid., 4, 26–29.

102. Ibid., 18; Fleger, interview.

103. Alberta Legislative Assembly, *Debates,* 27 March 1995, 839.

104. Alberta Advisory Council on Women's Issues, *A Decade of Challenge and Change: A Review of the Activities of the AACWI,* February 1996, 18–19.

105. Ibid., 2.

106. Ibid., 20.

107. Ibid., 21.

108. Ibid., 22.

109. ASWAC, board members to members, February 1993, ASWAC Resource Library, Edmonton.

110. Alberta Human Rights Review Panel, *Equality in Dignity and Rights,* June 1994, 34.

111. ASWAC, newsletter, February 1993, ASWAC Resource Library, Edmonton.

112. Umar, interview.

113. Ibid.

114. Tom Arnold, "Liberals offer amendments to new human rights act," *Edmonton Journal,* 3 April 1996: A7.

115. Alberta Human Rights Review Panel, 70 and 52.

116. The submissions of numerous women's groups to the review panel have been collected by Women Looking Forward, Calgary.

117. Poverty Focus Group, "Submission to the Human Rights Commission on the Individual Rights Protection Act and the Role of the Human Rights Commission in Alberta," 18 January 1994, Office of Women Looking Forward, Calgary.

118. Edmonton Working Women, "Submission to the Public Review of the Alberta Human Rights Commission and the Individual Rights Protection Act—Draft," February 1994, Office of Women Looking Forward, Calgary.

119. Alberta Human Rights Review Panel, 73.

120. Marta Gold, "Homosexuality a 'lifestyle'—Klein," *Edmonton Journal,* 20 March 1996: A3.

121. AFWUF, *The AFWUF Voice,* January/February 1993.

122. Ibid.

123. McGrath, interview.

124. Umar, interview.

125. Ibid.

126. Ibid.

127. Alberta Human Rights Review Panel, 68.

128. Ibid., 69.

129. Marta Gold, "Ghitter wants Mar gone; Minister 'has lost the confidence' of Albertans," *Edmonton Journal,* 25 May 1996: A7.

130. Sheldon Alberts, "Lukewarm reception to human rights review," *Calgary Herald,* 2 July 1994: A7.

131. Alberta Community Development, *Our Commitment to Human Rights: The Government's Response to the Recommendations of the Alberta Human Rights Review Panel* (Edmonton: December 1995), 4.

132. Ibid., 6.

133. Ibid., 16.

134. For a discussion of Ron Ghitter's bid for the leadership of the provincial Conservatives and his position on the appointment of an Advisory Council on Women's Issues see Chapter 3.

135. Stanford, interview. In co-ordinating the meeting with the Calgary caucus of the Conservative Party discussed below, Yvonne Stanford recounted her efforts to alleviate the fears of the more "establishment" members of the human rights coalition that they would be embarrassed by the behaviour of more radical groups. Representatives of mainstream groups were particularly concerned that their radical colleagues would catcall, walk out in anger, laugh inappropriately, storm the podium, or roll their eyes. Although Stanford agreed, for the purposes of this particular meeting, to ask all coalition members to refrain from such behaviour, she also made it clear that if future meetings were to be held, the more conservative members of the coalition might also be asked to modify their behaviour.

136. Ibid.

137. Ibid.

138. Ibid.

139. Ibid.

140. Ashley Geddes, "Only 'special interests' oppose rights bill—Klein," *Edmonton Journal,* 26 April 1996: A8.

141. Marta Gold, "Human rights 'not an issue,'" *Edmonton Journal,* 30 April 1996: A7.
142. Geddes, A8.
143. Coalition on Human Rights in Alberta, "A Response to the Government of Alberta's Bill 24: IRPA Amendment Act, 1996," April 1996.
144. Ibid.
145. Ibid.; Coalition on Human Rights in Alberta, "Backwards and Forwards for Human Rights in Alberta," 1996.
146. Tom Arnold, "Province to bar discrimination against the poor, but no move made on gay rights," *Edmonton Journal,* 16 May 1996: A1.
147. Gold, "Ghitter wants Mar gone," A7.
148. Stanford, interview.

6   Oil, Sex, and Power

1. The phrase "politics of stealth" has become common parlance within the study of Canadian social policy. Its first usage is attributed to Ken Battle, writing under the pseudonym Gratton Gray, "Social Policy by Stealth," *Policy Options* 11 (March 1990): 17–29.
2. Stanford, interview.

Bibliography

Books and Articles

Abramovitz, Mimi. *Regulating the Lives of Women: Social Welfare Policy from Colonial Times to the Present.* Boston: South End Press, 1989.

Adamson, Nancy, Linda Briskin, and Margaret McPhail. *Feminist Organizing for Change: The Contemporary Women's Movement in Canada.* Toronto: Oxford University Press, 1988.

Andersen, Gosta Esping. *The Three Worlds of Welfare Capitalism.* Princeton: Princeton University Press, 1990.

Andrew, Caroline, and Sandra Rodgers, eds. *Women and the Canadian State.* Montreal and Kingston: McGill-Queen's University Press, 1997.

Bakker, Isabella. *The Strategic Silence: Gender and Economic Policy.* London: Zed Books, 1994.

———. *Rethinking Restructuring: Gender and Change in Canada.* Toronto, University of Toronto Press, 1996.

Barrett, Michelle, and Mary McIntosh. *The Anti-Social Family,* 2nd ed. London: Verso, 1991.

Bashevkin, Sylvia. *Women on the Defensive: Living Through Conservative Times.* Chicago: University of Chicago Press, 1998.

Benhabib, Seyla, ed. *Democracy and Difference: Contesting the Boundaries of the Political.* Princeton: Princeton University Press, 1996.

————. "From Identity Politics to Social Feminism: A Plea for the Nineties." In David Trend, *Radical Democracy*.

Brodie, Janine. "Meso-Discourses, State Forms and the Gendering of Liberal-Democratic Citizenship." *Citizenship Studies* vol. 1, no. 2 (1997): 223–42.

————, ed. *Women and Canadian Public Policy*. Toronto: Harcourt Brace, 1996.

————. *Politics at the Margins: Restructuring and the Canadian Women's Movement*. Halifax: Fernwood, 1995.

————. "The Women's Movement Outside Quebec: Shifting Relations with the Canadian State." In Kenneth McRoberts, ed., *Beyond Quebec: Taking Stock of Canada*. Montreal and Kingston: McGill-Queen's University Press, 1995.

————, Shelley Gavigan, and Jane Jenson. *The Politics of Abortion*. Toronto: Oxford University Press, 1992.

Brown, Wendy. *States of Injury: Power and Freedom in Late Modernity*. Princeton: Princeton University Press, 1995.

Bruce, Christopher, Ronald Kneebone, and Kenneth McKenzie, eds. *A Government Re-invented: A Study of Alberta's Deficit Elimination Program*. Toronto: Oxford University Press, 1997.

Burt, Sandra, Lorraine Code, and Lindsay Dorney, eds., *Changing Patterns: Women in Canada*. Toronto: McClelland & Stewart, 1993.

Burt, Sandra. "The Women's Movement: Working to Transform Public Life." In James P. Bickerton and Alain G. Gagnon, eds., *Canadian Politics*. Peterborough: Broadview Press, 1994.

Caldarola, Carlo, ed. *Society and Politics in Alberta*. Toronto: Methuen, 1979.

Clarkson, Stephen, and Timothy Lewis. "The Contested State: Canada in the Post-Cold War, Post-Keynesian, Post-Fordist, Post-National Era." In Leslie Pal, ed., *How Ottawa Spends, 1999–2000*. Toronto: Oxford, 1999.

Clement, Wallace, ed. *Understanding Canada: Building on the New Canadian Political Economy*. Montreal and Kingston: McGill-Queen's University Press, 1997.

Cohen, Jean, and Andrew Arato. *Civil Society and Political Theory*. Cambridge, Mass.: MIT Press, 1992.

Cohen, Marjorie Griffin. "From the Welfare State to Vampire Capitalism." In Patricia Evans and Gerda Wekerle, eds., *Women and the Canadian Welfare State*. Toronto: University of Toronto Press, 1997.

————. "Democracy and the Future of Nations: Challenges for Disadvantaged Women and Minorities." In Robert Boyer and Daniel Drache, eds., *States Against Markets: The Limits of Globalization*. London: Routledge, 1996.

Corrigan, Philip, and Derek Sayer. *The Great Arch: English State Formation as Cultural Revolution*. Oxford: Basil Blackwell, 1985.

Dacks, Gurston. "From Consensus to Competition: Social Democracy and Political Culture in Alberta." In Larry Pratt, ed., *Essays in Honour of Grant Notley: Socialism and Democracy in Alberta*. Edmonton: NeWest Press, 1986.

Devigne, Robert. *Recasting Conservatism: Oakeshott, Strauss, and the Response to Postmodernism*. New Haven: Yale University Press, 1994.

Dobrowolsky, Alexandra. *The Politics of Pragmatism: Women, Representation, and Constitutionalism in Canada*. Toronto: Oxford University Press, 2000.

Dubinsky, Karen. *Lament for a Patriarchy Lost? Anti-Feminism, Anti-Abortion and R.E.A.L. Women in Canada*. Ottawa: Canadian Research Institute for the Advancement of Women, 1985.

Elton, David, and Arthur Goddard. "The Conservative Takeover, 1971–." In Carlo Caldarola, ed., *Society and Politics in Alberta*. Toronto: Methuen, 1979.

Evans, Patricia, and Gerda Wekerle, eds. *Women and the Canadian Welfare State*. Toronto: University of Toronto Press, 1997.

Findlay, Sue. "Facing the State: Politics of the Women's Movement Reconsidered." In Heather Jon Maroney and Meg Luxton, eds., *Feminism and Political Economy*. Toronto: Methuen, 1987.

Fraser, Nancy, and Linda Gordon. "A Genealogy of Dependency: Tracing a Keyword of the US Welfare State." *Signs* 19 (1994): 309–36.

Fraser, Nancy. "Gender Equity and the Welfare State: A Postindustrial Thought Experiment." In Seyla Benhabib, ed., *Democracy and Difference*. Princeton: Princeton University Press, 1996.

———. "Struggle Over Needs: Outline of a Socialist-Feminist Critical Theory of Late-Capitalist Political Culture." In Linda Gordon, ed., *Women, the State, and Welfare*. Madison: University of Wisconsin Press, 1990.

Fudge, Judy. "Fragmentation and Feminization: The Challenge of Equity for Labour Relations Policy." In Janine Brodie, ed., *Women and Canadian Public Policy*. Toronto: Harcourt Brace, 1996.

Gibbins, Roger. "Western Alienation and the Alberta Political Culture." In Carlo Caldarola, ed., *Society and Politics in Alberta*. Toronto: Methuen, 1979.

Gordon, Linda, ed., *Women, the State and Welfare*. Madison: University of Wisconsin Press, 1990.

———. "The Welfare State: Towards a Socialist-Feminist Perspective." In *The Socialist Register 1990*.

Gotell, Lise. "Policing Desire: Obscenity Law, Pornography Politics, and Feminism in Canada." In Janine Brodie, ed., *Women and Canadian Public Policy*. Toronto: Harcourt Brace, 1996.

Grewal, Inderpal, and Caren Kaplan, eds. *Scattered Hegemonies: Postmodernity and Transnational Feminist Practices*. Minneapolis: University of Minnesota Press, 1994.

Harrison, Trevor, and Gordon Laxer. "Introduction." In Trevor Harrison and Gordon Laxer, eds., *The Trojan Horse: Alberta and the Future of Canada*. Montreal: Black Rose Books, 1995.

Harrison, Trevor. "Making the Trains Run On Time: Corporatism in Alberta." In Trevor Harrison and Gordon Laxer, eds., *The Trojan Horse: Alberta and the Future of Canada*. Montreal: Black Rose Books, 1995.

Hornick, J.P., R.J. Thomlinson, and L. Nesbitt. "Alberta." In Jacqueline Ismael and Yves Vaillancourt, eds., *Privatization and Provincial Social Services in Canada*. Edmonton: University of Alberta Press, 1988.

Howlett, Michael, Alex Netherton, and M. Ramesh. *The Political Economy of Canada*. Toronto: Oxford, 1999.

Jenson, Jane. "Gender and Reproduction, or Babies and the State." *Studies in Political Economy* 20 (1986).

———. "'Different' but not 'exceptional': Canada's permeable fordism." *Canadian Review of Sociology and Anthropology* 26(1) 1989: 69–94.

———, and Susan Phillips. "Regime Shift: New Citizenship Practices in Canada." *International Journal of Canadian Studies* 14 (1996): 111–36.

Jessop, Bob. "Towards a Schumpetarian Workfare State? Post-Fordist Political Economy." *Studies in Political Economy* 40 (1993): 7–40.

Kabeer, Naila, and John Humphrey. "Neoliberalism, Gender and the Limits of the Market." In Christopher Colclough and James Manor, eds., *States or Markets? Neoliberalism and the Development Policy Debate*. Oxford: Clarendon Press, 1991.

Leadbeater, David, ed. *Essays on the Political Economy of Alberta*. Toronto: New Hogtown Press, 1984.

Lisac, Mark. *The Klein Revolution*. Edmonton: NeWest Press, 1995.

Luxton, Meg, ed. *Feminism and Families: Critical Policies and Changing Practices*. Halifax: Fernwood Publishing Co., 1997.

Lyotard, Jean-François. *The Postmodern Condition: A Report on Knowledge*. Minneapolis: University of Minnesota Press, 1984.

MacKinnon, Catherine. *Toward a Feminist Theory of the State*. Cambridge, Mass.: Cambridge University Press, 1989.

Magnusson, Warren. *The Search for Political Space*. Toronto: University of Toronto Press, 1996.

Mahon, Rianne. "Canadian public policy: The unequal structure of representation." In Leo Panitch, ed., *The Canadian State: Political Economy and Political Power*. Toronto: University of Toronto Press, 1977.

Mansell, Robert, and Michael Percy. *Strength in Adversity: A Study of the Alberta Economy*. Edmonton: University of Alberta Press, 1990.

Marino, Jim. "Clearcutting in the Groves of Academe." In Trevor Harrison and Gordon Laxer, eds., *The Trojan Horse: Alberta and the Future of Canada*. Montreal: Black Rose Books, 1995.

Maroney, Heather Jon, and Meg Luxton, eds. *Feminism and Political Economy*. Toronto: Methuen Publications, 1987.

McBride, Stephen, and John Shields. *Dismantling a Nation: The Transition to Corporate Rule in Canada*. 2nd ed., Halifax: Fernwood Publishing Co., 1997.

McMillan, Melville, and Allan Warrack. "One-Track (Thinking) Towards Deficit Reduction." In Trevor Harrison and Gordon Laxer, eds., *The Trojan Horse: Alberta and the Future of Canada*. Montreal: Black Rose Books, 1995.

McRoberts, Kenneth, ed. *Beyond Quebec: Taking Stock of Canada*. Montreal and Kingston: McGill-Queen's University Press, 1995.

———. "Federal Structures and the Policy Process." In Michael Atkinson, ed., *Governing Canada: Institutions and Public Policy*. Toronto: Harcourt Brace, 1993.

Murphy, Jonathan. "Workfare will make you free." In Trevor Harrison and Gordon Laxer, eds., *The Trojan Horse: Alberta and the Future of Canada*. Montreal: Black Rose Books, 1995.

Murray, Robin. "The State after Henry." *Marxism Today*, May 1991.

Myles, John. "When Markets Fail: Social Welfare in Canada and the United States." In Gosta Esping-Andersen, ed., *Welfare States in Transition*. London: Sage, 1996.

O'Connor, James. *The Fiscal Crisis of the State*. New York: St. Martin's Press, 1973.

Offe, Claus. *Contradictions of the Welfare State*. London: Hutchinson, 1984.

Orloff, Anne Shola. "Restructuring Welfare: Gender, Work and Inequality in Australia, Canada, the United Kingdom and the United States." Paper presented at "Crossing Borders: An International Dialogue on Gender, Social Politics and Citizenship." Stockholm, May 1994.

Palmer, Howard, and Tamara Palmer. *Alberta: A New History*. Edmonton: Hurtig Publishers, 1990.

Pateman, Carole. "The Patriarchal Welfare State." In Linda McDowell and Rosemary Pringle, eds., *Defining Women: Social Institutions and Gender Divisions*. Cambridge: Polity Press, 1992.

Petchesky, Rosalind. *Abortion and Women's Choice: The State, Sexuality and Reproductive Freedom*. Revised ed., Boston: Northeastern University Press, 1990.

Phillips, Anne. *Democracy and Difference*. University Park, Penn.: University of Pennsylvania Press, 1993.

———. *Engendering Democracy*. University Park, Penn.: University of Pennsylvania Press, 1991.

Phillips, Susan. "Meaning and Structure in Social Movements: Mapping the Network of National Canadian Women's Organizations." *Canadian Journal of Political Science* 24 (December 1991).

Pierson, Ruth Roach. "The Mainstream Women's Movement and the Politics of Difference." In Ruth Roach Pierson, Marjorie Griffin Cohen, Paula Bourne, and Philinda Masters, eds., *Canadian Women's Issues: Volume 1: Strong Voices, Twenty-five Years of Women's Activism in English Canada.* Toronto: Lorimer, 1993.

Piven, Frances Fox. "Ideology and the State: Women, Power and the Welfare State." In Linda Gordon, ed., *Women, the State and Welfare.* Madison: University of Wisconsin Press, 1990.

Pratt, Larry, and Ian Urquhart. *The Last Great Forest: Japanese Multinationals and Alberta's Northern Forests.* Edmonton: NeWest Press, 1994.

Pratt, Larry, ed. *Essays in Honour of Grant Notley: Socialism and Democracy in Alberta.* Edmonton: NeWest Press, 1986.

———. "The Political Economy of Province Building: Alberta's Development Strategy, 1971–81." In David Leadbeater, ed., *Essays on the Political Economy of Alberta.* Toronto: New Hogtown Press, 1984.

Prince, Michael J. "From Health and Welfare to Stealth and Farewell: Federal Social Policy, 1980–2000." In Leslie Pal, ed., *How Ottawa Spends, 1999–2000.* Toronto: Oxford, 1999.

Randall, Vicki, and Georgina Waylen, eds., *Gender, Politics and the State.* London: Routledge, 1998.

Renouf, Simon. "Chipping Away at Medicare: 'Rome Wasn't Sacked in a Day'." In Trevor Harrison and Gordon Laxer, eds., *The Trojan Horse: Alberta and the Future of Canada.* Montreal: Black Rose Books, 1995.

Richards, John, and Larry Pratt. *Prairie Capitalism: Power and Influence in the New West.* Toronto: McClelland & Stewart, 1979.

Robertson, Heather-Jane, and Maude Barlow. "Restructuring from the Right: School Reform in Alberta." In Trevor Harrison and Gordon Laxer, eds., *The Trojan Horse: Alberta and the Future of Canada.* Montreal: Black Rose Books, 1995.

Rose, Nikolas. "The death of the social? Re-figuring the territory of government." *Economy and Society* 25 (August 1996): 327–56.

Scott, Joan. "Deconstructing Equality-Versus-Difference: Or, the Uses of Poststructuralist Theory for Feminism." In Marianne Hirsch and Evelyn Fox Keller, eds., *Conflicts in Feminism.* New York: Routledge, 1990.

Shaffer, Ed. "Oil, Class, and Development in Alberta." In Larry Pratt, ed., *Essays in Honour of Grant Notley: Socialism and Democracy in Alberta.* Edmonton: NeWest Press, 1986.

————. "The Political Economy of Oil in Alberta." In David Leadbeater, ed., *Essays on the Political Economy of Alberta.* Toronto: New Hogtown Press, 1984.

Taft, Kevin. *Shredding the Public Interest: Ralph Klein and 25 Years of One-Party Government.* Edmonton: University of Alberta Press and Parkland Institute, 1997.

Tremblay, Manon, and Caroline Andrew, eds., *Women and Political Representation.* Ottawa: University of Ottawa Press, 1998.

Trend, David, ed. *Radical Democracy: Identity, Citizenship and the State.* New York: Routledge, 1996.

Trimble, Linda. "The Politics of Gender in Modern Alberta." In Allan Tupper and Roger Gibbins, eds., *Government and Politics in Alberta.* Edmonton: University of Alberta Press, 1992.

Tupper, Allan, and Roger Gibbins, eds., *Government and Politics in Alberta.* Edmonton: University of Alberta Press, 1992.

————, Larry Pratt, and Ian Urquhart. "The Role of Government." In Allan Tupper and Roger Gibbins, eds., *Government and Politics in Alberta.* Edmonton: University of Alberta Press, 1992.

————. "Opportunity and Constraint: Grant Notley and the Modern State." In Larry Pratt, ed., *Essays in Honour of Grant Notley: Socialism and Democracy in Alberta.* Edmonton: NeWest Press, 1986.

Ursel, Jane. *Private Lives, Public Policy: 100 years of State Intervention in the Family.* Toronto: Women's Press, 1992.

Vickers, Jill. "Bending the Iron Law of Oligarchy: Debates on the Feminization of Organization and Political Process in the English Canadian Women's Movement, 1970–1988." In Jeri Dawn Wine and Janice Ristock, eds., *Women and Social Change: Feminist Activism in Canada.* Toronto: J. Lorimer, 1991.

Waring, Marilyn. *Three Masquerades: Essays on Equality, Work and Human Rights.* Auckland: Auckland University Press, 1996.

Watkins, Ernest. *The Golden Province: A Political History of Alberta.* Calgary: Sandstone Publishing, 1980.

Yeatman, Anna. *Postmodern Revisionings of the Political.* New York: Routledge, 1994.

————. "Voice and representation In the politics of difference." In Sneja Gunew and Anna Yeatman, eds., *Feminism and the Politics of Difference.* Boulder: Westview Press, 1993.

Young, Iris Marion. "Polity and Group Difference: A Critique of the Ideal of Universal Citizenship." In *Throwing Like a Girl and Other Essays.* Bloomington: Indiana University Press, 1990.

————. *Justice and the Politics of Difference.* Princeton: Princeton University Press, 1990.

Women's Groups and Community Organizations

Alberta Federation of Women United for Families (AFWUF). "A Response to the Department of Education's Discussion Paper, 'Partners in Education'." 11 March 1985. Women's Secretariat Records, Provincial Archives of Alberta, Edmonton.

———. *The AFWUF Voice.* December 1982, September 1984, December 1987, April/May 1989, May/June 1990, November 1990, January/February 1993, Summer 1993, September/October 1993, May/July 1994. Women's Secretariat Resource Library, Edmonton: March 1983, Spring 1986, Winter 1987. Personal papers of Julie Anne Le Gras, Provincial Archives of Alberta, Edmonton: August 1983, September 1984. Women's Secretariat Records, Provincial Archives of Alberta, Edmonton: Jan.–Feb. 1994, Sept.–Oct. 1994, Nov.–Dec. 1995, Spring 1996, Summer 1996, Sept.–Oct. 1996, Nov.–Dec. 1996, Jan.–Feb. 1997, Aug.–Sept. 1997, Nov./Dec. 1997–Jan./Feb. 98, Summer 1998, Jan./Feb. 1999, Spring 1999. Alberta Human Rights and Citizenship Commission Library, Edmonton.

———. Submission to the Alberta Human Rights Commission, 5 February 1987.

———. Submission to the City of Edmonton Re: Daycare, 12 February 1985. Women's Secretariat Records, Provincial Archives of Alberta, Edmonton.

———. Conference Resolutions. 1983. Women's Secretariat Records, Provincial Archives of Alberta, Edmonton.

———. Position papers (ca. 1983?). Women's Secretariat Resource Library, Edmonton.

———. "History." In *Good Citizens, Good Government.* Women's Secretariat Resource Library, Edmonton.

———. "What Humanism can do to your Child," pamphlet, n.d. ASWAC Resource Library, Edmonton.

Alberta Society of Obstetricians and Gynecologists. Position paper on elective abortions, 1981. Alberta Status of Women Action Committee, ASWAC Resource Library, Edmonton.

ASWAC. Documentation and clarification (re: interactions between ASWAC and pro-life organizations) (ca. December 1981). ASWAC Resource Library, Edmonton.

———. Annual Reports 1977–78, 1979–80, 1981–82. ASWAC correspondence and issue files, Provincial Archives of Alberta, Edmonton.

———. Conference program. November 1987. ASWAC Resource Library, Edmonton.

———. "Equal Pay for Work of Equal Value: Prospects for Alberta." A brief presented to the Canadian Human Rights Commission by ASWAC. 19 March 1980. ASWAC Resource Library, Edmonton.

———. Newsletter. May 1980, May 1984, August 1985, January 1986, March 1986, May 1986, December 1986, March 1987, June 1987, August 1987, September 1987, October 1987, January 1988, March 1988, May/June 1988, July/August 1988, December 1989, March 1990, May 1990, June 1991. ASWAC Collection, Provincial Archives of Alberta, Edmonton; February 1993. ASWAC Resource Library, Edmonton.

———. "Organizational Review Update: Report to the Secretary of State Women's Program." June 1992. ASWAC Resource Library, Edmonton.

———. "Organizational Review Update: Report to the Secretary of State Women's Program." March 1992. ASWAC Resource Library, Edmonton.

———. *Joint Initiatives: A Goal for Women and Government in Alberta.* Edmonton: ASWAC, October 1976.

———. *Women Against Poverty.* Edmonton: ASWAC, 1992; 2nd ed., 1996. Calgary Birth Control Association. Annual Report 1973. Calgary Birth Control Association Collection, Glenbow Archives, Calgary.

———. "A Brief in Response to the anti-Calgary Birth Control Association Brief" (ca. 1976). Calgary Birth Control Association Collection, Glenbow Archives, Calgary.

———. "History of the Abortion Information Centre" (ca. 1972?) Calgary Birth Control Association Collection, Glenbow Archives, Calgary.

Calgary Committee for an Alberta Council on Women's Affairs. Newsletter. Fall 1984. Provincial Coalition for a Council on Women's Affairs Collection, Glenbow Archives, Calgary.

Calgary Local Council of Women. "Resolution on the Division of Property Between Spouses" (ca. 1974). Calgary Local Council of Women Collection, Glenbow Archives, Calgary.

Calgary Status of Women Action Committee. Position update. 10 May 1983. Calgary Status of Women Action Committee Collection, Glenbow Archives, Calgary.

———. "Review of Calgary Status of Women Action Committee 1976–77" (ca. fall 1977). Calgary Status of Women Action Committee Papers 1974–78, Glenbow Archives, Calgary.

Calgary YWCA. "The Calgary YWCA and the Alberta Advisory Council on Women's Issues—A Brief History." October 1994. Private papers of Dale Hensley, Calgary.

———. Social Issues Committee. "Report Concerning Recommendations and Activities of the Alberta Advisory Council on Women's Issues." March 1988. Alberta Advisory Council on Women's Issues Collection, Provincial Archives of Alberta, Edmonton.

Campaign Life. Press release, 16 November 1981. Women's Secretariat Records, Provincial Archives of Alberta, Edmonton.

Coalition on Human Rights in Alberta. "A Response to the Government of Alberta's Bill 24: IRPA Amendment Act, 1996." April 1996.

———. "Backwards and Forwards for Human Rights in Alberta." 1996.

Edmonton Options for Women Council. Societies Act (ca. 1974). Options for Women (OFW) Collection, Provincial Archives of Alberta, Edmonton.

Edmonton Social Planning Council. "Where Did These Laws Come From?" 15 March 1976. OFW Collection, Provincial Archives of Alberta, Edmonton.

Edmonton Social Planning Council for OFW. "Maternity Leave in Alberta." 10 May 1975. OFW Collection, Provincial Archives of Alberta, Edmonton.

Edmonton Women's Place. Newsletter. January 1976. OFW Collection, Provincial Archives of Alberta, Edmonton.

Edmonton Working Women. "Submission to the Public Review of the Alberta Human Rights Commission and the Individual Rights Protection Act—Draft," February 1994. Office of Women Looking Forward, Calgary.

Freeland, Halyna. *Matrimonial Property: The New Legislation.* Edmonton: Alberta Law Foundation, 1977.

Friends of Medicare. "Background to the Issues and Policy Statement." ASWAC Resource Library, Edmonton.

Glenora Parent-Teacher Association. "Fact Sheet on Kindergarten." 1996. Private papers of Sheila Greckol, Edmonton.

———. "Submission to the Edmonton and District Council of Churches on the Framework for Funding School Boards." 14 March 1995. Private papers of Sheila Greckol, Edmonton.

———. "Submission of the Glenora PTA to the Edmonton Public School Board." 16 May 1994. Private papers of Sheila Greckol, Edmonton.

———. "Submission to the MLA Implementation Team and Advisory Committee on the Framework for Funding School Boards." 1995. Private papers of Sheila Greckol, Edmonton.

———. "Submission to the Edmonton Public School Board." 1994. Private papers of Sheila Greckol, Edmonton.

Lawrence, Patricia. *Supports for Independence and the Cost of Living in Alberta: Regional Differences.* Edmonton: Alberta Council of Women's Shelters, 2000.

Le Gras, Julie Anne. *Pushing the Limits: Reflections on Alberta Women's Strategies for Action.* Edmonton: Unique Publishing Association, 1984.

———. "Council on Women's Affairs, Background Paper." 15 January 1983. ASWAC Resource Library, Edmonton.

———. Notes on first annual conference of Alberta Federation of Women United for Families. 19–20 November 1982.

Institute of Law Research and Reform. *Matrimonial Property Report.* Edmonton: Institute of Law Research and Reform, 1975.

OFW. Newsletter. February 1978. OFW Collection, Provincial Archives of Alberta, Edmonton.

———. "Information for Women" (ca.1975). OFW Collection, Provincial Archives of Alberta, Edmonton.

Planned Parenthood Alberta. "Position of Federal, Provincial and Municipal Governments Re: funding of Planned Parenthood Alberta" (ca.1983). Women's Secretariat Records, Provincial Archives of Alberta, Edmonton.

Poverty Focus Group. "Submission to the Human Rights Commission on the Individual Rights Protection Act and the Role of the Human Rights Commission in Alberta." 18 January 1994. Office of Women Looking Forward, Calgary.

Provincial Coalition for a Council on Women's Affairs. Newsletter. 22 February 1985. Provincial Coalition for a Council on Women's Affairs Collection, Glenbow Archives, Calgary.

———. "Workshop on the White Paper Proposals." Third annual conference. Autumn 1984. Private collection of Linda Trimble, Edmonton.

RATJAM, ad hoc committee of ASWAC. "Alberta Adoption Foundation Act." Draft. 3 February 1982. ASWAC Resource Library, Edmonton.

Source: Alberta Women's Newsletter, 1 (spring 1974).

"Summary of the Activities of the Calgary Status of Women Action Committee." Accession file to the Calgary Status of Women Action Committee Papers, Glenbow Archives, Calgary.

Tremblay, Mariette, and Bonnie McEwan. "ASWAC Position Paper on Child Care." Presented to the Special Committee on Child Care, 2 June 1986. ASWAC Resource Library, Edmonton.

United Nurses of Alberta. "Brief Submitted to the Standing Committee on Public Affairs." 22 April 1983. Library of the Alberta Legislature, Edmonton.

University Women's Club of Calgary. "Brief on Maternity Leave." 26 April 1976. University Women's Club of Calgary Collection, Glenbow Archives, Calgary.

———. "Brief on Reform to Matrimonial Property Legislation." October 1974. University Women's Club of Calgary Collection, Glenbow Archives, Calgary.

Women Looking Forward. "Calendar." January 1996. Office of Women Looking Forward, Calgary.

———. "Final Report, Annual General Meeting." 1993. Office of Women Looking Forward, Calgary.

———. "Final Report, Annual General Meeting." 1992. Office of Women Looking Forward, Calgary.

———. "Activity Report 1989–90." Office of Women Looking Forward, Calgary.

Women of Unifarm. "Submissions to the Provincial Cabinet by Women of Unifarm." 1973–78. Legislative Library, Alberta Legislature, Edmonton.

Wright, Pat. Speech at press conference on matrimonial property. 17 October 1977. Women's Secretariat Records, Provincial Archives of Alberta, Edmonton.

Government Reports, Legislative Records

Alberta Advisory Council on Women's Issues. *A Decade of Challenge and Change: A Review of the Activities of the Alberta Advisory Council on Women's Issues.* February 1996.

———. *Breadmakers and Breadwinners ... The Voices of Alberta Women.* February 1996.

———. *Desperately Seeking Certainty: Assessing and Reducing the Risk of Harm for Women Who Are Abused.* October 1995.

———. *Differential Impact and the Alberta Advantage.* October 1995.

———. *The Economic Situation of Women Over 55, Present and Projected.* June 1994.

———. "Supports for Independence and its Effects on Women." April 1992.

———. Annual Report. 1989–90. Private papers of Linda Trimble, Edmonton.

———. Press release. 20 February 1990. ASWAC Resource Library, Edmonton.

———. "Review of the Maintenance Enforcement Program." 27 January 1989. Resource Library of the Alberta Women's Secretariat, Edmonton.

——— et al. "Submission to the Premier's Commission on Future Health Care for Albertans." November 1988. Resource Library of the Alberta Women's Secretariat, Edmonton.

———. "Recommendations to the Government of Alberta." June 1988. Legislature Library, Alberta Legislature, Edmonton.

———. "Midwifery in Alberta: A Discussion Paper." May 1988. Resource Library of the Alberta Women's Secretariat, Edmonton.

———. Annual Report. 1 April 1987–31 March 1988.

———. "Summary of Public Input, Lethbridge Public Meeting." 25 February 1988. Alberta Advisory Council on Women's Issues Collection, Provincial Archives of Alberta, Edmonton.

———. *The Newsmagazine by Alberta Women.* November/December 1987. Alberta Advisory Council on Women's Issues Collection, Provincial Archives of Alberta, Edmonton.

———. Press release. 13 October 1987.

———. "Response to the Alberta Government's 'Caring and Responsibility: A Statement of Social Policy for Alberta.'" (ca. 1987). Alberta Advisory Council on Women's Issues Collection, Provincial Archives of Alberta, Edmonton.

Alberta Communications Network. Press release. 9 February 1988.

Alberta Community Development. Annual Reports 1993–96.

———. *Our Commitment to Human Rights: The Government's Response to the Recommendations of the Alberta Human Rights Review Panel.* December 1995.

Alberta Family and Social Services. *One Step at a Time: Supports for Independence.* 1991.

———. "Alberta Day Care Programs." Pamphlet. 1991.

———. "Alberta Day Care Licensing Reforms." Pamphlet. July 1990.

———. "Alberta Day Care Reforms: A fairer, better system for Albertans." July 1990.

Alberta Health. *Getting Started: An Orientation for RHAs.* Calgary: Health Plan Coordination Project, 1994.

Alberta Human Rights Commission (AHRC). Press release, 24 July 1984. AHRC Collection, Provincial Archives of Alberta, Edmonton.

———. "Background Paper on the Inclusion of Sexual Orientation as a Prohibited Grounds for Discrimination." 25 April 1984. AHRC Collection, Provincial Archives of Alberta, Edmonton.

——— Chairman. "*Introductory Remarks* of news conference." 5 February 1980. AHRC Collection, Provincial Archives of Alberta, Edmonton.

———. Press release. 15 October 1979. AHRC Collection, Provincial Archives of Alberta, Edmonton.

———. April public agenda. 3 April 1979. CSWAC Collection, Glenbow Archives, Calgary.

———. Press release. 11 May 1978. CSWAC Collection, Glenbow Archives, Calgary.

———. Annual Reports 1974–75.

———. "Summary of a Report Submitted to the AHRC on Occupational Segregation and its Effects: A Study of Women in the Alberta Public Service." AHRC Collection, Provincial Archives of Alberta, Edmonton.

AHRC, Gay and Lesbian Awareness Society of Edmonton, CLAGPAG, and Gay Lines of Calgary. "A Study of Discrimination Based on Sexual Orientation." December 1992. Legislature Library, Alberta Legislature, Edmonton.

Alberta Human Rights Journal. 1 (spring 1983), 1 (winter 1983), 2 (fall 1984), 3 (June 1985), 5 (November 1987), 6 (summer 1988).

Alberta Human Rights Review Panel. *Equality in Dignity and Rights.* June 1994.

Alberta Legislative Assembly. *Debates.* 25 March 1983, 12 May 1983, 17 April 1984, 1 November 1984, 8 June 1988, 9 June 1988, 10 June 1988, 13 June 1988, 17 May 1993, 28 September 1993, 30 September 1993, 6 October 1993, 7 March 1994, 2 November 1994, 7 November 1994, 22 February 1995, 1 March 1995, 8 March 1995, 27 March 1995.

Alberta Women's Bureau. *Alberta Labour Legislation of Interest to Women in the Paid Workforce.* July 1977.

Alberta Women's Secretariat. "Update! Alberta Plan for Action for Women." April 1990.

———. "Person to Person: An Alberta Dialogue on Economic Equity for Women." January 1989.

———. "Impact on Women of Alberta Government Fiscal Restraint Measures." June 1987. Alberta Women's Bureau Collection, Provincial Archives of Alberta, Edmonton.

———. "Background Paper: Barriers to Educational and Training Opportunities for Women in Alberta." July 1986. Private papers of Elizabeth McClintock, Edmonton.

———. "Summary of AFWUF's Presentation to the Interdepartmental Committee on Women's Issues." 27 March 1985. Women's Bureau Collection, Provincial Archives of Alberta, Edmonton.

———. "Brief on Protection Against Discrimination on the Basis of Pregnancy." August 1984. Ministry of Labour Collection, Provincial Archives of Alberta, Edmonton.

Annual Conference of First Ministers. "Towards a Labour Force Strategy: A Framework for Training for Women: Progress Reports. Alberta Submission." Ottawa: 9–10 November 1989. Legislature Library, Alberta Legislature, Edmonton.

Bagley, Chris. "Child Care in Alberta." 1985. ASWAC Resource Library, Edmonton.

Blough, Ann. (Calgary City Councillor) "A Brief to the Government of Alberta Re: Grants to the Calgary Birth Control Association." 3 December 1975. Calgary Birth Control Association Collection, Glenbow Archives, Calgary.

Calgary Regional Health Authority. "Laundry: where are we at?" 20 February 1998, 31 July 2000. On-line at www.crha-health.ab.ca/publicaffairs/news/laundry.htm.

Citizens' Advisory Board. "An Interim Report on the Status of Women in Alberta." Edmonton: 1972.

Cookson, Jack, MLA. "Progressive Conservative Position on the Status of Alberta Women." OFW Collection, Provincial Archives of Alberta, Edmonton. n. d.

Ellis, Phyllis. "Summary of Second Annual Meeting of the Provincial Committee for a Council on Women's Affairs." 9 November 1984. Women's Secretariat Records, Provincial Archives of Alberta, Edmonton.

———. "Report of Meeting of Southern Alberta Women's Organizations, Calgary." 30 November 1981. Women's Secretariat Records, Provincial Archives of Alberta, Edmonton.

Government of Alberta. "Right on the Money: Alberta's Debt and Deficit 1993." 1993.

———. "Working Together to Prevent Family Violence." 1992.

———. Press release. 1 August 1989. Women's Bureau Collection, Provincial Archives of Alberta, Edmonton.

———. "Alberta Plan for Action for Women: A Proud History, A Bright Future." July 1989.

———. "Response to Alberta Advisory Council on Women's Issues, June 1988 Recommendations." 1988. Legislature Library, Alberta Legislature, Edmonton.

———. Press release. 7 April 1988. Alberta Advisory Council on Women's Issues Collection, Provincial Archives of Alberta, Edmonton.

———. "Cabinet Response to the 1987 Recommendations of the Alberta Advisory Council on Women's Issues." Legislature Library, Alberta Legislature, Edmonton.

———. "Alberta's Statement on Equality for Women." Conference of First Ministers on the Economy, 2nd Annual Conference. Vancouver, B.C.: 21–22 November 1986.

———. Press release. 15 April 1985. Women's Bureau Collection, Provincial Archives of Alberta, Edmonton.

———. Press release. 28 February 1984. Women's Bureau Collection, Provincial Archives of Alberta, Edmonton.

———. "Ministerial Statement and Action Plan for Promoting Tolerance and Understanding" (ca. 1983). Calgary Status of Women Action Committee Collection, Glenbow Archives, Calgary.

Horner, Hugh. "An Address by Hon. Dr. Hugh M. Horner, Deputy Premier and Minister of Transportation, Government of Alberta, to ASWAC." 29 October 1976. ASWAC Resource Library, Edmonton.

Premier's Council in Support of Alberta Families. *Perspectives on Family Well-Being.* Edmonton: Government of Alberta, 1993.

———. *Albertans Speak Out About Families.* Edmonton: Government of Alberta, 1992.

———. *Directions for the Future.* Edmonton: Government of Alberta, 1992.

———. *Family Policy Grid.* Edmonton: Government of Alberta, 1992.

Shearer, Renate. "Review of ASWAC and Women's Programme, Secretary of State, Alberta." 15 April 1986. ASWAC Collection, Provincial Archives of Alberta, Edmonton.

Young, Les. "Potential Opening Remarks Re: Affirmative Action." Meeting of Ministers Responsible for Human Rights. 8–9 September 1983. Women's Bureau Collection, Provincial Archives of Alberta, Edmonton.

Minutes of Meetings

ASWAC. Minutes from a meeting to examine the widows' pension program. April 1985. ASWAC Resource Library, Edmonton.

———. Minutes of the inaugural meeting of ASWAC. 27 September 1975. Calgary
Status of Women Action Committee Papers 1974–78, Glenbow Archives,
Calgary.
Calgary Committee for the Proposed Council on Women's Affairs. Minutes. 15
November 1983. Calgary Committee for a Council on Women's Affairs
Collection, Glenbow Archives, Calgary.
Calgary Local Council of Women. Minutes of executive meeting. 14 April 1992 and 1
September 1992. Calgary Local Council of Women Collection, Glenbow
Archives, Calgary.
Calgary Status of Women Action Committee. Board meeting minutes. 20 January
1977, 18 January 1978, 14 December 1978, 8 January 1979, 17 May 1979.
———. "Proceedings: Women in a Violent Society Conference." 21–23 April 1978.
CSWAC Collection, Glenbow Archives, Calgary.
Edmonton Committee of the Provincial Committee for a Council on Women's
Affairs. Minutes. 7 May 1984. Women's Secretariat Records, Provincial
Archives of Alberta, Edmonton.
Edmonton OFW. Minutes, general meeting. 7 October 1976. OFW Collection,
Provincial Archives of Alberta, Edmonton.
Interdepartmental Committee on Women's Issues. Minutes. 15 March 1985.
Women's Bureau Collection, Provincial Archives of Alberta, Edmonton.
———. Minutes. 29 October 1984. Women's Bureau Collection, Provincial Archives
of Alberta, Edmonton.
Options for Women Coordinating Committee. Minutes. 18 December 1975. OFW
Collection, Provincial Archives of Alberta, Edmonton.
Options for Women. Minutes of the Co-ordinating Committee. 3 June 1975. OFW
Collection, Provincial Archives of Alberta, Edmonton.
———. Minutes of founding meeting. 13 October 1973. OFW Collection, Provincial
Archives of Alberta, Edmonton.
Provincial Committee for a Council on Women's Affairs. Minutes. 7 May 1983.
Women's Secretariat Records, Provincial Archives of Alberta, Edmonton.
Women Looking Forward. Minutes of round table and annual general meeting. 1991.
———. Minutes of round table. 23 February 1982, 28 September 1989, 4 September
1992. Office of Women Looking Forward, Calgary.

Newspapers and Magazines

"3rd rights staffer quits; stays mum." *Edmonton Journal,* 19 July 1980: B1.
"Alberta may stop funding abortions: Intense debate likely in caucus." *Globe and
Mail,* 20 July 1995: A1.
"Alberta PCs face tough test." *Globe and Mail,* 7 March 1996: A7.

"Health-care coffers refilled by Klein: election not a factor, Tories say." *Globe and Mail*, 26 November 1996: A1.

"In Calgary, the report is just 'ho hum.'" *Calgary Herald*, 8 December 1970: 61.

"Klein's stock soaring, party gets thin skin." *Globe and Mail*, 3 April 1995: A1.

"Minister says women's group won't get axe." *Calgary Herald*, 29 March 1989: A1.

"Women's council strong." Editorial. *Calgary Herald*, 20 June 1989.

"Women's groups winning." *Edmonton Journal*, 22 October 1984: B1.

Alberta Report, 2 May 1988: 44–45.

Alberts, Sheldon. "Lukewarm reception to human rights review." *Calgary Herald*, 2 July 1994: 7.

Armstrong, Luanne. Letter to the Editor. *Camrose Canadian*, November 1987. Women's Secretariat Records, Provincial Archives of Alberta, Edmonton.

Arnold, Tom. "Province to bar discrimination against the poor, but no move made on gay rights." *Edmonton Journal*, 16 May 1996: A1.

———. "Liberals offer amendments to new human rights act." *Edmonton Journal*, 3 April 1996: 7.

Barnett, Vicki. "Women's council head vows she will be heard." *Calgary Herald*, 21 April 1989: B2.

Braungart, Susan. "40,000 women back campaign." *Calgary Herald*, 14 March 1983: B6.

Byfield, Ted. "'Family values' do count for something." *Financial Post Daily*, 15 June 1992: 3.

Camrose Canadian. Editorial. 18 November 1987. Women's Secretariat Records, Provincial Archives of Alberta, Edmonton.

Canadian News Facts, 1–15 January 1993; 1–15 September 1993; 1–15 January 1994; 16–30 June 1994; 16–31 October 1994; 16–30 June 1995.

Cohen, Cheryl. "Women's issues to get boost." *Edmonton Journal*, 19 October 1983: A15.

Cooney, Roman. "MLA promises change for women." *Calgary Herald*, 13 September 1983: B1.

Dempster, Lisa. "Halls of Learning: Teachers, students facing a strange new world." *Calgary Herald*, 30 June 1994. A5.

Geddes, Ashley. "Only 'special interests' oppose rights bill—Klein." *Edmonton Journal*, 26 April 1996: A8.

———. "Women's council interim head named." *Calgary Herald*, 4 April 1989: B3.

———. "McCoy will push help for women." *Calgary Herald*, 19 January 1989: A1.

Gold, Marta. "Ghitter wants Mar gone; Minister 'has lost the confidence' of Albertans." *Edmonton Journal*, 25 May 1996: A7.

———. "Human rights 'not an issue.'" *Edmonton Journal*, 30 April 1996: A7.

———. "Homosexuality a 'lifestyle'—Klein." *Edmonton Journal*, 20 March 1996: A3.

Goyette, Linda. "Zeroing in on the real enemy." *Edmonton Journal*, 16 June 1986: A7.

Harris, Kelly. "New law to ban same-sex marriage." *Calgary Herald*, 16 March 2000: A1.

Helm, Richard. "Boycott women's advisory body, prospective members told." *Edmonton Journal*, 7 May 1986: B1.

Johnsrude, Larry. "Gov't looks at building 'fences' to limit fallout from court ruling." *Edmonton Journal*, 10 April 1998: A5.

———. "A little relief on the way: Klein to spend some of that $570 million surplus." *Edmonton Journal*, 30 January 1996: A1.

Kent, Gordon and Graham Thomson. "Healthcare workers set to strike." *Edmonton Journal*, 22 November 1995: A1.

Kerr, Kathy, and Sheila Pratt. "Women annoyed only Ghitter will attend forum." *Calgary Herald*, 3 October 1985: A9.

Laghi, Brian. "Right turn for the Tories?" *Edmonton Journal*, 9 September 1995: A1.

Lisac, Mark. "Multi-Corp caper leaves troubling trail." *Calgary Herald*, 17 November 1995: A14.

Livingstone, Barb. "McCoy under attack over advisory role." *Calgary Herald*, 20 February 1988: C1.

Locherty, Lorraine. "Critics tell women's council to prove its worth." *Calgary Herald*, 17 November 1986: A9.

———. "Koziak and Getty camps anger women." *Edmonton Journal*, 24 August 1985: B1.

———. "Time's up, women tell Tories." *Edmonton Journal*, 3 July 1985: B1.

Lunman, Kim. "City firm fighting for hospital laundry deal." *Edmonton Journal*, 11 January 1996, A1.

McGrath, Anne, and Dean Neu. "Washing our blues away." *Our Times*, 15 (March/April 1996).

McLeod, Kim. "Women seek answers from Getty." *Edmonton Journal*, 21 February 1989: B4.

———. "Balance views, Real Women told." *Edmonton Journal*, 28 November 1987: B5.

Mitchell, Alanna. "Loss of jobs doesn't wash with populace." *Globe and Mail*, 24 November 1995: A2.

Morningstar, Lasha, and Duncan Thorne. "Future of women's council in doubt." *Edmonton Journal*, 9 March 1989: B1.

Moysa, Marilyn. "Council 'not working' for women in Alberta." *Edmonton Journal*, 5 June 1989: F5.

———. "Feminists slam new women's council chairman." *Edmonton Journal*, 21 April 1989: B1.

———. "Leahey leaves war-weary but wiser." *Edmonton Journal*, 2 April 1989: B1.

———."Alberta women's council urged." *Edmonton Journal*, 27 April 1981: B2.

Norwood News, March 1982. ASWAC Resource Library, Edmonton.

Nugent, Patrick. "Marriage bill not proper use of notwithstanding clause." *Edmonton Journal*, 27 March 2000: A11.

The Other Alberta Report, July 6–September 6, 1986, 7 September–18 October 1986, 19 October–14 November 1986, 15 November–28 December 1986, 29 December 1986–18 February 1987, 19 February– 2 April 1987, 3 April–31 May 1987, 1 June–15 July 1987, 16 July–11 September 1987, 12 September–5 November 1987, 6 November–31 December 1987, 1 January–14 February 1988, 16 February–31 March 1988, 16 May–30 June 1988, 1 July–15 August 1988, 1 October–13 November 1988, 14 November–31 December 1988, 15 February–31 March 1989.

Pommer, Dave. "Dirty laundry helps to define labor history." *Calgary Herald*, 26 November 1995: A3.

———. "Labor board orders laundry staff to end illegal walkout." *Calgary Herald*, 17 November 1995: B2.

Pratt, Sheila. "Women's council bill favoured." *Calgary Herald*, 2 August 1986: A7.

———. "Ghitter draws fire on advisory council plan." *Calgary Herald*, 6 October 1985: A3.

Tompkins, John. "Women move closer to equality in work." *Edmonton Journal*, 9 November 1972: 18.

Walker, Robert. "Authority backed on laundry." *Calgary Herald*, 12 December 1995: B1.

———. "Membership claim challenged." *Calgary Herald*, 28 February 1985: B4.

Zwarun, Suzanne. "Feminist group explores its future, raison d'etre." *Calgary Herald*, 28 February 1983: B4.

———. "Blitz continues quest for provincial women's council." *Calgary Herald*, 14 January 1983: B5.

Correspondence

Adair, Al "Boomer," to CSWAC, 13 December 1977. Calgary Status of Women Action Committee Collection, Glenbow Archives, Calgary.

ASWAC board members, to members, 18 April 1997. Private papers of Lois Harder.

———, to members, February 1993. ASWAC Resource Library, Edmonton.

———, to Elaine McCoy (Minister responsible for women's issues), 6 March 1989. ASWAC Collection, Provincial Archives of Alberta, Edmonton.

———, to member groups of Coalition for a Council on Women's Affairs, 31 January 1983. Women's Secretariat Records, Provincial Archives of Alberta, Edmonton.

————, to Myrna Coombs (Social Development Officer, Secretary of State), 5 January 1982. ASWAC Collection, Provincial Archives of Alberta, Edmonton.

Alberta Union of Provincial Employees, to ASWAC, 30 June 1982. ASWAC Resource Library, Edmonton.

Antonio, Marlene (Chair of AHRC), to Les Young (Minister of Labour), 22 June 1984. Department of Labour Collection, Provincial Archives of Alberta, Edmonton.

Calgary Birth Control Association, to Helen Hunley (Minister of Social Services and Community Health), 12 February 1976. Calgary Birth Control Association Collection, Glenbow Archives, Calgary.

————, to Members of the Legislative Assembly, 6 September 1973. Calgary Birth Control Association Collection, Glenbow Archives, Calgary.

————, to Calgary Inter-Faith Community Action Committee, 23 January 1973. Calgary Birth Control Association Collection, Glenbow Archives, Calgary.

————, to Supporters, September 1975. Calgary Birth Control Association Collection, Glenbow Archives, Calgary.

————, to various doctors, (ca. 1973). Calgary Birth Control Association Collection, Glenbow Archives, Calgary.

Calgary Status of Women Action Committee, to Jim Foster (Attorney General of Alberta), 13 February 1978. CSWAC Papers, Glenbow Archives, Calgary.

Calgary YWCA, to Ralph Klein (Premier of Alberta), 6 April 1993. Private papers of Dale Hensley, Calgary.

————, to women's groups, 10 November 1981. Women's Secretariat Records, Provincial Archives of Alberta, Edmonton.

Chabillion, Dave (Executive Director, Career Development Sector), to Randy Fischer (Executive Assistant to the Minister, Advanced Education and Manpower), 22 June 1982. Women's Secretariat Records, Provincial Archives of Alberta, Edmonton.

Chairman of the Board of the Calgary Birth Control Association, to supporters of the association, September 1975. Calgary Birth Control Association Collection, Glenbow Archives, Calgary.

Chichak, Catherine, MLA, to Julie Anne Le Gras, 26 April 1982. ASWAC Resource Library, Edmonton.

Clarke, Robert (Executive Director, Alberta Medical Association), to Shelley Smith (Co-ordinator, ASWAC), 28 January 1981. ASWAC Resource Library, Edmonton.

Cooper, Pat, (Calgary YWCA), to Les Young, 12 November 1981. Women's Secretariat Records, Provincial Archives of Alberta, Edmonton.

————, to Phyllis Ellis (Alberta Women's Bureau), 16 October 1981. Women's Secretariat Records, Provincial Archives of Alberta, Edmonton.

Dean, Meaghan, to Calgary Status of Women Action Committee members, 14 January 1983. Calgary Status of Women Action Committee Collection, Glenbow Archives, Calgary.

DeZutter, Pat, to Helen Wilson, 19 November 1987. Women's Secretariat Records, Provincial Archives of Alberta, Edmonton.

Ellis, Phyllis (Director, Alberta Women's Bureau), to Mary LeMessurier, 20 June 1983. Women's Secretariat Records, Provincial Archives of Alberta, Edmonton.

———, to Mary LeMessurier (Minister of Culture), 18 March 1983. Women's Secretariat Records, Provincial Archives of Alberta, Edmonton.

———. "Information Letter to Alberta Women's Groups" (ca. 1975?). ASWAC Collection, Canadian Women's Movement Archives, Morisette Library, University of Ottawa, Ottawa.

Ethier, Margaret (President, United Nurses of Alberta), to Norma Farquharson, 12 December 1983. Personal papers of Sylvia McKinley, Edmonton.

Farquharson, Norma, to Dick Johnston (Minister Responsible for Women's Issues), 23 October 1984. Women's Secretariat Records, Provincial Archives of Alberta, Edmonton.

———, to members of Provincial Coalition for a Council on Women's Affairs, 12 March 1984. Women's Secretariat Records, Provincial Archives of Alberta, Edmonton.

Foster, Jim (Attorney General), to OFW, 26 May 1977. OFW Collection, Provincial Archives of Alberta, Edmonton.

Getty, Don (Premier of Alberta), to the Calgary Status of Women Action Committee, 22 December 1987. Women's Secretariat Records, Provincial Archives of Alberta, Edmonton.

Hall, Ann, to Lou Hyndman (Deputy Premier), 22 February 1977. Women's Secretariat Records, Provincial Archives of Alberta, Edmonton.

Higgins, Kathleen (President, Alberta Federation of Women United for Families), to Maureen Towns (Co-chair, Provincial Committee for a Council on Women's Affairs), 3 May 1983. Women's Secretariat Records, Provincial Archives of Alberta, Edmonton.

———, to Peter Lougheed, 22 February 1983. Women's Secretariat Records, Provincial Archives of Alberta, Edmonton.

Hobbs, Harry, Deputy Minister Executive Council, to L. Hyndman, N. Crawford, J. Horsman, B. Bogle, and L. Young, 18 May 1979. Women's Secretariat Records, Provincial Archives of Alberta, Edmonton.

Hunley, Helen, to all Preventive Social Service Board chairmen, 16 March 1976. Calgary Birth Control Association Collection, Glenbow Archives, Calgary.

Hyndman, Lou, to Ann Hall, 3 March 1977. Women's Secretariat Records, Provincial Archives of Alberta, Edmonton.

Jackson, Donna, to Peter Lougheed (Premier of Alberta), 22 January 1985. Women's Bureau Documents, Provincial Archives of Alberta, Edmonton.

Johnston, Dick, to Lorna Lagrange, 30 July 1985, Women's Bureau Collection, Provincial Archives of Alberta, Edmonton.

———, to Pat Thompson, 20 December 1984. Women's Secretariat Records, Provincial Archives of Alberta, Edmonton.

———, to Peter Lougheed, 26 September 1984. AHRC Collection, Provincial Archives of Alberta, Edmonton.

———, to Norma Farquharson, 25 May 1984. Private collection of Sylvia McKinley.

———, to Norma Farquharson (ca. April 1984). Women's Secretariat Records, Provincial Archives of Alberta, Edmonton.

Kennedy, Al (Assistant Deputy Minister, Ministry of Labour), to Les Young, 11 September 1984. AHRC Collection, Provincial Archives of Alberta, Edmonton.

———, to Les Young, 25 March 1982. Women's Secretariat Records, Provincial Archives of Alberta, Edmonton.

Koper, Janet, to Norma Farquharson, 28 February 1984. Personal collection of Sylvia McKinley, Edmonton.

Lagrange, Lorna, to Jim Horsman (Minister of Federal and Intergovernmental Affairs), 2 April 1985. Women's Bureau Collection, Provincial Archives of Alberta, Edmonton.

Langeslag, Flores, to potential contributors, February 1985. Women's Secretariat Records, Provincial Archives of Alberta, Edmonton.

Le Gras, Julie Anne, to Dick Johnston, 27 July 1984. Women's Secretariat Records, Provincial Archives of Alberta, Edmonton.

———, to Ian Reid (Minister of Labour), 27 June 1988. Private papers of Julie Anne Le Gras, Provincial Archives of Alberta, Edmonton.

———, to Ian Reid, 29 March 1988. Private papers of Julie Anne Le Gras, Provincial Archives of Alberta, Edmonton.

Le Rougetel. Amanda, to Sylvia McKinley, 3 June 1985. ASWAC Resource Library, Edmonton.

Leahey, Margaret (Chair, Alberta Advisory Council on Women's Issues), to Rick Orman (Minister of Career Development and Employment), 23 December 1987. Alberta Advisory Council on Women's Issues Collection, Provincial Archives of Alberta, Edmonton.

McCoy, Elaine (Minister of Consumer and Corporate Affairs), to Julie Anne Le Gras, 30 June 1989. Private papers of Julie Anne Le Gras, Provincial Archives of Alberta, Edmonton.

———, to Margaret Leahey, 15 December 1988. Alberta Advisory Council on Women's Issues Collection, Provincial Archives of Alberta, Edmonton.

———, to Ken Rostad (Solicitor General), 17 December 1987. Women's Secretariat Records, Provincial Archives of Alberta, Edmonton.

———, to Dennis Anderson (Minister Responsible for Women's Issues), 2 July 1987. Women's Bureau Collection, Provincial Archives of Alberta, Edmonton.

———, to Dennis Anderson, 4 June 1987. Women's Bureau Collection, Provincial Archives of Alberta, Edmonton.

McKinley, Sylvia, and Norma Farquharson, to Dennis Anderson, 14 November 1986. Private collection of Sylvia McKinley, Edmonton.

Olson, Linda, to Ken Rostad, 15 November 1987. Women's Secretariat Collection, Provincial Archives of Alberta, Edmonton.

Oman, Ed (Chair of Calgary Progressive Conservative Caucus), to Doreen Blitz, 8 September 1982. Women's Secretariat Records, Provincial Archives of Alberta, Edmonton.

OFW, to Neil Crawford (Minister of Social Services), 22 December 1975, OFW Collection, Provincial Archives of Alberta, Edmonton.

Orman, Rick, to Julie Anne Le Gras, 26 October 1988. Private papers of Julie Anne Le Gras, Provincial Archives of Alberta, Edmonton.

———, to Margaret Leahey, 1 February 1988. Alberta Advisory Council on Women's Issues Collection, Provincial Archives of Alberta, Edmonton.

Osterman, Connie (Minister of Social Services), to Julie Anne Le Gras, 23 February 1988. Private papers of Julie Anne LeGras, Provincial Archives of Alberta, Edmonton.

Payne, Annette (Director, Policy and Program Development Branch, Department of Housing), to Eslin Eling (Executive Assistant to Deputy Minister of Labour), 5 September 1984. Ministry of Labour Collection, Provincial Archives of Alberta, Edmonton.

President of the Calgary Birth Control Association, to S.E. Blakely (Director, Preventive Social Services), 23 October 1978. Calgary Birth Control Association Collection, Glenbow Archives, Calgary.

Reid, Ian, to Julie Anne Le Gras, 8 August 1988. Private papers of Julie Anne Le Gras, Provincial Archives of Alberta, Edmonton.

———, to Julie Anne Le Gras, 3 May 1988. Private papers of Julie Anne Le Gras, Provincial Archives of Alberta, Edmonton.

Rendle, Gwen, to various recipients, August 1986. ASWAC Resource Library, Edmonton.

Rostad, Ken, to Elaine McCoy, 18 November 1987. Women's Secretariat Records, Provincial Archives of Alberta, Edmonton.

Ruffo, Susan, to Jim Foster (Attorney General), February 1978. Women's Secretariat Records, Provincial Archives of Alberta, Edmonton.

Shone, Margaret (Institute of Law Research and Reform), to Phyllis Ellis, 28 December 1977. Women's Secretariat Records, Provincial Archives of Alberta, Edmonton.

Simken, Ruth, to Lou Hyndman, 6 December 1977. Calgary Status of Women Action Committee Papers 1974–78. Glenbow Archives, Calgary.

Smith, Keith (Executive Director, Research and Education Services, Workers' Health, Safety and Compensation), to Jack Freebury (Associate Director, Planning and Research, Alberta Labour), 12 September 1984. Ministry of Labour Collection, Provincial Archives of Alberta, Edmonton.

Smith, Shelley, to Robert Clarke, 17 March 1981. ASWAC Resource Library, Edmonton.

Stevens, Greg, to Peter Lougheed, 22 August 1979. AHRC Collection, Provincial Archives of Alberta, Edmonton.

Sykes, Ron (Mayor of Calgary), to Helen Hunley (Minister of Social Services and Community Health), 16 February 1976. Calgary Birth Control Association Collection, Glenbow Archives, Calgary.

Thompson, Pat, to Dick Johnston, 3 December 1984. Women's Secretariat Records, Provincial Archives of Alberta, Edmonton.

Tieman, Lynne (Editor of *Calgary Women's Newspaper*), to the board, Calgary Status of Women Action Committee, July 1980. Calgary Status of Women Action Committee Papers 1974–78. Glenbow Archives, Calgary.

Towns, Maureen (Chair, Provincial Committee for a Council on Women's Affairs), to coalition members, 22 February 1985. Private Collection of Sylvia McKinley, Edmonton.

Warren, Catherine, to Helen Hunley (Minister without Portfolio), 14 June 1973. Calgary Status of Women Action Committee Papers 1974–78, Glenbow Archives, Calgary.

Webber, Neil (Minister of Social Services and Community Health), to Gwen Rendle, 11 July 1984. ASWAC Resource Library, Edmonton.

White, Sharon (Senior Employee Relations Officer, Personnel Administration), to Albert Kennedy, 11 September 1984. Department of Labour Collection, Provincial Archives of Alberta, Edmonton.

Wilson, Roy (MLA), to Helen Milone, 22 January 1975. University Women's Club of Calgary Collection, Glenbow Archives, Calgary.

Wynn, Sheila (Senior Intergovernmental Officer, Social and Cultural Affairs Division, Department of Federal and Intergovernmental Affairs), to members of the Interdepartmental Committee on Women's Issues, 7 January 1986. Women's Bureau Collection, Provincial Archives of Alberta, Edmonton.

———, to Dick Johnston, 4 October 1985. Women's Bureau Collection, Provincial Archives of Alberta, Edmonton.

———, to Lorna Lagrange, 24 April 1985. Women's Bureau Collection, Provincial Archives of Alberta, Edmonton.

———, to Dick Johnston, 28 March 1985. Women's Bureau Collection, Provincial Archives of Alberta, Edmonton.

———, to Janina Vanderpost, 27 March 1985. Women's Bureau Collection, Provincial Archives of Alberta, Edmonton.

———, to Dick Johnston, 26 February 1985. Women's Secretariat Records, Provincial Archives of Alberta, Edmonton.

———, to Richard Dalon, (Executive Director, Social and Cultural Affairs Division), 22 February 1982. Women's Secretariat Records, Provincial Archives of Alberta, Edmonton.

Young, Les, to Gwen Rendle, 4 September 1984. ASWAC Resource Library, Edmonton.

———, to Betty Galatiuk (Calgary YWCA), 20 July 1982. Women's Secretariat Records, Provincial Archives of Alberta, Edmonton.

———, to Al Kennedy, 1 March 1982. Women's Secretariat Records, Provincial Archives of Alberta, Edmonton.

———, to Pat Cooper, Mary Collins, and Monica Sloan, 21 August 1981. Calgary Committee for a Council on Women's Affairs Collection, Glenbow Archives, Calgary.

Interviews

Ackerman, Sheryl. Interview with Sheila Dunphy, 3 August 1989. Northern Alberta Women's Archives Project, Provincial Archives of Alberta, Edmonton.

Adams, Francis. Interview with Sheila Dunphy, 15 August 1989. Northern Alberta Women's Archives Project, Provincial Archives of Alberta, Edmonton.

Anderson, Melanie. Interview with author, 10 January 1997, Calgary. Tape recording.

Blakeman, Laurie. Interview with author, 22 June 2000, Edmonton.

Boynton, Pat. Interview with author, 14 January 1997, Edmonton. Tape recording.

Bray, Cathy. Interview with Sheila Dunphy (ca. summer 1989). Northern Alberta Women's Archives Project, Provincial Archives of Alberta, Edmonton

Chapman, Arlene. Interview with author, 28 June 2000, Edmonton.

Fleger, Marilyn. Interview with author, 13 December 1996, Edmonton. Tape recording.

Fox, Susan. Personal communication, 13 January 1997. Edmonton.

Freeland, Halyna. Interview by Sheila Dunphy, 28 June 1989, Northern Alberta Women's Archives Project, Provincial Archives of Alberta, Edmonton.

Gordon, Marie. Interview with author, 13 January 1997, Edmonton. Tape recording.

Greckol, Sheila. Interview with author, 6 January 1997, Edmonton. Tape recording.

Krause, Pam. Interview with author, 10 January 1997, Calgary. Tape recording.

Laing, Marie. Interview by author, 8 January 1997, Edmonton. Tape recording.

Langford, Nanci. Interview with author, 12 December 1996, Edmonton. Tape recording.

Langford, Nanci. Personal communication, 3 January 1996, Edmonton.

Le Gras, Julie Anne. Interview with author, 19 December 1996, Vancouver. Tape recording.

———. Interview with Sheila Dunphy, 26 July 1989. Northern Alberta Women's Archives Project, Provincial Archives of Alberta, Edmonton.

Margets, Jenny, Interview with Sheila Dunphy, August 1990. Northern Alberta Women's Archives Project, Provincial Archives of Alberta, Edmonton.

McCoy, Elaine. Interview with author, 16 December 1996, Calgary. Tape recording.

McGrath, Anne. Interview with author, 10 January 1997, Calgary. Tape recording.

Miller, Nancy. Interview with author, 10 January 1997, Calgary. Tape recording.

Richardson, Trudy. Interview with Sheila Dunphy, 16 August 1989. Northern Alberta Women's Archives Project, Provincial Archives of Alberta, Edmonton.

Riddle, Marie. Interview with author, 7 January 1997, Edmonton. Tape recording.

Scharf, Mark. Telephone interview with author, 11 May 1998, Calgary.

Smith, Mair. Interview with Sheila Dunphy, 15 July 1989. Northern Alberta Women's Archives Project, Provincial Archives of Alberta, Edmonton.

Stanford, Yvonne. Interview with author, 15 December 1996, Calgary. Tape recording.

Umar, Amal. Interview with author, 10 January 1997, Calgary. Tape recording.

Williams, Mimi. Interview with author, 23 June 2000, Edmonton.

Wynn, Sheila. Interview with author, 19 December 1996, Victoria. Tape recording.

Miscellaneous Unpublished Material

Bélanger, Pauline, and Laverne Booth, "ASWAC: The History of a Women's Organization 1976–1980." Course paper, University of Alberta, 1981. ASWAC Resource Library, Edmonton.

Blais, Monica. "Feminist Politics in Alberta in the 1980s." MA thesis, University of Alberta, 1990.

Bray, Cathy. "Government and the Women's Movement: The ASWAC Example." Course paper, University of Alberta, 1983. ASWAC Resource Library, Edmonton.

Index

AACWI *See* Alberta Advisory Council on Women's Issues

Aboriginal people xi, 26, 51, 76, 80, 105, 106, 110, 144–45, 169 n. 62

abortion 13, 22, 54–55, 60–61, 84, 93, 95–96, 98, 110, 116, 122, 123–38, 137, 159, 180 n. 62, 185–86 n. 18, n. 26, n. 29

Abortion By Choice 54

Abramovitz, Mimi 14

ACWS *See* Alberta Council of Women's Shelters

Adair, Al "Boomer" 35, 168 n. 55

advisory councils on women's issues 3, 23, 29–32, 36, 49, 58–67, 77, 141

affirmative action 38–42, 48, 64, 68, 72–73, 86, 88, 90, 145, 146, 156, 169 n. 62

AFWUF *See* Alberta Federation of Women United for Families

agriculture xii, 2, 33, 145, 147

AHRC *See* Alberta Human Rights Commission

Alberta Advisory Council on Women's Issues (AACWI) 3–4, 12, 18, 66–67, 77, 78, 80, 86, 114, 116, 122, 138–39, 155–156, 158

demise of 123, 140–42

recommendations 98, 104–7, 111, 140–142

relationship with government 98, 105, 107–11

relationship with women's groups 86, 93–94, 104–6, 110–11, 141

Alberta Civil Liberties Research Centre 88

Alberta Coalition for Universal Health Care 97

Alberta Council of Women's Shelters
(ACWS) 121, 128–29
Alberta Federation of Women United
for Families (AFWUF) 11, 53–57,
60–61, 66, 81, 91–94, 139, 140,
145, 155. *See also* abortion,
sexual orientation
establishment 53–55
Good Citizens Good Government 91
and liberal pluralism 11, 46, 52,
55–57, 91
meeting with Interdepartmental
Committee on Women's Issues
75–77
and neoliberalism 121, 123–25
Alberta Human Rights Commission
(AHRC) 5, 37–42, 52, 68–75,
100–101, 138–39, 140, 147, 149.
See also Individual Rights
Protection Act
approach to sexual harassment
40–41, 145
human rights review panel 143–47
Alberta Institute of Law Research and
Reform 2, 33–36
Alberta Labour Relations Board 135
Alberta Medical Association (AMA)
95, 97, 98, 127, 180 n. 59, n. 62
Alberta Multiculturalism Commission
139
Alberta Pacific Terminals 118
Alberta Report 125
Alberta Status of Women Action
Committee (ASWAC) 11, 28, 43,
48, 52, 53, 76, 93, 108, 116–17, 121,
122, 184 n. 8
and Alberta Federation of Women
United for Families 54–56, 171 n.
26
demise of 122–23, 137, 158

government view of 51–52, 83–85
Joint Initiatives 29–33, 48–49
maintenance enforcement 52–53
matrimonial property 33, 35–36
organizational innovations 49–52,
82–83
and Provincial Coalition for a
Council on Women's Affairs 58,
59
and racism 89–90
radical feminism within 48–49, 82
Women Against Poverty (WAP)
85–87
Alberta Union of Public Employees
(AUPE) 134–135
Alberta Women in Support of
Agriculture 93
Alberta Women of Worth 55. *See also*
Alberta Federation of Women
United for Families
Alberta Women's Secretariat 4, 51,
62–63, 68–70, 77–78, 80–81,
98–99, 102, 122, 139, 155
and Alberta Advisory Council on
Women's Issues 105
and Alberta Federation of Women
United for Families 11, 76–77, 94
AMA *See* Alberta Medical Association
Anderson, Dennis 61, 97, 109
anti-feminism 48, 53, 117. *See also*
Alberta Federation of Women
United for Families, conserva-
tive women's groups
Antonio, Marlene 68, 72
Arthurs, Catharine 140–41
ASWAC *See* Alberta Status of Women
Action Committee
Attorney General 24, 32, 52–53
AUPE *See* Alberta Union of Public
Employees

Barrett, Michelle 14
Betkowski (MacBeth), Nancy 96, 119,
	184 n. 1
birth control 13, 93, 95–98, 107, 116, 156
Bow Valley Centre 134–137, 188 n. 81
Business and Professional Women's
	Association 128

cabinet 4, 27, 30, 32, 39, 42, 48, 59, 74,
	80–81, 85, 90, 96–97, 99, 101,
	102, 104, 108, 110–11, 114, 121, 138,
	155, 177 n. 3
Cabinet Committee on Social
	Planning 31, 56
Cabinet Committee on Women's
	Issues 11, 29–31, 62, 75, 77, 176
	n. 113
Calgary, feminist activism in 25,
	87–90, 126–27. See also specific
	organizations
Calgary Birth Control Association 93
Calgary Board of Education 88
Calgary General Hospital 96. See also
	Bow Valley Centre
Calgary Immigrant Women's Centre
	88
Calgary Local Council of Women
	92–93
Calgary Public School Board 131
Calgary Regional Health Authority
	133–34, 136
Calgary Status of Women Action
	Committee (CSWAC) 23–25,
	34–35, 43, 48–49, 89–90
Calgary Women of Colour Collective
	89–90
Calgary Women's Health Collective
	88

Calgary Women's Newspaper 23–25,
	49
Calgary YWCA 90, 93
	Social Issues, Committee of 57,
	104–06
Campaign Life 54–55
Camrose 83–84
Canada Assistance Program 102
Canadian Advisory Council on the
	Status of Women 9, 42, 59, 61
Canadian Union of Public Employees
	(CUPE) 134–135
capitalism (capitalist economy) 10, 93,
	153, 158, 162
Catholic Women's League 61, 128
Changing Together 90
Charter of Rights and Freedoms
	46–48, 68, 71, 73, 95, 124, 143
charter schools 131, 186 n. 40
child care 7, 15, 28, 48, 52, 55, 71, 76, 84,
	89, 92–93, 102, 104–05, 132, 156
Christianity x, 84, 92
Committee to End Tax Funded
	Abortions 125, 127, 185 n. 18
Common Front 130
Conservative Party (Alberta) 4, 13,
	19–20, 48, 64–65, 67, 87, 104,
	109, 116, 119, 125–28, 132, 140–41,
	143–44, 156
	caucus 5, 34, 62, 114, 121, 123, 125–27,
	139, 141, 145, 147, 148–49. See
	also cabinet
	leadership selection 65–66, 110–20,
	174 n. 77, 184 n. 1
conservative women's groups 82, 90,
	92–94, 111, 121, 123, 164 n. 16. See
	also specific groups
Constitution of Canada xi, 62, 92, 95,
	124. See also Charter of Rights
	and Freedoms

Index 221

Section 33 (notwithstanding clause) 5, 71, 124, 150
Corrigan, Phillip 6–7
CSWAC *See* Calgary Status of Women Action Committee
CUPE *See* Canadian Union of Public Employees

Day, Stockwell 112–113
Department of Community Development 129, 139–41, 144, 146–47
    Human Rights and Citizenship Branch 138
Department of Education 75, 131
Department of Family and Social Services 139
"Dialogue on Economic Equity" 86
Dignity Foundation 147–48
Dinning, Jim 113
divorce and separation 2–3, 7, 22, 33–36, 52–53, 112–13. *See also* matrimonial property, maintenance enforcement
domestic violence 15, 88, 92, 102–5, 112–13, 128–29. *See also* women's shelters

economic conditions 13, 16, 22, 45, 62, 75, 79, 80, 86, 101, 115, 120–21, 141, 143, 154, 160
    boom 20–22, 37, 153, 154
    boom-bust cycle 1, 22, 153
    deficit and debt 15, 57, 97, 102–3, 117, 120–22, 125, 128, 130, 157
    fiscal crisis 13, 16, 18, 57, 98–99, 117–18, 140, 143, 153

surplus 15, 18, 97, 120–21, 125–26, 160
Edmonton 87, 95, 127, 134, 180 n. 62,
Edmonton Public School Board 131
Edmonton Working Women 145
education 8, 15, 17, 28, 39–40, 48, 55, 72, 75, 101, 106, 115, 122, 130–31, 154, 157, 158. *See also* charter schools, kindergarten, sex education
    public education 28, 35–36, 50, 52, 86, 88–89, 106, 144, 146, 149
electoral politics 13, 18, 47–48, 56, 66, 84–85, 112, 154, 155–56, 160, 184 n. 1
    1971 election 19
    1984 election (federal) 47
    1986 election 77–67, 81
    1989 election 81, 108, 109–10, 113
    1993 election 120, 126
    1997 election 136
    elected representatives ix, 11, 22, 30, 56, 58, 64, 78, 89, 91, 99–100, 116, 126
    electorate 10, 121, 123, 127, 154
    women in 64, 85
employment equity. *See* affirmative action
Employment Standards Act 68–69
equality 9, 13, 16, 17, 20–21, 23, 26, 28–30, 32, 35–36, 43, 46, 54, 56, 61, 64, 96, 98, 103, 107, 111–12, 116, 140, 156–57, 159, 162. *See also* Alberta Human Rights Commission, affirmative action, Individual Rights Protection Act, pay equity
    formal x, 17, 20, 30–31, 43, 47–49, 58, 77, 117, 120

sameness/difference 14–15, 20, 27,
43, 46, 68–70, 74–75, 84, 101,
139, 145, 158, 160–61
struggle for 10, 12, 18, 22, 27, 33, 37,
43, 49, 79, 120, 151, 162

family 3, 8, 13–14, 22, 28–29, 73, 84, 91,
94, 98, 101–2, 105, 107–8, 110,
112–15, 117, 135. *See also* Alberta
Federation of Women United
for Families, Premier's Council
in Support of Alberta Families
Family Day 13
family values 4–5, 13, 57, 64, 80, 103,
112–17, 123, 132, 156
family violence. *See* domestic
violence, women's shelters
Famous Five xi
federal government x, 9, 12, 20–21, 42,
47, 57, 80, 102, 110, 116, 120, 122,
154, 157, 184 n. 8, 185–86 n. 29.
See also Secretary of State
federal-provincial relations xii, 21, 45,
47–48, 96, 103, 113, 155
Fraser, Fil 147
Fraser, Nancy 7, 43
Fraser Institute 101
Financial Administration Act 56
fiscal restraint. *See* economic condi
tions
Foothills Hospital 135
Framework for Action on Family
Violence 103
funding of women's organizations 11,
12, 21, 50–51, 54–57, 80, 82–85,
102, 106, 108–9, 116–17, 120,
122–23, 128–29, 139, 142, 157, 159,
165–66 n. 9, 184 n. 8, 185 n. 26.
See also Secretary of State

fundraising 24, 51, 83, 128

Gainers Meat-Packing 118
gambling x, 24–25, 113, 142, 166 n. 14
Getty, Don 4, 64, 66, 81, 94, 108, 111–13,
118–19, 143
Ghitter, Ron 65, 147–48, 174 n. 77
Glenora Parent Teacher Association
130–32
Government of Alberta. *See* cabinet,
caucus, Conservative Party of
Alberta, specific departments

health care 123. *See also* Medicare
Health Sciences Association of
Alberta 135
Higgins, Kathleen 60
Horner, Hugh 3, 30–31, 35, 167 n. 35
Human Rights, Citizenship, and
Multiculturalism Act 148–49
Hyndman, Lou 31, 32

immigrant women 76, 81, 90, 104–7,
110, 134, 136, 144
Immigrant Women's Centre 90
Individual Rights Protection Act
(IRPA) 26, 37, 41. *See also* sexual
orientation
amendments 38–39, 42, 68–74,
147–49
exceptions to 27, 42, 74, 147, 169
pregnancy 26–27, 68–70, 74
sexual orientation 5, 17, 38, 68,
70–72, 74, 124, 140, 143–47,
149–50, 159

individualism x, 8, 13, 16, 21, 26–27, 29,
37–38, 41, 43, 57, 70, 72–75, 99,
101, 127, 159, 162
Industrial Relations Board 27, 37
Interdepartmental Committee on
Women's Issues 11, 29–30, 62,
67, 75–77, 155, 176 n. 113
intergovernmental relations (federal-
provincial) 47–48, 103
International Women's Year 9, 27
IRPA *See* Individual Rights Protection
Act

Jewish Women's Groups 59–60
Johnston, Dick 62–64, 168 n. 44, 173
n. 55, 176 n. 113
*Joint Initiatives: A Goal for Women and
Government in Alberta* 48–49

K-Bro Linen Systems Inc. 134–35, 137
Kids First 92, 93
Kindergarten 18, 122, 130–33, 136
Klein, Ralph 5, 17–18, 119–26, 128,
131–33, 135–36, 139–41, 144, 148,
158, 184 n. 1, 190 n. 20
Koziak, Julian 65

Labour Relations Act 26–27
Labour Relations Board 135
Langeslag, Flores 51
laundry workers 130, 133–37
Leahey, Margaret 4, 66, 107–09, 111
legitimacy, women's political 6–8,
10–11, 13, 16, 20–21, 43, 47, 55, 57,
61, 67, 77, 80–81, 85, 90, 92,
111–12, 116–17, 120, 138, 155–56,
162, 164 n. 16

Lethbridge and District Pro-Life 93
Lethbridge Immigrant Women's
Association 93
Liberal Party (Alberta) 99, 138, 148
liberal pluralism (pluralist politics)
10–13, 15, 17, 22, 43, 46–47, 49,
55–57, 78, 84–85, 94, 101, 112, 117,
120, 143, 155, 157
Lieutenant Governor's Conference on
the Family 110–11
Lisoski, Ernestine 61
Lougheed, Peter 19–20, 30, 32, 36–37,
64, 65, 75, 99, 176 n. 113

MacPherson, C. B. x
MagCan 118
Mahoney, Kathleen 147
maintenance enforcement 48, 52–53
Mar, Gary 144, 146
maternity leave 14, 26–28, 43, 69–70
matrimonial property 2–3, 26, 31,
33–36, 43, 49
McCoy, Elaine 85, 97, 98, 107–09, 111
Media 32, 35, 39, 84, 88, 92, 125, 126, 142
Medicare (health insurance) 95, 96,
97–98, 107, 116, 121, 127–28
Mertick, Elva 109–11
Minister of Community Development
129, 138, 140–141, 146, 149
Minister of Labour 32, 38, 59, 68, 71, 72,
73
Minister responsible for women's
issues 11, 29–33, 48, 51–52, 56,
61–63, 66–67, 77, 84–85, 97,
104, 106–10, 116, 122, 138–139,
156, 168 n. 44, 173 n. 55
Mirosh, Dianne 5, 140, 144, 147, 188 n.
91
Moore, Marvin 95–98

Multicorp 135
Murdoch, Irene 2, 33–35

National Action Committee on the
    Status of Women 88, 136
National Energy Program 47
neoconservatism 13, 17, 46, 83–85, 98,
    117, 121, 123–28, 150, 158–59, 161.
    See also Alberta Federation of
    Women United for Families,
    conservative women's groups,
    family, Individual Rights
    Protection Act: sexual orienta-
    tion
neoliberalism 6–9, 11, 16–18, 120–51,
    153, 157–58, 160–62
New Democratic Party 24, 85, 99, 188
    n. 91
Northern Alberta Women's Archive
    Project 82
Norwood Women's Collective 35
Novatel 118

oil and gas (energy) x, 9–10, 20–21, 23,
    37, 45, 57, 61–62, 78–80, 116, 121,
    153–154, 168 n. 55
    pricing 10, 16, 20–23, 43, 45, 47, 80,
    133, 155
O'Neill, Jack 144
OPEC See Organization of Petroleum
    Exporting Countries
Options for Women 25–28
Organization of Petroleum Exporting
    Countries (OPEC) 20
Organized labor 60, 80, 130, 133, 135.
    See also laundry workers,
    specific unions

Oxfam Human Rights Initiative 148,
    190 n. 135

Palmer, Howard 22
Palmer, Tamara 22
pay equity 4, 39–40, 42, 46–48, 52, 64,
    68, 72–73, 75, 88, 98–101, 116,
    140, 145–46, 156, 159, 188 n. 91
Plan for Action for Alberta Women 4,
    13, 86, 101–04, 116, 156
Planned Parenthood Alberta 76,
    126–27, 180 n. 62, 185 n. 26
Planned Parenthood Edmonton 95, 127
pluralism. See liberal pluralism
pornography 13, 15, 57, 84
poverty x, 22, 38, 71, 102, 106, 110–11,
    122, 129, 145, 149, 161, 178 n. 23.
    See also Alberta Status of
    Women Action Committee
Premier's Council in Support of
    Alberta Families 4, 13, 94, 102,
    108, 112–15, 123, 179 n. 45
    Family Policy Grid 102, 181 n. 91
Premier's Council on the Status of
    People with Disabilities 140
privatization 8, 17, 112, 121, 130–31, 134,
    136, 154, 162, 185–86 n. 29
Progressive Conservative Party
    (federal) 47
Provincial Coalition (Committee) for
    a Council on Women's Affairs
    49, 58–67

Quebec 47

Index 225

race and racism x, 12, 14, 80, 89–90,
100–101, 106, 139, 154, 160–61,
186 n. 40
REAL Women 57
Regional Authorities for Child and
Family Welfare 129
regional health authorities (RHAs)
133–34
RHAs *See* regional health authorities
Robert's Rules of Order 50, 83
Rostad, Ken 83–85
Royal Alexandra Hospital 96
Royal Commission on the Status of
Women 19, 23, 26, 28, 33, 37

Sayer, Derek 6–7
Schlafly, Phyllis 55
Secretary of State Women's Program
9, 21, 28, 50–51, 57, 82, 85, 87, 117,
123
Seniors' Secretariat 140
sex education 55, 75, 76, 124. *See also*
birth control
sexual orientation 76, 83–84, 114,
123–24, 130, 140, 150, 159. *See
also* Individual Rights
Protection Act
single mothers 8, 112–13
social assistance 1, 78, 52–53, 75, 80,
86, 90, 108, 113, 122, 128–129, 139,
159
social conditions x, 7, 14, 20–23, 53,
79–80, 96–98, 101, 112–13,
116–17, 127, 129, 151, 154, 160–61
social consensus x, 6, 9, 10, 16, 21, 43,
45–47, 78, 154
Social Credit Party 19–20, 33, 36
social justice 9–10, 21, 37, 45, 122, 137,
143, 157, 159, 161

social policy 4, 9–10, 12, 15, 22, 28, 81,
90, 94, 110, 113, 117, 120–123, 126,
128, 151, 162, 191 n. 1
special interests 2, 7, 11, 17, 123, 128, 132,
140, 145, 148, 158, 161
state form. *See* neoliberalism, welfare
state
sterilization 13, 95–98, 107, 116, 150, 156
Supreme Court of Canada 2, 5, 17, 33,
96, 124, 160, 175 n. 88

Teen Aid 93
Therapeutic Abortion Committees
95–96, 180 n. 59
Toth, Kathleen 54–55

United Church of Canada 70–71
United Nations Convention on the
Rights of the Child 123
United Nations Convention to
Eliminate All Forms of
Discrimination Against
Women 46–47
United Nurses of Alberta 60

Vencap 134

WAP *See* Women Against Poverty
welfare state (interventionism) 6–12,
16, 20–23, 37, 43, 49, 75, 79, 81,
115, 117, 121, 138, 143, 153, 157, 160
Western Accord 47
widows' pension program 52, 73, 106
Women Looking Forward 87–89, 144
Women of Colour 81, 89–90, 105

Women's Bureau 9, 37, 62, 140,
168 n. 58
Women's Secretariat 29–31. *See also*
Alberta Women's Secretariat
Women's Secretariat Act 66
women's shelters 13, 102, 106, 108, 120,
128–29, 156, 186 n. 36
Women's Unit of the Anglican Church
88
work 7–9, 15, 21, 26–28, 71, 93, 101, 115,
151, 159. *See also* affirmative
action, pay equity

paid 3, 13, 35–37, 40–43, 60, 72–73,
92, 98–99, 102, 104, 115, 129, 145,
147
unpaid 2–3, 8, 15, 33, 48, 55, 64, 72,
91, 114, 117, 120, 122, 157
Wynn, Sheila 63, 173 n. 55

Yeatman, Anna 16–17
Young, Iris 11, 43
Young, Les 56, 73–74
YWCA 93. *See also* Calgary YWCA